HOW INFORMATION MATTERS

Titles in the Series

HOW INFORMATION MATTERS

Networks and Public Policy Innovation

KATHLEEN HALE

Georgetown University Press / Washington, D.C.

Georgetown University Press, Washington, D.C. www.press.georgetown.edu

Library of Congress Cataloging-in-Publication Data

Hale, Kathleen.
    How information matters : networks and public policy innovation / Kathleen
Hale.
        p. cm.—(Public management and change series)
    Includes bibliographical references and index.
    ISBN 978-1-58901-700-9 (pbk. : alk. paper)
    1. Policy networks—United States.   2. Information networks—United
States.   3. Policy sciences.
I. Title.
JK468.P64H35   2011
320.60973—dc22

                                                                        2010036895

15 14 13 12 11   9 8 7 6 5 4 3 2
First printing

Printed in the United States of America

CONTENTS

ILLUSTRATIONS

Figures

ACKNOWLEDGMENTS

This research would not have been possible without the voluntary assistance of nonprofit leaders, state administrators, and others practicing public policy throughout the United States. Executive directors, board members, and public policy specialists were willing to talk freely about their organizations and their work within the criminal justice system. These key stakeholders did not always agree; in fact, all were careful to delineate the missions and policy positions of their respective organizations and to distinguish their organizations from other groups. Each organization shared deep commitment to the policy process and to accomplishing policy change, and yet all were respectful of the roles of other organizations in the national network. It would not have been possible to define a national nonprofit information network or to examine the use of information within the states without their participation.

State administrators were also essential. Their willingness to take part in the national survey and to talk about their programs added greatly to the richness of my understanding of the ground-level implementation of drug court policy. Special thanks are also due to the state drug court administrators in Alabama, Georgia, Florida, Indiana, Missouri, and Tennessee for opening their doors to me. I continue to be inspired by the dedication, energy, and enthusiasm of these offices; I am confident that their work is representative of the efforts of many others across the country. In particular, their discussions about the challenges of operation and measurement suggest a degree of diligence in accomplishing public goals that is not often reflected in research about public programs. Key informants and survey respondents were assured anonymity, and I regret that it is not possible to properly acknowledge their patience in answering questions and their attention to detail. I am also indebted to the many individuals who forwarded my messages, returned my calls, and generally pointed me in the right direction within various state bureaucracies.

I gratefully acknowledge the support that I received from Karen Moss-berger as my chief mentor in the formative stages of this project, as well as the important suggestions made by Beryl Radin, Don Jacobs, and the anonymous reviewers at Georgetown University Press. Jack Gargan and Caroline Tolbert also provided insights and direction that contributed sub-stantially to the work overall. I also want to acknowledge the University Fellowship assistance from the Department of Political Science at Kent State University, which provided support for me in the formative stages of the project. I appreciate the collegial support and encouragement I have received from the faculty and staff of the Department of Political Science and the Master's of Public Administration Program at Auburn University, and the support from the Department and the College of Liberal Arts that gave me the time and resources to conduct additional research.

The efforts of several others deserve special mention. Caroline Cooper at the Office of Justice Programs Drug Court Clearinghouse housed at American University provided previously published data about drug court programs in an electronic format. West Huddleston at the National Associ-ation of Drug Court Professionals provided archived data on board mem-bership as well as contextual background for the drug court movement. Jean Cochet at the National Center for State Courts provided archived copies of the organization's annual reports. The staff members of each of these organizations were extraordinarily helpful as well. The usual caveats apply; I hope this research contributes to the collaborative work between public administrators and nonprofit organizations in advancing public purposes, and to our understanding of its importance.

Introduction

INFORMATION RELATIONSHIPS AND INNOVATION

This is a book about how information matters to public administrators in the process of policy change. In this book the concept of information is defined as specific knowledge or data that reflects the expertise and judgment of professionals engaged in a particular policy realm. Information is more sophisticated than a random collection of facts; information includes the values and ideologies reflected in an area of public concern, how problems are defined, how solutions are crafted, how policy is put into action, and how to decide whether particular solutions are worthwhile. Public administrators looking for information are essentially looking for knowledge and data to assist them in making decisions about whether to make policy changes and, if so, how best to go about it. In education policy, for example, information includes whether and how to institute various types of alternatives to traditional public education, such as charter programs, vouchers, and home schooling. In the realm of elections, information includes the range of methods of voter identification at the polls, the effect of early voting methods or different ballot designs, and new technologies for conducting elections. Information about environmental sustainability includes the limits of natural resources, the benefits of various conservation methods, and the relative consumption of resources by humans, agriculture, and industry. These examples only scratch the surface of the rich range of knowledge that is reflected in the term "information," and yet they convey the reality that the value of information extends far beyond the raw data.

Public administrators acquire information from a vast array of sources; this book focuses on the information they acquire from a national information network of nonprofit organizations. This book is about how this type of information *matters* in bringing about policy innovation in the contemporary intergovernmental environment. It is the story of how a national information network of nonprofit organizations influenced and supported state and local administrators in their efforts to implement and institutionalize a policy innovation as a new approach to some very old problems. It is also the story of how the nonprofit sector and public sector connected synergistically to develop a new capacity for addressing public problems and delivering public service.

A central consideration in intergovernmental relationships today is whether and how organizations outside the state can make a difference in policy implementation and policy outcomes in comparison with other factors that shape policy decisions, such as citizen needs, ideology, and the partisan nature of the public policy process. The overarching purpose of this book is to explore some of the emerging questions about the influence of information in intergovernmental relationships. Its goal is to identify and analyze the influence of information relationships and the information tools and processes disseminated by information networks on policy implementation efforts and policy outcomes. Ultimately, the concern here is whether those states that are more "informed" by an information network undertake more extensive state implementation efforts and whether this information improves policy outcomes. The central argument is that states can achieve a greater degree of success in policy implementation by utilizing the information relationships, tools, and processes that information networks provide, and that this success builds capacity for future policy initiatives.

The information environment that informs public administrators is framed in this book as an intersectoral policy environment, which is the web of policy communication relationships between the public and nonprofit sectors in a particular policy area. This intersectoral framing is important because it presents the intergovernmental environment as public administrators actually experience it—as a web of multiple, layered jurisdictions and authorities within government proper that interact with each other and with nonprofit organizations in myriad formal and informal relationships. This intersectoral concept calls attention to the intersection of the sectors and to the contributions that each can make in building and sustaining solutions to public problems. Across the spectrum of public policy, today's practice of public administration involves extensive work with organizations that are not constituted as public bureaucracies. The questions posed in this book beg the larger question of how best to optimize relationships between the public and nonprofit sectors in designing and implementing public policy.

The influence of the information that is disseminated in this intersect-oral policy environment is organized using several interrelated concepts. One is a national nonprofit information network and the information relationships that developed between these organizations and public administrators in state and local governments. Through these relationships, information tools such as best practices, model programs, and evaluative research provided administrators with a synthesis of multiple experiences. Information decision-making processes fostered collaboration and synthesis across professions, layers of government, and sectors. New informal and institutional relationships formed as a result; these relationships and institutions represent new administrative capacity that can be brought to bear on the policy question at hand. Moreover, these relationships and institutions will extend into new intergovernmental relationships and policy questions.

The book illustrates the influence of one information network on the diffusion and institutionalization of a policy innovation by examining the spread of drug courts as an innovation in judicial administration and criminal justice policy. The drug court concept blends public safety and public health principles through a highly structured system of judicial intervention coupled with a cross-professional, interjurisdictional therapeutic approach to drug treatment. The goal of the program is to reduce drug use in the criminal justice population by breaking the cycle of addiction and reducing the level of criminal activity presumed to be associated with drug use and drug-seeking behavior.

The drug court concept provides a rich opportunity for exploring the influence of an information network of administrators and nonprofit organizations on policy change. First, the drug court policy initiative is widely considered to be successful. Second, drug court policy evolved as the result of the interaction of diverse values and beliefs about drugs and crime that cross professional boundaries and that engage different levels and branches of government. As an innovation in criminal justice reform and judicial administration, the concept of drug courts was diffused rapidly as one policy response to pressures from mandatory sentencing policies and penalties for drug crimes. A national network comprising many types of nonprofit organizations—including professional associations, research groups, and other groups—brought a range of ideologies and values to bear on the question of drug court policy. Through missions unique to each individual group, the national nonprofit organizations assumed different information positions in the network that reflected their individual ideologies and missions, as well as the extent to which their work was aligned with a particular strategy for policy change. These organizations communicated policy information about drug courts through information tools such as best practices, model programs, and evaluation research about drug courts and other criminal justice policy options. The network also fostered processes for local, state, and intergovernmental decision making that synthesized interests across professions and jurisdictions. Together, these forms of information, relationships, and processes influenced state and local administrative decisions about drug court policy as a method of reform.

The legacy of the intersectoral information network is a new network of local, state, and intergovernmental relationships, tools, and processes that sustains drug court policy and new policy initiatives. These relationships, tools, and processes also illustrate a much broader narrative about the contemporary intergovernmental environment and how public-sector policy choices are shaped by actors outside the state. A persistent theme surrounding the legacy of devolution is that it has fostered or even ossified an incompetent public sector by promoting complex and interdependent arrangements within and outside government. The increasing interdependency and diffuse accountability that characterize these relationships appear to work against the ability of government to accomplish its goals.

The thesis presented here takes a more optimistic view of the consequences of complexity and interdependence and argues that these relationships can be leveraged for public benefit—that the information relationships between public administrators and nonprofit organizations are a vital dimension of the capacity of government to solve public problems. An examination of the capacity that can be created by these information relationships helps move the conversation about government–nonprofit relationships beyond service contracts and the potential perils of issue advocacy. By studying these information relationships, we learn more about how policy is diffused in the intergovernmental system beyond adoption into implementation. We also learn more about intersectoral information relationships as both a collection of content and of processes, and we examine forms of information and information processes that may play strategic roles in institutionalizing support within local communities and across the intergovernmental system. The study of these information relationships also helps us assess whether the information disseminated by nonprofit organizations to state administrators actually has any impact on the efforts of states to implement innovative policies or on the policy outcomes themselves.

The Approach to Analysis

The central theme of this book is that the information relationships between the nonprofit sector and government agencies create a synergy that develops new capacity for government to address public problems. These relationships and the influence of the information tools and decision-making processes that flow from the national information network of nonprofit organizations are illustrated in a study of the drug court experience from its genesis in 1989 to its present-day status as a mature policy initiative.

To construct the analysis, data were drawn from information relationships pertaining to drug court policy in the American states beginning with the inception of the program in 1989. Data were collected in several stages, and both quantitative and qualitative methods were used in the analyses. Additional information about the methodology is briefly provided throughout the chapters that follow; the research stages are described more fully in the appendix. An exploratory round of interviews with leaders of national nonprofit organizations provided a foundation for describing a national network of nonprofit organizations devoted to alternatives to incarceration and drug policy reform in the criminal justice system and the kinds of information they developed and shared with public administrators. Original data were collected using a national survey of state drug court administrators and drug court personnel to identify the types of information that administrators sought from nonprofits about drug court programs and the information they found most useful. The survey also collected data about how states were organizing their administrative efforts to institutionalize and support local drug court programs. Multivariate statistical methods were used to test the influence of information on the diffusion of drug courts throughout local courts and in state governments from the beginning of the program in 1989 through 2004. Additional interviews were conducted with the staffs of six states, which were selected because they represented a range of earlier and later adopters and illustrated varying approaches to institutionalizing drug courts within state government.

An Outline of the Presentation

This book has seven chapters. Chapter 1 establishes the significance of the study within several major literatures that pertain to the work of public administrators in the intergovernmental arena. The intergovernmental relations literature and emerging network literature demonstrate the importance of networks to those responsible for implementing policy. The policy diffusion literature provides a foundation for understanding how information facilitates the diffusion of innovation and why some policy innovations spread widely across the states. The nonprofit literature expands upon the implications of relationships between government and nonprofit organizations, which are woven throughout the layers of the intergovernmental system. These relationships contribute to the interdependence and complexity that affect the ability of public administrators to demonstrate accountability and performance. The conceptual framework for the book is outlined in terms of relationships between information, implementation, and policy change. The concept of an "information position" is proposed as a method for organizing the information network. A typology of information positions categorizes the organizations in the national nonprofit information network as champions, challengers, supporters, and bystanders. The chapter concludes with an outline of the study's major findings.

Chapter 2 turns the focus toward drug courts as a policy innovation and the parameters of a national nonprofit information network concerned with this policy reform. The ideological debate about criminal drug use and the various policy alternatives that have evolved over time are linked to the information positions of organizations in the information network. These positions illuminate a rich competition of ideas and values across the network regarding the drug court innovation. The missions and policy positions of particular organizations are reflected in the types of information that nonprofits disseminated in their relationships with state and local administrators.

Chapter 3 demonstrates the national influence of the information network on the diffusion of drug court programs and the growth of institutional support across the states during the programs' history. Enduring information relationships between administrators and nonprofit organizations were formed on the basis of service on national governing boards and state professional associations. These relationships fostered sustained interaction between state offices and local programs and were instrumental in the development of new information links among states, local programs, and national organizations. These relationships are also associated with improved state policy outcomes.

Chapter 4 highlights the information tools that administrators found within the information network and adapted to institutionalize the drug court concept in their states. These information tools synthesize multiple experiences and provide a sort of information strategy for administrators. State and local experiences with a policy template, a package of policy experiences, and research information were particularly valuable. Examples of state and local practices illustrate the influence of these types of strategic information on the spread of the drug court program and the synthesis that can be achieved through government–nonprofit relationships.

Chapter 5 examines two dimensions of the information environment that combined to generate new collaborative processes for state and local administrators. One dimension was the collaborative process that flowed from the creation of a new profession of drug court administrators within the broader field of public administration. Another dimension was the collaborative information processes that were prompted by the use of the policy template of best practices. Both dimensions combined to forge a consensus among diverse professional constituencies and layers of government. These processes produced new platforms for information exchange in multijurisdictional intergovernmental environments; in turn, new information, new institutions, and new relationships emerged that were based on the drug court concept. From these processes, states learned to develop standards and certification programs and design methods to navigate the balance of power between state and local governments.

Chapter 6 illustrates the continuing cycle of the information network as it expanded to encompass new institutions and actors. The network engaged new organizations and needs, which provided additional opportunities to negotiate policy content across political jurisdictions and diverse constituencies. The information relationships, tools, and collaborative processes that evolved based on the drug court concept were extended to address new questions in criminal justice and judicial administration. This chapter also illustrates aspects of the information network that may be unique to this policy realm.

Chapter 7 generalizes the information relationships, tools, and collaborative processes into a strategic framework of information connections between public and nonprofit organizations. Key aspects of the information network are generalized to suggest the value of the information network for state and local programs across policy domains. The roles of nonprofit organizations as champions, challengers, supporters, and bystanders are generalized to the broader policy community and public administrators across policy areas.

The perceptions of public administrators are a centerpiece of this book; vignettes are used to illustrate their perceptions about information relationships, tools, and processes as they encountered decision points in adopting and institutionalizing the new drug court policy. These vignettes are based on real situations but are written in a fictional style. Throughout, illustrations from the states describe how public administrators have integrated information from the national network into their strategies for developing state-level programs and institutionalizing state support for local efforts. These examples also illustrate how the national information network has assisted state administrators in developing state institutional support for programs with local origins and strong local ties.

1

Intergovernmental Relationships, Information, and Policy Change

The significance of networks in the American intergovernmental environment is now widely acknowledged (Agranoff 2007; Agranoff and McGuire 2003; Kickert, Klijn, and Koppenjan 1999; O'Toole 1997; Provan and Milward 1995, 2001).[1] What we commonly discuss as an intergovernmental system of federal, state, and local institutions that suit a range of general and special purposes is actually a network of interdependent relationships that include both public and nongovernmental organizations. Networks have become a prominent dimension of the way that the public sector operates as a consequence of several broad themes about public policy and the role of government that have evolved and intertwined during the past fifty years.

In general terms, the expansion of federal welfare policy into local communities in the 1960s and 1970s generated new relationships among federal and local governments and new local agencies, many of which were newly formed nonprofit groups that provided public services under new federal programs (Salamon 1995; Smith and Lipsky 1995). Policies focused on large-scale change in social conditions and took a comprehensive stance in defining "public" problems. Beginning with the War on Poverty, sweeping policy changes have been encompassed under popular labels such as urban renewal, welfare reform, and the war on drugs. Each of these intractable (or "wicked") problems attracted participation across disciplines and from both public and private organizations.[2]

Alongside this expansion of government programs, the concept of intergovernmental relations emerged to reflect a new system of funding relationships and contacts among federal, state, and local units of government

(Wright 1988). New federal funding relationships typically revolved around cross-sector and interdisciplinary collaboration and advanced the participation of multiple actors and constituencies. In the 1980s and 1990s devolution shifted a significant measure of policymaking authority and fiscal responsibility from the federal level to the states, particularly in the area of social welfare services (Conlan 1998; Kettl 2002; Salamon 2002). Together with devolution, the reinvention initiatives of the 1990s (e.g., Gore 1993) further shifted the provision of direct social welfare and other public services to the private sector. Reinvention stimulated public organizations to flatten internal hierarchies and decentralize, pushing responsibility down from the federal level to the states and from state to local governments, and out from government at all levels to private nonprofit organizations (Kettl 1995; Osborne and Gaebler 1992).

From the 1970s forward, the nonprofit sector has expanded dramatically in conjunction with these policy shifts. In part, the expansion of the nonprofit sector has occurred in response to the expanded need for direct public services and related government support; and in part it has also grown to accommodate the formation of voluntary groups interested in pursuing specific missions for civic engagement and policy change. As devolution has matured, nonprofit organizations have followed the transfer of responsibility away from the federal government and have established new and stronger ties with state and local governments (DeVita and Twombly 2006). Technological change has also contributed to the current networked arrangement in and around government programs. The rise of the Internet and new methods of electronic information exchange in the first years of the twenty-first century have made it exponentially easier to gather and share information, to collaborate in decision-making processes, and to incorporate broad involvement across groups of individuals and organizations (Goldsmith and Eggers 2004).

As a consequence, the modern public administrator now operates at the intersection of these trends, in an environment filled with networks. These networks are commonly defined as interdependent interorganizational arrangements that involve "all or part of multiple organizations where one unit is not merely the formal subordinate of the other in some larger hierarchical arrangement" (O'Toole 1988, 414). Conceptually, networks can be informal arrangements or can be more formally constituted based on a common goal, a legal structure such as a grant or charter or contract, or some other organizing principle. Within the broad concept of a network, research demonstrates that not all networks are alike, and some are more different than others. As research in the area has grown, several distinct network arrangements have emerged as the focus for study. The work of Kickert, Klijn, and Koppenjan (1999) has focused on the policy network as a unit of decision making for governance and public management questions. Provan and Milward (1995, 2001) have examined human services networks to discover various conditions of centrality that contribute to network effectiveness; their findings identify distinct layers of effectiveness that are related to distinct layers of network constituencies at the individual level, the network level, and the community level. Agranoff and McGuire (1998, 2003) have focused on the difficulties of managing under the collaborative conditions of local governments.

In a study of fourteen midwestern networks that range across policy areas and purposes, Agranoff (2007, 3) establishes the concept of public management networks as the "intergovernmental entities that emerge from interactions among formal organizations." Within this concept, public management networks are differentiated by function into four primary types: information networks, developmental networks, action networks, and outreach networks. The function of each public management network has implications for its involvement in public policy. Another form of network arrangement has been specified for federal grant relationships. Identified as "articulated vertical networks of third parties," this network form has been defined to encompass the grant relationship between the federal government and other units of government or nongovernmental organizations as third parties (Frederickson and Frederickson 2006).

The network arrangement has consequences. Networks bring to the table multiple stakeholders with overlapping and competing missions, varying degrees of commitment, and varying levels of resources. Network participants may align with one another on the basis of a broad common goal such as community development or the coordination of some type of service, but the missions of the organizations remain unique. Constituent organizations may choose to participate in networks for widely different reasons. Some may participate to pursue a goal common to the group. Others may use participation in a network primarily to advance their own missions.

One theme running through the study of networks is that complexity and interdependence impede policy success by diffusing the authority and accountability mechanisms typically associated with bureaucratic hierarchy. The essential characteristics of networks frustrate the ability of public administrators to exercise sufficient authority in the management of public programs. Complexity and interdependence are heightened, and accountability for results is diffused (Agranoff and McGuire 1998, 2003; Kettl 2002;

Kickert, Klijn, and Koppenjan 1999; Provan and Milward 2001; Radin 2006). Networks also have implications for the sovereign role of government. In networks, government authority tends to dissipate as various responsibilities are assumed by multiple constituencies and can result in a condition of "governance without government" (Rhodes 1996, 1997). Principal–agent analysis of management responsibilities suggests that the actions of networks, and of their constituent organizations, can be co-opted away from government objectives, creating management difficulties for public-sector administrators (e.g., McGuire 2002; O'Toole and Meier 2004; Milward and Provan 1998b). Networks can assume an autonomous character that challenges the central sovereign responsibilities and governing imperative of the public sector (Kettl 2002). The challenge posed by network arrangements to government sovereignty creates a concern that policy decisions will be made outside the realm of political accountability and that policies will be implemented in ways that do not reflect legitimate government authority. Nonprofit organizations that enter into contracting relationships with government may encumber some level of legal accountability under the principles of agency; however, many network relationships are decidedly informal and do not compel nonprofit organizations to align with government purposes.

This challenge to sovereignty also challenges the overall capacity of governments to deliver public policy. In some quarters there is concern that government institutions may lack essential capacity to navigate the complexities and interdependencies of the current environment (Hula, Jackson-Elmore, and Reese 2007; Kettl 2005). Interdependencies between public agencies and private nonprofit organizations, where each is responsible for some portion of an effort but none are responsible for or capable of the whole, pose important questions about responsibility for performance and democratic accountability to citizens.

In spite of the difficulties associated with networks, they remain an entrenched aspect of the reality of public administration and have positive dimensions. Public management networks, as one example, added value to the programs that government agencies implemented (Agranoff 2007, 4). More broadly, networks of public and nongovernmental actors have the potential to improve the design and delivery of public policy in ways that cannot be accomplished by government and markets alone. Another appeal is that networks have the potential to create a synergy among participants that is greater than the sum of the individual parts (Mandell 1994, 1999; Milward and Provan 1998a; Townsend 2004). Rather than a prescription for failure, the idea of a network may be an attribute of intergovernmental success. A wide range of scholarship implies that network arrangements are an element of effective government operations, and that it is desirable for government organizations to have a clear mission of public service that is widely shared with, and endorsed by, the general public and specific stakeholder constituencies (Rainey 2003, 400; Rainey and Steinbauer 1999).

Further, the fragmented nature of public-sector decision making suggests that public organization initiatives will tend, more often than not, toward efforts that are diffuse rather than specific (Page 2004; Wildavsky 1972). The differences between nonprofit organizations and government in their missions and normative approaches to serving the public good suggest that network arrangements between public administrators and nonprofit organizations are inherently either inefficient or ineffective, or both. But the information network and information relationships examined in this book argue for a different conclusion: that an information network of nonprofit organizations can enhance the performance of government programs when the missions of both are closely aligned or intersect in some significant way. Government organizations can expect to realize gains in the form of synergy when they form partnerships with organizations based on a common mission. In the case of community development, for example, nonprofit community foundations can enhance public-sector performance because their goals and missions are similar (Carman 2001, 2007). A common goal may eliminate or reduce the effect of some differences between constituent organizations in networks; it may also suggest methods for combining efforts across sectors in pursuit of effective public policy.

Information Diffusion and Policy Change

One way to approach the relationship between an information network and policy decisions is through the framework of information diffusion. Information connections between governmental and nongovernmental actors are a fundamental aspect of the framework within which state decisions about public policy are made. The seminal work of Jack Walker (1969) demonstrates that states accomplish innovation through networks of state officials and professional organizations; in these networks, states share information about policy ideas, problems, and solutions. State decisions to adopt particular policy innovations have been influenced by the information gained by state administrators through interactions with other states, organizations of state officials, professional associations, and other groups (Balla 2001; Cigler 1999; Mintrom and Vergari 1998). Patterns of adoption shift according to the policy area (Gray 1973; Savage 1985). Further, states tend to adopt policies by emulating either neighboring states or states in the same region (Berry and Berry 1990; Mintrom 2000; Mooney 2001; Mooney and Lee 1995).

Today, we understand that state policy change is influenced by multifaceted patterns of information exchange. In the intergovernmental environment, these information patterns encompass horizontal information exchanges between the states and vertical information exchanges between the states and the federal government. The information flow through these multiple channels can be conceptualized as a process of polydiffusion, which includes vertical channels between the federal and subnational governments and horizontal channels between the states, as well as information channels between that states and various types of nongovernmental organizations (Mossberger 2000). Polydiffusion incorporates the concept of point-source diffusion (Eyestone 1997), whereby an idea that promotes state policy change diffuses from a point source such as the federal government; however, in the point-source model, states or other subnational units react to the federal impetus but not to one another. The premise of polydiffusion is that policy experiences and information are shared in all directions across a network of public and nonpublic actors that spans all levels of the intergovernmental system. In polydiffusion, federal funding outlets act as stimuli for the involvement of states and other groups through, for example, grant support or the demand for information. Theoretically, polydiffusion can be seen as a form of bounded rationality for state decision makers; the costs of seeking and evaluating information can be reduced by communicating with other states and with nongovernmental groups (Simon 1986; Mossberger 2000).

Research about patterns of information diffusion in the American intergovernmental system has identified some differences in the types of information that state administrators seek from governmental organizations and nongovernmental, nonprofit organizations. For instance, best practices and the experiences of other states influenced the spread of the enterprise zones across the states (Mossberger 2000) and the state implementation of school-to-work policy (Mossberger and Hale 2002). Further, in a national comparative study of state school-to-work policy, Mossberger and Hale (2002) found that state administrators sought different types of information from different types of organizations within a national information network. State administrators looked to the federal government to provide information about grants and program requirements; however, states looked to nonprofit organizations for synthesized information about best practices, model programs, and program evaluation.

In that experience, nonprofit organizations were seen by administrators as providing synthesized information as a type of information "software" that held particular value for state administrators, over and above the information "hardware" that was available from public sources (Mossberger and Hale 2002, 399). This information software is essentially interpretive information that brought meaning to other forms of information such as grant applications and legal requirements. As a whole, these studies support Walker's hypothesis that state policymakers use information from networks of national and state professional associations and from other states in making decisions to adopt new policies.

Information and information exchange are also essential aspects of the capacity of public organizations. Specific types of information such as technical assistance and training were noted among some of the earliest discussions of methods to enhance the capacity of local governments to implement federal programs (Burgess 1975; Honadle 1981). The capacity of public organizations reflects both organizational competency and the ability to influence competency more broadly, beyond the organization. In early work on the concept, Honadle (1981, 577) defines an almost heroic list of attributes associated with public-sector capacity, including the "ability to anticipate and influence change, make informed intelligent decisions, develop programs and implement policy, attract and absorb resources, manage resources, and evaluate current activities to guide future actions." Important to this equation is the "ability to forge effective links with other organizations, processes for solving problems, coordination among disparate functions and mechanisms for institutional learning" (Honadle 1981, 579). Capacity in public organizations is also linked to the ability to accommodate local preferences (Gargan 1981; Honadle 1981).

Information in a networked setting should also contribute to successful implementation. Successful policy implementation has been linked in part to effective exchange of information both within various agencies and within levels of government (Frederickson and Frederickson 2006; Rhodes 1997). Implementation studies of education policy (Roderick, Jacob, and Bryk 2000) and welfare-to-work programs (Riccio, Bloom, and Hill 2000) illustrate that information is centrally important to efforts to evaluate implementation and policy success. Further, in collaborative environments, information exchanges can build the trust that is essential for communication and understanding among diverse participants and for the success of networked arrangements (Mandell 1994, 1999).

In studying the influence of information, it is important to add a caveat about the contestable nature of information itself. As a policy instrument, information is a tool of influence and an instrument of the process that exists in a political context (Weiss 2002). Within and surrounding public programs, information is always value laden, always intertwined with the ideologies and interests of its producers and consumers (Radin 2000, 2006; Stone 1997; Weiss 1983; Weiss 2002). Information brings a political dimension to all stages of the public policy process. Policy problems are defined through information derived from values and normative beliefs; the dominant beliefs that are translated into policy are also the product of a political process based on majority rule (Stone 1997). The criteria that are used to define policy success are also determined and measured politically. In seeking to understand how information may influence implementation and subsequent policy success, it is important to explore the sources of information that flow to state administrators, why they want it, whether there are constituencies that advocate particular aspects of it, and where in the policy process the information attaches (Radin 2006).

This volume extends the influence of information relationships in public policy to examine the relationship between an information network, policy implementation, and policy outcomes. Information is conceptualized on the basis of a national nonprofit information network. This information network is constructed from the experiences of public administrators based on one area of criminal justice reform. The national nonprofit information network includes the national organizations upon which public administrators in state and local governments relied for information about whether and how to institute policy change. This is a network that produced knowledge about a series of public questions, and through which public administrators found information relationships, information tools, and decision-making processes that helped them focus on particular policy solutions. The national nonprofit information network is also interactive; together with organizations in the information network, administrators developed synergistic processes that fostered new institutions and further collaboration.

The national nonprofit information network presented in this book is not a public management network as described by Agranoff (2007). The organizations in this network, however, reflect the range of policy activities that fall within the public management network framework, including information exchange, policy solutions, advocacy, and action. The influence of the national nonprofit information network extends directly into policy implementation and is linked directly to government agency action through a series of professional memberships in the national professional associations that form the national nonprofit information network. Figure 1.1 portrays the relationships between the national nonprofit information network, implementation, and policy outcomes that are explored further in this book.

Why and What Nonprofits Contribute

A central premise underlying this study is that information relationships between nonprofit organizations and public administrators can enhance the ability of the public sector to deliver its responsibilities. This premise derives from several factors, including the tradition of nonprofit engagement in public life in connection with government policies, the relative autonomy of the sector, the tradition of the sector in working with diverse constituencies to produce common value, and the sustained voluntary commitment that the sector represents.

Americans have a long tradition of forming organizations to engage broadly in public life. The widespread associationalism that de Tocqueville (1835/1945) observed in the early 1800s is still heralded today as uniquely American. As the nation grew, public interest in civic engagement and personal voluntary fulfillment expanded into philanthropic and charitable service sectors (e.g., Dowie 2001; Hall 1992; Hammack 1998). Today, the nonprofit sector includes more than 1.2 million organizations and represents approximately 10 percent of the American workforce (Steuerle and Hodgkinson 2006). These nonprofit organizations have been formed to raise money, to provide charity to those in need, to provide opportunities for social interaction, to build community support, to educate the public on topics of interest, and to advocate for a multitude of causes.

In recent decades, nonprofits have evolved alongside the forces that shaped the current complex and interdependent intergovernmental environment. The growth of the nonprofit sector and its intertwining relationship with government have contributed to the rise of complexity and interdependence in intergovernmental relationships. A wide range of studies reflect concern with the blurring of lines between public and private actors in service-contracting relationships. These studies observe the potential loss of democratic accountability or public responsiveness when nonprofit organizations are used by government agencies as vehicles for public service provision (e.g., Braddock, Hemp, and Richards 2008; Salamon 1995; Smith and Lipsky 1995; Sosin et al. 2009). One consequence

Figure 1.1 Conceptual Relationships between Information, Implementation, and Public Policy Outcomes

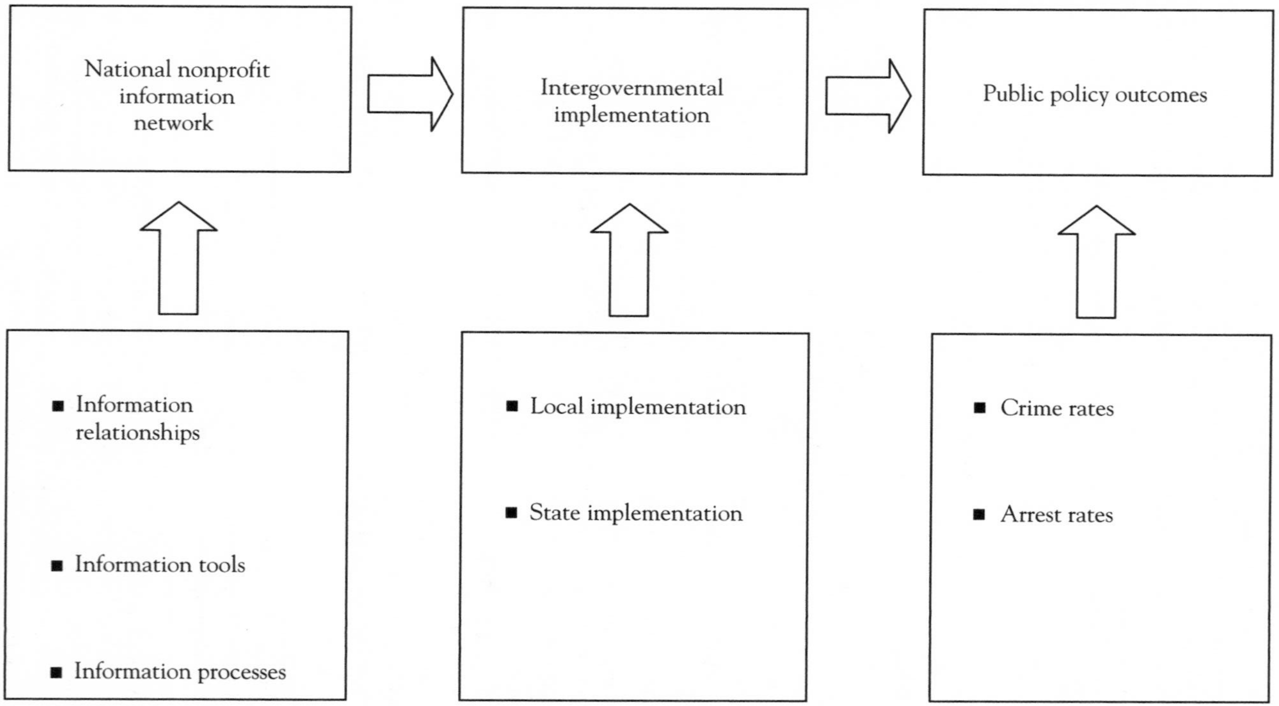

of the financial partnership between government and nonprofit organizations is the growth of the nonprofit sector itself (Boris 2006; DeVita 1999; Salamon 2002; Smith 2006; Steuerle and Hodgkinson 2006). National patterns also demonstrate an increase in government funding support for the nonprofit sector for social services overall. Starting in the 1960s, historical data demonstrate permanent shifts in social service delivery from the government to nonprofit organizations in various regions of the country (Salamon 1995; Smith and Lipsky 1995).

The prolonged interconnected funding relationship between the sectors is not necessarily benign for the nonprofit sector or for government policy initiatives. Nonprofit organizations that rely increasingly on public funds may lose the independence and autonomy that comes with private contributions. Government social spending may actually discourage private philanthropy in some policy areas (Brooks 2000). Nonprofits may also assume the characteristics of the large public bureaucracies that provide funding (Anheier, Toepler, and Sokolowski 1997). On the other side of the equation, government relationships with nonprofit organizations may frustrate public interests in transparency given the private status of nonprofit organizations. The extent of government funding for nonprofit service provision differs across policy areas; however, in all areas where government funding represents a significant portion of nonprofit program revenue, nonprofits are challenged to make up losses in government funding through program fees and voluntary contributions. This funding relationship can be quite complex, and the loss of government funding may result in the elimination of programs that have grown up around dedicated revenue streams (e.g., Braddock, Hemp, and Richards 2008; and the case of developmental disabilities in the states).

The nonprofit element of the network calculus, however, may offer a unique contribution to finding the way forward in identifying information tools and processes for information exchange and decision making. At the heart of it, nonprofits conjure up images of service, community, and commitment to a cause or social goal. Although these causes and goals vary widely, all nonprofit organizations have several elements in common (Salamon 2002). Nonprofits are essentially private, voluntary organizations. They exist outside the state and are formed voluntarily by groups of individuals to pursue a mission. Organizations are self-governed through boards of volunteers, and in most cases some of the organization's work is accomplished by volunteers. Further, nonprofit organizations are not intended to generate revenue to distribute to shareholders; surplus revenue is returned to the organization to further its mission.

These defining characteristics have generated several strengths for the nonprofit sector relative to government. Nonprofits have considerable independence and autonomy as a result of their voluntary character and dedication to a particular mission. Nonprofit organizations use their own criteria for developing missions and making connections with client populations and communities. Nonprofits can define their missions narrowly or broadly; if nonprofits choose to provide services, they can also choose to exclude people or groups that are expensive or difficult to serve. In doing so, nonprofits are not limited by the equity considerations that fall upon government. Further, nonprofits are more likely to operate in contentious or innovative policy fields, and they have a greater relative ability than the public sector to experience and assume risk. Nonprofits are also less likely to operate in rule-driven environments than are present in the typical government agency (Light 1998). As a whole, the nonprofit sector is a "prototyping test bed" and a form of "social risk capital" that simultaneously promotes associational life along with individual diversity (Light 1998; Ott 2001; Smith 1973). Nonprofit organizations provide a voice for the views and needs of minority groups. One reason that nonprofit organizations are formed is to address individual and group needs that are not satisfied by government and to advocate for minority viewpoints that are not reflected through the framework of majority rule (Salamon 2002; Young 2006). These needs and views may be unpopular with majority interests and involve marginalized or dependent constituencies such as criminal offenders, addicts, poor people, and minority or ethnic groups.

Nonprofit organizations foster a process of civic engagement that is inherently collaborative and involves multiple stakeholders and community-based interactions. Civic engagement is essential to the formation of the social capital that is a critical element in developing and sustaining vital communities (Putnam 2001; Van Til 2000). These organizations knit together diverse constituencies as they assemble governing boards, acquire resources, and work to fulfill their missions. As a consequence, nonprofit organizations tend to be guided by community and client responsiveness, whereas government agencies tend to be concerned about whether the distribution of public resources is perceived to be fair and politically feasible (Smith 2006, 234). As a mirror image of the collaborative process, nonprofits have long been at the forefront of strategies to demonstrate performance to diverse constituencies (Brooks 2004; Chait, Holland, and Taylor 1996). Cross-sector collaborations between nonprofit and for-profit organizations demonstrate that common missions, or common elements within missions, provide a platform for external relationships that are valuable to the participants; further, the benefit of these external relationships increases with the accumulation of experience and interaction (Austin 2000). Nonprofits value collaboration with external groups as a method of seeking opportunities for innovation and of strengthening their organizations; the importance of collaboration persists regardless of organizational age, size, or budget (Light 1998, 2004).

Nonprofit governing boards and managers recognize the need to demonstrate accountability to multiple constituencies within their communities by identifying desirable community outcomes and measuring program activities against them. The strategic choice to demonstrate performance to diverse constituencies is illustrated in the increased use of program evaluation protocols in nonprofit human service organizations across the country (Hoefer 2000). Programs to engage social service agencies in the process of program evaluation and outcomes measurement have been instituted in many United Way organizations across the country (Hatry, Cowan, and Hendricks 2004; Light 2000). Although nonprofits themselves may not implement performance measurement and evaluation programs evenly or with great sophistication in some cases (e.g., Carman 2009), the concept is now familiar to nonprofit organizations that participate in community funding streams.

Further, nonprofits tend to demonstrate a sustained *voluntary* energy and enthusiasm for the mission and purpose of the organization. This energy and enthusiasm for mission is an important aspect of the potential contribution that nonprofit organizations may be able to offer to the work of public agencies. And this mission orientation can provide sustained stability and focus toward accomplishing a particular program or goal. In contrast, changes in partisan political control are inevitable across the intergovernmental system. These changes are accompanied by shifts in ideology and policy priorities. As a consequence, sustained commitment to particular programs is difficult (or impossible) to achieve within government as a political environment.

One underlying rationale for this project is to contribute to our knowledge about solutions that address the potential lack of capacity of public organizations to deliver public policy in today's highly complex, networked environment. The central proposition of this book is that an information network of nonpublic actors contributes substantially to the capacity of government to implement policy. The pressures of devolution and complex policy approaches compel states to pursue collaborative, networked strategies for policy implementation. Understanding the contributions of a national nonprofit information network can help state administrators identify and utilize beneficial information relationships. Moreover, a greater understanding of productive information relationships can contribute to administrators' ability to establish programs that enhance public-sector capacity; and this understanding can also contribute to administrators' ability to operate in networked environments in ways that advance public goals.

Conceptualizing a National Nonprofit Information Network

As I explored the influence of an information network of national nonprofit organizations on the decisions of state and local administrators concerned with a particular area of policy innovation, the research project that led to this book posed several questions:

1. What does the information network look like? What kinds of nonprofit organizations are communicating with public administrators?
2. What do administrative contacts with the information network look like? What nonprofit organizations do administrators use as information sources? Are certain types of information more valuable than others? Is synthesized information (e.g., best practices, model programs, research, or evaluation findings) more useful to administrators than other types of information?
3. What is the influence of the national nonprofit information network on implementation efforts and policy outcomes? Is the scope of implementation more extensive in states with more extensive participation in the information network? Do states with higher levels of implementation also experience better policy outcomes?
4. What are the implications of the diffusion of information through nonprofit organizations? Does information from nonprofit organizations enhance states' capacity for policy implementation? Does information from sources outside the public sector matter in comparison with other factors?
5. How does information from the national information network influence the administration of local programs and state offices?

To address these questions, I conceptualized the nonprofit information network in this book as an unchartered information environment of national nonprofit groups organized informally around ideas for policy innovation. These organizations reflect varying ideologies, missions, and constituencies, and they interact with one another and with public administrators across the intergovernmental spectrum. In the information network, organizations develop information about policy options and ideas for reform that are consistent with their missions and goals. Through contacts in the information network, public administrators access this information and use it to design and implement policy change. This national nonprofit information network is an important area for study because it reflects the very real encounter of public administration with the forces of policy innovation. The information relationships between administrators and the nonprofit information network cross sectors, professions, disciplines, and jurisdictions.

The information that is diffused to public administrators via the national information network is organized on the basis of a typology of information positions. These information positions flow from various views about solving public problems and reflect the ideological and mission orientation of each organization. The information position of an organization reflects the degree to which an idea is aligned with the ideology and mission of the organization and whether that idea represents an opportunity for action. Essentially, the concept of an information position reflects the extent to which an organization embraces a policy innovation and is committed to its success. The conceptual typology of information positions and a national nonprofit information network is diagrammed in figure 1.2. In the typology, nonprofits operate primarily as champions, challengers, supporters, or bystanders with respect to particular initiatives for policy change.

Champions

Champion organizations are highly engaged in and highly supportive of a particular policy solution. For champion organizations, the organizational mission is bound up with an idea or group of ideas about policy reform. Champions are catalysts for change. Champions provide sustained motivation and energy for policy change over time, as well as a strong measure of consistency and continuity in a particular policy direction. In an information network, champions generate information to promote change toward their preferred solutions. Champion organizations provide a rich set of information tools and decision processes. Champions design opportunities to engage with public administrators to promote their ideas for change. Champions provide vehicles for collaboration and synthesis between nonprofit groups and government and between different levels and branches of

Figure 1.2   The Information Position Typology

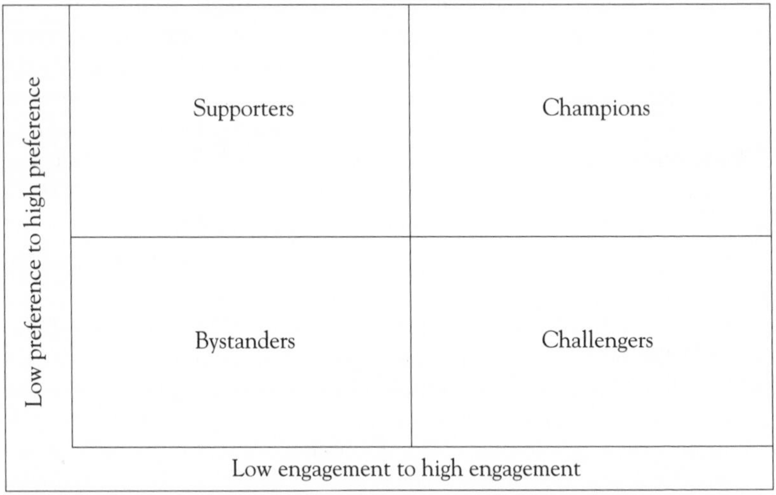

government. Champions also design information tools and institutions that facilitate information exchange and promote the adoption and implementation of their preferred ideas. Within the information network, other nonprofits support and challenge this collaboration and synthesis in different ways.

Supporters

Supporter organizations engage administrators on the basis of ideas that further their organizational missions. Supporters foster the implementation and institutionalization of champion ideas, but in ways that are directed at furthering the various missions of supporters. A new policy idea may provide an opportunity for a supporter organization to provide its core services with a fresh perspective. An organization devoted to research, technical assistance, or education, for example, can adopt an idea for policy change as a strategy for providing new services to its members or the public. Supporters might link their research projects, for example, to a new policy idea; organizations that take a supporter position may also link to this new idea by providing educational programs for their members or technical assistance to government offices. A new policy idea provides an opportunity for supporters to advance their own missions by aligning their work with the idea. Champions and supporters can reinforce an idea for policy reform through a cross-fertilization of ideas. From supporters, administrators can gain information that links a policy innovation to existing programs or practices. This kind of information can help administrators see how, or why, adopting a particular innovation would be beneficial.

Challengers

Challenger organizations are equally involved alongside champions in addressing questions of policy reform. Challengers, however, do not necessarily define policy problems in the same way, or support the same solutions as do champions. In fact, challengers may define a particular policy problem quite differently from other organizations in the information network. Challengers may actively advocate against an innovation, or they may work to draw distinctions between their approach and the innovative idea favored by champions. In some way challengers view the innovation as an impediment to their organizational mission. Challengers are not simply obstructionist groups; the challenger information position challenges champions to address specific critiques and clarify the value of the innovation relative to other options. Challenger information keeps champions and supporters honest about the need for policy change and the merits of particular policy solutions.

Bystanders

At the opposite end of the interest spectrum, bystander organizations do not devote significant effort to promote or defeat a particular policy initiative and do not express particular preferences about policy change. For bystanders the innovation is simply not part of the mission of the organization. However, bystanders are experts in the field. Bystanders are well informed about proposals for change and how those proposals fit into the broader policy environment. Bystanders do not perceive any present need or interest in acting in any particular way about an innovation. These organizations may determine that the innovation does not pose a threat or does not offer an advantage to their mission. Bystanders can become interested in the future as events change and may shift their orientation toward a different information position.

How Information Mattered in Innovation

The information relationships between national nonprofit organizations and public administrators that were studied in researching this volume showcased the relative strengths of the nonprofit sector. A collection of national organizations served as an incubator for policy strategies that addressed drug use and related criminal activity. A rich mix of ideas percolated throughout the unique missions of these organizations, which ran the gamut from developing administrative practices for state courts to decriminalizing some forms of drug use. Organizations shared these ideas and strategies with state and local administrators as states and localities looked for solutions to rising rates of incarceration and rising costs of criminal justice administration. From that environment of competing ideas and values, the drug court experiment emerged to address a specific set of problems within the criminal offender population.

The information network contributed to the development of public-sector capacity by providing information relationships, tools, and processes that fostered implementation and institutionalization. The information network provided continuity and stability as well as an architecture for synchronizing interests and actions within local communities and within states. The information environment created by these national organizations helped diffuse the drug court experiment across local courts. The National Association of Drug Court Professionals (NADCP) emerged to champion the idea early in the history of the program. As the champion, the NADCP developed several tools that provided stability and consistency for government administrators who became interested in drug courts as federal grants to local programs came online. One of these was the development and dissemination of forms of information that synthesized the experiences of multiple programs and diverse environments, such as best practices, model programs, and evaluative information. These forms of synthesized information became a type of interpretive information software for public administrators. Here, these forms of information were particularly valuable to public administrators as they made decisions about how to develop a drug court program in their local court jurisdictions. Conceptually, the use of synthesized information supported the findings of other studies on information exchange (e.g., Mossberger and Hale 2002).

The NADCP also facilitated diffusion of the drug court concept through the development of a collaborative, professionalized field of public service. This organization established and promoted the idea of a cross-professional drug court team that collaborated to make decisions about drug court participants. It also initiated a process of professionalization for drug court teams and drug court administrators that were typically responsible for coordinating team activities. And it conducted training programs and held conferences to solidify the drug court professional as a distinct position in public administration. Today the "drug court professional" is an established occupation alongside other positions in court administrative offices and criminal justice programs across the country.

The NADCP also provided continuity for the diffusion of the drug court concept by publishing a set of guiding principles for the design and operation of drug courts. These principles became a policy template under which local programs evolved. The principles provided a skeletal outline of drug court program concepts, but they took on real meaning only through interpretation by various collaborations of stakeholders. The NADCP's guiding principles and the multidisciplinary drug court team concept provided a framework for building new collaborations within state court administrations and state criminal justice policy offices to tackle the development of standards for drug court operation within states and of methods for measuring successful performance.

During the twenty years that drug courts have been operating, other organizations in the information network moved in and out of supporting roles as drug court activity raised questions that were more germane to their particular missions. For example, the National Center for State Courts was extensively involved in consultations with state judicial administrators about questions of court organization and administration that encompassed the drug court program. Other organizations, such as the Vera Institute of Justice, conducted extensive research studies on criminal justice reform and sentencing practices across the country and in particular states, and also published their findings. The Justice Policy Institute and the Sentencing Project published numerous research studies on the racial implications of various sentencing strategies and other criminal justice practices in play in the states. Other organizations in the information network challenged the assumptions of the drug court movement. The Drug Policy Alliance and the Open Society Institute, for example, challenged the criminalization of certain drug offenses. Both organizations have been active in supporting state ballot initiatives to decriminalize low levels of drug possession and other related aspects of drug use. Across the national information network, other nonprofit organizations also assumed roles as supporters and challengers; the efforts of all these groups combined to contribute to the development of the drug court idea, its diffusion, its implementation, and its institutionalization across state and local governments.

The sustained commitment of the NADCP to the drug court mission was an important factor in the diffusion and implementation of drug court programs at the local level and in state government during a period of twenty years. The NADCP initiative illustrated one type of relationship between nonprofit organizations and government that combined innovation, flexibility, collaboration, and local involvement with general government grant support. The broad parameters of this relationship suggest a model that may be useful in other policy initiatives, and particularly in initiatives that seek to blend local support with accountability and to bring policy innovations to scale. Sustained motivation has long been observed to be a critical element of implementation, but it is not easily found within government agencies or in the chains of organizations that ultimately become involved in implementation (e.g., Pressman and Wildavsky 1984). In addition, the process of synthesis that was fostered by the NADCP's guiding principles supported the development of new relationships and administrative capacity. The principles took on real meaning only through the interpretations and practices of local drug courts. Similarly, state institutionalization efforts were tied to the principles and came to life only through a combination of state and local efforts.

The National Center for State Courts played a similar role in fostering the institutionalization of the drug court concept through its commitment to excellence in state court administration. The tools and supports developed by the NADCP and the information generated by other organizations made a positive difference in the spread of drug courts across the country and in the institutionalization of the concept within state criminal justice systems. Moreover, in states that were more extensively involved with this information network, criminal justice policy outcomes seem to have improved, at least according to large-scale measures.

The national nonprofit information network fostered synergy across state and local programs and provided a sustained source of information and relationships that enhanced implementation and aligned states with better outcomes. The information relationships between nonprofit organizations and public administrators illustrated that the national nonprofit information network has much to offer in the form of strategies and tools that government organizations can leverage to build capacity to accomplish public goals. Here, nonprofits helped government agencies build capacity by building new relationships and new collaborations, and by supporting those new information exchanges with new skills and new tools that institutionalized the innovation. These skills and tools were useful in the immediate situations facing public administrators. They were also portable, and thus they have been used to bring resources to bear on other problems and have become a springboard for additional collaboration.

Notes

1. See Agranoff (2007) for a detailed review of the evolution of the study of networks in American public administration.

2. Detailed discussions of wicked problems are presented by Harmon and Mayer (1986) and Rittel and Webber (1973).

From Information to Innovation

THE DRUG COURT EXPERIENCE

Twenty years ago, the idea of a therapeutic judicial process for non-violent drug offenders was just that—an idea. Today the drug court idea has grown to encompass more than two thousand drug court programs in cities and counties across the country. From the first program in 1989 to the present day, the diffusion and institutionalization of drug courts has come about through a series of interactions between state and local administrators and an extensive information network of national nonprofit organizations. In all fifty states, public administrators designed and implemented drug court programs by using information relationships, tools, and processes that were developed in and nurtured by the intersectoral policy information network (box 2.1).

In this chapter I trace the drug court innovation as a policy innovation that has been shaped and influenced by an information network and its interactions with public administrators. This information environment has long been a rich environment of competing values, perspectives, and ideas about incarceration, drugs, and crime. Throughout this policy environment, public administrators across the country have had access to multiple sources of information and points of view that have shaped their interest in adopting and supporting new programs. These different perspectives have provided a context for understanding the wide range of ideas and sources of information that have been available to public administrators and the emergence of drug courts as a public policy innovation.

The chapter first introduces the drug court concept in the context of the information environment that surrounds drug use and criminal justice policy. Next, the information environment that surrounds this innovation is explored in terms of several broad themes that have been intertwined in the policy debate about criminal punishment and drugs during the past

BOX 2.1

Judge James Norwood

Judge James Norwood took his seat on the express train, en route to a national conference sponsored by the National Center for State Courts. Judge Norwood had recently been named by his state's Chief Justice to head a statewide judicial task force charged with making recommendations about drug offenders in the state's criminal justice system. Judge Norwood had seen some dramatic shifts in his Midwestern county courtroom during his three decades on the bench. State sentencing standards became tougher and defendants were sentenced for longer periods of time. The alternatives to incarceration that the state legislature approved several years back had done little to stop the flow of drug offenders through his court docket. A ballot initiative backed by national groups was slated to come before the voters in the November general election to decriminalize marijuana. Prison crowding had some in the legislature talking about treatment or reduced sentences for nonviolent drug crimes.

Judge Norwood turned his attention to the conference brochure. The conference panel on judicial administration alternatives for drug offenders had sparked his interest in the conference. The four panelists represented widely divergent views; it was sure to be an interesting presentation. One of the panelists represented a new national organization called the National Association of Drug Court Professionals. Judge Norwood had heard of this group from some of his colleagues in other states. Another panelist represented the Drug Policy Alliance. This national group was one of the sponsors of the upcoming ballot initiative to legalize marijuana; Judge Norwood had read about their work on similar initiatives in other states. Judge Norwood recognized the third speaker as a judge whom he had met at a judicial education session conducted by the National Judicial Conference; this judge was a leader in designing judicial education to meet emerging needs in judicial administration. The fourth speaker on the panel was from the Vera Institute of Justice; Judge Norwood knew that Vera was actively involved in research about state criminal justice programs. Judge Norwood was keenly interested in learning more about how he might lead his colleagues in sorting out a new approach; he hoped that while he was at the conference he would learn more about what other jurisdictions were doing.

several decades, and the national nonprofit organizations that have formed in response to those themes. These themes include an increase in criminalization, a rise in the use of alternatives to incarceration, and shifting public opinion in favor of drug treatment and rehabilitation as criminal justice policy goals. The national information network is examined through the relative perspectives of the national nonprofit organizations that have generated and shared information with public administrators and with each other across the information network. The missions and general purposes of these organizations provide the basis for the information they generate and the positions they assume within the information network as relative champions, supporters, challengers, or bystanders regarding the drug court concept.

The Drug Court Concept: Innovation from Competing Ideas and Perspectives

The Bureau of Justice Assistance of the U.S. Department of Justice defines the drug court initiative as "a specially designed court calendar or docket, the purposes of which are to achieve a reduction in recidivism and substance abuse among nonviolent substance abusing offenders and to increase the likelihood of successful habilitation through early, continuous and intense judicially supervised treatment, mandatory periodic drug testing, community supervision, and use of appropriate sanctions and other habilitation services" (Bureau of Justice Assistance 2005, 3).

The drug court concept is an innovation in the classic sense of the Rogers (1995) definition: that is, an idea or practice that is considered to be new by those who adopt it. More important, drug courts also deliver a substantive shift in policy that is more than a symbolic name change. The substantive aspects of the innovation include a new theoretical philosophy or creed, an interdisciplinary approach, and a nonadversarial process that changed the orientation of judges and other professionals participating in the program.

The drug court concept emerged from ideas that spread throughout an information network of competing values, policies, and public opinion about incarceration, drugs, and crime that has been evolving for decades. The evolution of these competing perspectives is important for at least two reasons. The first is that the drug court initiative evolved by blending various elements of these distinctly different perspectives to achieve its unique approach among alternatives to jail or prison. The second is that the organizations engaged in this information environment brought distinctly different values and perspectives to the mix. These values and perspectives in turn shaped the production of information that was disseminated to public administrators and that continues to influence administrative efforts in the fifty states today.

A key factor in the evolution of the drug court concept was the pressure experienced by local courts from crowded facilities and the revolving door of high recidivism (Belenko 1999b; Nolan 2001). The influence of drug use (and abuse) on the criminal justice system has been both substantial and persistent since the 1980s; various estimates suggest that 50 percent of the prison and jail population is either drug abusing or drug dependent (Bhati, Roman, and Chalfin 2008; Boyum and Kleiman 2002; Karberg and James 2005; Mumola and Karberg 2006). Since the late 1970s, states have substantially increased the population under supervision in the criminal justice system through "tough-on-crime" policies, including mandatory sentencing, three-strikes laws, and truth-in-sentencing policies. Criminal penalties for behavior associated with crack cocaine use were particularly harsh and inflexible. State mandatory sentencing schemes were applied most commonly to drug offenses, which tended to increase both the number of drug offenders who were sentenced and the length of their sentences. The pressure created by these policies was substantial. State prison populations exploded. African Americans in particular were arrested for drug possession and sentenced for drug-related offenses at a rate disproportionate to that of whites (King and Mauer 2002; Mauer 1999; Wilson 2002). By 2008 more than one in every hundred adults was confined in an American jail or prison, including one in thirty-one men between the ages of twenty and thirty-four years; at the same time, among men of age twenty to thirty-four, approximately one in ten African American men were in jail, prison, or otherwise under criminal justice supervision (Pew Center on the States 2008, 2009).

In the states traditional criminal justice approaches were unable to accommodate a substantial drug treatment component or to curb drug addiction among offenders (Hennessey 2001; Nolan 2002). The systemic pressures created by these policies presented opportunities to experiment with new approaches to drug treatment. Consequently, alternatives to incarceration gained popularity as more effective, more efficient, or more humane options (DiMascio et al. 1997; Marion 2002; Nolan 2001; Tonry 1998; Turner and Petersilia 1996). Broadly, alternatives to incarceration are different forms of sanction or punishment along a graduated continuum between traditional prison and traditional probation. Typical alternatives include reporting centers, halfway houses and other housing arrangements, various levels of human or electronic supervision, and monitoring for drug and/or alcohol use (Leone, McCarthy, and McCarthy 2007; Tonry 1998).

Alongside the range of alternatives to incarceration, civil commitment emerged as a strategy for imposing drug treatment through the criminal justice process. Civil commitment confined offenders for treatment itself and for noncompliance with court-imposed treatment requirements. Over time, coercive treatment gained attention as a policy strategy. Civil commitment programs related to drug addiction were limited in scope, and scholars disagree about the ultimate efficacy of early programs. However, civil commitment programs that enforced treatment through law enforcement professionals and that used incarceration as a sanction for relapses were more successful than those with less severe sanctions and those that relied on social workers for supervision (Nolan 2001; Wilson 1983, 1990). The use of these approaches has been supported by shifts in public opinion that favor treatment and rehabilitation for drug offenders rather than incarceration or other forms of punishment alone (Hart and Associates 2002; Hartney and Marchionna 2009; Krisberg and Marchionna 2006).

The national drug court movement began modestly through a handful of local programs established by local judges in response to the strain of drug-related caseloads on the criminal justice system. Although some local jurisdictions had adopted alternative programs to address increasing caseloads and to incorporate treatment into case administration, the net effect of alternatives did not reduce the growth of either the prison population or judicial caseloads (Goldkamp 1999; Nolan 2002; Terry 1999). Judges were interested in reducing the sheer size of their judicial dockets, but they were also seeking new policy solutions that could be used to successfully intervene in the strong relationship between drug use and crime and the recidivism of drug-involved offenders.

The Dade County (Miami) drug court was established in 1989 as the first in the country. Federal grant support under the Violent Crime Control and Law Enforcement Act of 1994 (PL 103–322) encouraged the expansion of the drug court concept through competitive federal grants to local jurisdictions. Support came primarily from grants through the Drug Court Program Office (DCPO) of the U.S. Department of Justice for planning, implementing, and enhancing drug court operations (U.S. General Accounting Office 1997).[1] Figure 2.1 shows the total number of DCPO

Figure 2.1   Federal Grant Awards for Local Drug Courts, 1995–2003

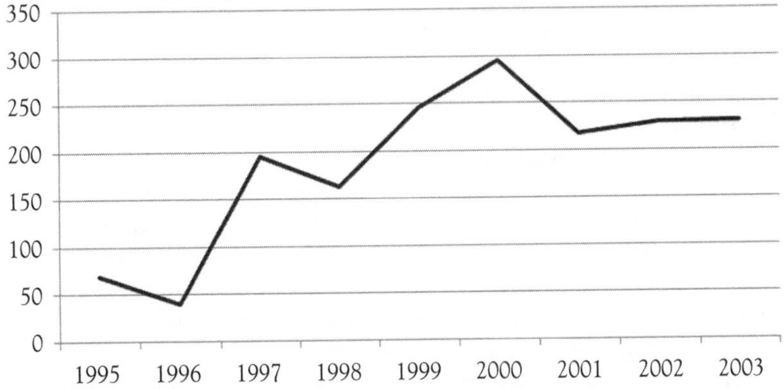

Note: Drug Court Program Office grant awards for local drug court planning, implementation, and enhancement activities, federal fiscal years 1995–2003.

Source: Compiled by the author from data from Office of Justice Programs 2003, 2004b, 2004c.

grants awarded to local programs from 1995 through 2003. One year after the DCPO grant program began, the number of operational drug courts more than doubled, and that number has steadily increased every year. By 2007 more than 2,100 drug courts were operating across all fifty states, and the number of local drug courts increased more than 30 percent from 2004 to 2008 (Huddleston, Marlowe, and Casebolt 2008).

The drug court philosophy represented an innovative theoretical approach to crime in the form of therapeutic jurisprudence (Berman and Feinblatt 2005; Hennessey 2001; Nolan 2002; Rosenthal 2002; Wexler 2004).[2] The drug court approach blends efforts to protect public safety, promote personal accountability, and provide public health services through treatment (U.S. Government Accountability Office 2005). This blended approach created innovation in the way professional public servants do their jobs. Drug courts operated through an interdisciplinary team of professionals, including law, treatment, law enforcement, and judicial administration. This "drug court team" operated together in a nonadversarial process that focused on the benefits that the team delivered to those participating in the program. To function in this nonadversarial fashion, the various members of a drug court team stepped outside their traditional professional roles. For example, the prosecutors and defense counsel working in drug courts no longer functioned as adversaries but instead worked together with treatment providers and the drug court judge to focus on health promotion, disease prevention, and behavioral changes that would benefit participant offenders (Nolan 2001; Steen 2002).

This nonadversarial, interdisciplinary team model also challenged the long-standing legal and ethical roles of judges and lawyers and their approaches to professional responsibility, effective legal representation, and advocacy. The drug court approach stretched the boundaries of the judicial function by giving drug court judges the authority to make decisions about treatment and criminal conduct that were typically the responsibility of the executive branch (Bean 2002; Boldt 1998; Nolan 2001). Some judges saw these decisions as an appropriate exercise of judicial discretion, a measure of which had been reduced in the swing to mandatory and determinant sentencing practices (Gebelein 2000) and other "tough-on-crime" policies. Others believed that, by imposing medical treatment, they were performing the executive branch function of implementing the law rather than the judicial function of interpretation (Hoffman 2000, 2002).

The Perspectives of National Nonprofit Organizations

The national information environment that surrounded the drug court movement was influenced by national nonprofit organizations with different perspectives about drug use, ranging from legalization to incarceration. Organizations such as the Sentencing Project worked for changes in sentencing practices to mediate or reverse the consequences of state sentencing and incarceration policies. Groups like the Vera Institute for Justice and the Urban Institute's Justice Policy Center conducted research to identify new policy solutions. Organizations such as the National Judicial College, the National Conference of Juvenile and Family Court Judges, and the National Legal Defender Association represented those in the traditional professions who were involved in the operation of the criminal justice system—judges, attorneys, and state court administrators. Organizations also represented members of various professional constituencies that emerged based on particular interests and functions in the criminal justice system; these included treatment professionals, probation or parole offices, and now drug court professionals.

These different orientations and professional alignments were important, given the contestable nature of information in the public policy process (Radin 2006; Stone 1997). Within and surrounding public programs, the idea of "perfect" neutral information is a myth; rather, information is always value laden, and always intertwined with ideologies and interests (Radin 2006; Weiss 1983). Information has both "cognitive and normative content" and is selected to promote or diffuse some ideas and not others (Weiss 2002, 219). Information always has a point of view—it is never benign; consequently, the values and ideas that shape organizations will also shape the information they provide.

Organizations can be expected to develop and distribute information that will promote their mission. Within the information environment surrounding drug use and crime, a variety of communities of expertise have evolved with different perspectives about problem definition; consequently, these organizations have very different perspectives on the appropriate elements of policy solutions and the data that will demonstrate success. Some organizations favor the status quo. Other groups favor some form of incremental reform that builds on current practices to improve program outcomes and operating efficiencies. Still others favor more radical change through fundamental shifts in policy such as decriminalization. Law enforcement professionals involved with specific aspects of criminal justice such as probation or parole favor the policy strategies associated with their professions. Treatment professionals favor approaches that recognize drug problems as medical conditions. Similarly, judges, prosecutors, and defense counsel respond to the professional and ethical considerations of the legal profession.

Collecting Data about a National Information Network Related to Drug Courts

To gain insight into the views and values of nonprofit organizations on the issues pertaining to the development and expansion of drug court programs and the extent to which these views and values have informed state administrators, data were collected about national nonprofit organizations that were likely to be involved with issues of criminal justice reform, alternatives to incarceration, and drug policy. Data were collected through semistructured interviews and a review of public documents. Semistructured interviews were conducted with key informants (Bernard 2000) in national nonprofit organizations who identified themselves as highly familiar with and/or responsible for the information disseminated by their organizations to state administrators and similar officials responsible for public policy.[3]

An initial group of organizations was selected purposively (Schutt 1999, 130–31) as likely to be knowledgeable about alternatives to incarceration, reform initiatives related to drug policy, and other contemporary proposals for criminal justice reform related to drug use. The first interviews were conducted with representatives of the American Correctional Association, the National Association of Drug Court Professionals, the National Association of State Sentencing Commissions, and the Drug Policy Alliance. These organizations were chosen to represent diverse viewpoints about drugs and crime and to provide a diverse starting point for identifying other groups through interviews using a snowball technique (Rubin and Rubin 1995; Schutt 1999). The American Correctional Association was founded in 1870 as the National Prison Association and is the oldest organization devoted to corrections methods. Its work includes the accreditation of a wide range of criminal justice approaches, including prisons, jails, and other programs. The National Association of State Sentencing Commissions was formed in 1984 along with the advent of the U.S. Sentencing Commission; these groups represent state sentencing commissions in the national conversation about sentencing practices. The National Association of Drug Court Professionals was formed in 1994 by members of the first twelve drug courts; its mission is to promote and professionalize the drug court concept across the country. Also established in 1994, the Drug Policy Alliance promotes alternatives to the "drug war" that reflect the rights of individuals to control their own bodies. Interviews continued with new informants until the interviews did not identify additional organizations and became substantially repetitive in terms of information (Rubin and Rubin 1995, 72–73; Schutt 1999, 131).

Key informants were asked a series of open-ended questions to identify national nonprofit organizations involved in alternatives to incarceration generally—including drug courts, community-based corrections programs, and other reforms—and to identify the types of information that they used to communicate with state administrators on these issues. Interview questions were based on case study research on professional associations that disseminate information to state administrators that promotes the use of research ideas and the use by state administrators of federal statistical information (Yin and Andranovich 1986, 1987). Interview data were supplemented with public data about basic organizational missions and resources collected from organizational websites and public information sources. As the result of an analysis based on pattern matching, a core group of nineteen organizations emerged to constitute an ongoing information network with the mission, resources, and intention to communicate with state policymakers about alternatives to incarceration and policy alternatives for criminal drug use.

Data about the participation of state policy administrators in the national nonprofit information network were collected by survey. Administrators from each of the fifty states identified national nonprofit organizations that were sources of information about drug courts, and provided data about the types of information that they sought from these organizations and how that information was used. The survey contained a list of core organizations identified by key informants; respondents were also asked to identify additional nonprofit organizations that were sources of information about drug courts. The survey also collected data about the types of information that administrators found most useful, and the frequency with which they sought information. Finally, the survey collected data about the state-level activities that states have taken to support drug court operations, including establishing various types of legislation, state conferences, advisory councils, standards, and other measures. All respondents reported active engagement in drug court operations at the state level and reported significant responsibility for state-level implementation efforts, including policy leadership and administrative support. The complete interview questions, survey questions, and additional details about the methodology are reproduced and explained in the appendix.

A Wealth of Information

The information network that administrators identified was a fluid collection of diverse national organizations that worked in different ways and with different perspectives about alternatives to incarceration and criminal justice reform. Organizations had varying perspectives about drug court policy within the larger framework of reform strategies to address the intersection of drug use and crime. The national nonprofit organizations that participated in this broader conversation with administrators are listed in table 2.1, which also summarizes the mission of each group and the year in which the group was established.[4]

The information network reflected major trends in public opinion and major shifts in public policy about drugs and crime that evolved over time. Until the 1960s the nonprofit organizations that dealt with these questions

Table 2.1 Descriptions and Missions of Nonprofit Organizations in the National Information Network

Name	Year Founded	Organizational Description and Mission Information
American Correctional Association	1870	Professional organization for individuals and groups, both public and private that share a common goal of improving the justice system. Oldest association specifically for correctional system practitioners; originally the National Prison Association.
National Legal Aid and Defender Association	1911	Represents legal aid and defender programs as well as individual advocates, advocates for attorneys, and other equal justice professionals engaged with low-income clients and their families and communities. Began as National Alliance of Legal Aid Societies.
National Council of Juvenile and Family Court Judges	1937	Founded by a group of judges dedicated to improving the effectiveness of the nation's juvenile courts. Mission is "to improve courts and systems practice and raise awareness of the core issues that touch the lives of many of our nation's children and families." Members include judges, referees, commissioners, masters, and other juvenile and family law professionals.
Vera Institute of Justice	1961	Mission is "making justice systems fairer and more effective through research and innovation." Conducts research, demonstration projects, and reform initiatives in partnership with local, state, or national officials. Independent, nonpartisan, nonprofit center for justice policy and practice.
National Judicial College	1963	Professional judicial education. Mission is to provide "leadership in achieving justice through quality judicial education and collegial dialogue."
International Community Corrections Association	1964	International membership organization that acts as the representative voice for residential and other community corrections programs. Began as the International Halfway House Association in 1964 and has also been known as the International Association of Residential and Community Alternatives.
National Center for State Courts	1971	Mission is "to improve the administration of justice through leadership and service to state courts, and courts around the world." Purposes include creation and dissemination of new knowledge about judicial administration, applying knowledge to help courts solve problems and meet future needs, and supporting the projects and policies of state courts and state court associations.

National Association of State Alcohol and Drug Abuse Directors	1971	Purpose is "to foster and support the development of effective alcohol and other drug abuse prevention and treatment programs throughout every State." Members include state drug agency and alcoholism agency directors.
American Probation and Parole Association	1975	International association of members involved with probation, parole, and community-based corrections; constituents include all levels and branches of government. Mission is "to serve, challenge, and empower our members and constituents by educating, communicating and training; advocating and influencing; acting as a resource and conduit for information, ideas and support; developing standards and models; and collaborating with other disciplines."
National Center for Institutions and Alternatives	1977	Mission is to "help create a society in which all persons who come into contact with human service or correctional systems are provided with the care necessary to live their lives to the best of their abilities." Operates facilities and provides sentencing advocacy, capital case mitigation services, parole release advocacy; works with public defenders, probation officers, and other court staff.
National Association of Probation Executives	1981	Professional organization representing the chief executive officers of local, county, and state probation agencies. Dedicated to "enhancing the professionalism and effectiveness in the field of probation by creating a national network for probation executives, bringing about positive change in the field, and making available a pool of experts in probation management, program development, training, and research."
American Prosecutor's Research Institute	1984	Arm of the National District Attorneys Association. National interdisciplinary resource center for research and development, technical assistance, training and publications for the prosecutorial profession. Mission is "to provide state and local prosecutors knowledge, skills, and support to ensure that justice is done and the public safety rights of all persons are safeguarded."
National Association of State Sentencing Commissions	1984	Affiliated with the United States Sentencing Commission, which is an independent agency in the judicial branch of government. Mission is "to facilitate the exchange and sharing of information, ideas, data, expertise, and experiences and to educate on issues related to sentencing policies, sentencing guidelines, and sentencing commissions."

Table 2.1 Descriptions and Missions of Nonprofit Organizations in the National Information Network (Continued)

Name	Year Founded	Organizational Description and Mission Information
Sentencing Project	1986	Works for fair and effective criminal justice system by promoting reforms in sentencing law and practice and alternatives to incarceration. Founded to provide defense lawyers with sentencing advocacy training and to reduce the reliance on incarceration. The Sentencing Project is dedicated to changing the way Americans think about crime and punishment.
Open Society Institute	1993	Mission is to "build vibrant and tolerant democracies whose governments are accountable to their citizens." Works to "shape public policies that assure greater fairness in political, legal, and economic systems and safeguard fundamental rights." Affiliated with Soros Foundation Network; challenges status quo drug policy.
Drug Policy Alliance	1994	Mission is to "advance those policies and attitudes that best reduce the harms of both drug misuse and drug prohibition, and to promote the sovereignty of individuals over their minds and bodies." Promotes alternatives to "drug war" that "no longer arrest, incarcerate, disenfranchise and otherwise harm millions of nonviolent people." Includes consideration of the "disproportionate impact of the drug war on people of color." A part of the Drug Policy Alliance Network; advocates for legalization of some forms of drug use.
Justice Policy Center	1994	Conducts nonpartisan research on crime, justice, and community safety. A research center of the Urban Institute; manages Federal Justice Statistics Center for the U.S. Department of Justice.
National Association of Drug Court Professionals	1994	Founded by members of the first twelve drug courts in the nation to promote, sustain, and professionalize the drug court concept. Research arm is National Drug Court Institute.
Justice Policy Institute	1997	Mission is "to promote effective solutions to social problems and to be dedicated to ending society's reliance on incarceration." Includes advocacy, research, and public education to "enhance public dialog" in support of treatment and community-based alternatives to jail and prison.

Note: This table is not an exhaustive list of national groups formed from 1870 concerned with issues related to drug use and crime.
Sources: Organization websites and organization reports filed with the Internal Revenue Service to document mission and activities.

were relatively few in number. The field was dominated by associations that represented a few major actors in the correctional system, such as the American Correctional Association, the National Legal Defender Association, and the National Council of Juvenile and Family Court Judges. New organizations formed over time to reflect the emergence of new specialties within the criminal justice system and trends toward increasing professionalization in public administration overall. The founding of the International Halfway House Association, now the International Community Corrections Association, reflected the growing institutional interest in alternatives to incarceration throughout the 1960s and 1970s. The founding of the National Center for State Courts and the National Judicial College in 1971 indicated a broad national interest in the professionalization of state court systems and judicial education.

Professional associations were founded to reflect an increasingly diverse array of specialized approaches to issues involving drugs and crime and the wide array of actors involved in addressing these issues. These organizations included the National Association of State Alcohol and Drug Abuse Directors and the American Probation and Parole Association; the National Association of Probation Executives and the American Prosecutor's Research Institute followed in the 1980s. State sentencing commissions and the Sentencing Project were formed in the mid-1980s to consider different perspectives about sentencing consistency and equity. State sentencing commissions facilitated many of the tough-on-crime policies established by the states at that time. The Sentencing Project, in contrast, focused on reducing reliance on incarceration and promoting systemic reform in that direction. In the 1990s new organizations formed to address different avenues of policy research in the field; the Justice Policy Center opened as a center of the Urban Institute. The Justice Policy Center, along with the Vera Institute of Justice and the Justice Policy Institute, generated research on state criminal justice systems. Within this web of organizations, the National Association of Drug Court Professionals carved out unique territory in 1994 as the first and only professional organization dedicated to drug courts as a specific policy initiative. Advocacy for systemic change was enhanced during the 1990s with the formation of the Drug Policy Alliance, the Open Society Institute, and the Justice Policy Institute.

The growth of the information network over time is illustrated in figure 2.2. The trend of growth in the 1960s and 1970s paralleled the general growth of the nonprofit sector during that period. The growth in the number of new nonprofit organizations during the 1990s, each with a specialized mission and constituency, suggested a growing diversity of ideas and points of view about drugs and crime and alternative policy solutions.

Figure 2.2   The Growth of the National Nonprofit Information Network

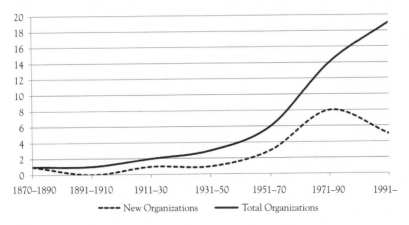

This national information network was especially capable of informing public administrators on questions about drugs and crime. The national nonprofits that constitute the information network were resource rich in comparison with the rest of the nonprofit sector. On the whole, nonprofit organizations in the information network had considerably greater financial resources than the average nonprofit organization. On the basis of annual revenue data reported on Internal Revenue Service Form 990 for 2003, all but one organization in the national information network reported annual revenue in excess of $1 million, and nearly half reported annual revenue in excess of $5 million. As a benchmark, fewer than 20 percent of all nonprofit organizations reported annual revenue of $1 million or more and fewer than 7 percent reported annual revenue of $5 million or more. Organizations in the information network generated their revenue primarily from fees charged for program services (about 60 percent) and government sources (about 25 percent); these proportions were similar to those for sources of revenue for human services nonprofit organizations overall (Boris 2006; Hodgkinson and Weitzman 1996; Steuerle and Hodgkinson 2006). Table 2.2 compares the aggregate revenue sources of the national nonprofit network with the revenue source profiles of common nonprofit classifications. Because organizations in the information network were generally wealthier than other nonprofits with similar missions, organizations in the information network appear to have had ample

Table 2.2   Revenue Sources for the National Information Network
Compared with the Nonprofit Sector

Revenue Source	National Network Revenue Share (% of total)	Revenue Share by NTEE Classification[a] (% of total)		
		Health	Human Services	Public/Societal Benefit
Government grants	25.0	2.3	24.4	16.5
Private contributions	12.0	3.3	19.1	38.4
Program services	56.0	89.3	46.4	27.7
Other	7.0	5.1	10.1	17.4
Total	100.0	100.0	100.0	100.0

Sources: National network data compiled by the author; NTEE data from *Nonprofit Almanac 1996/1997* (Hodgkinson and Weitzman 1996, 262–67).

[a] National Taxonomy of Exempt Entities; these classifications are derived from information reported by nonprofit organizations about their activities.

resources with which to develop information for use by public administrators.

The nonprofit organizations illustrated four areas of primary focus common to the sector: membership, research, education, and advocacy. It is important to note that these four areas were not functionally exclusive; nonprofit organizations typically provide some form of member services, conduct research and public education about their mission, and advocate for particular points of view in furtherance of a cause. Rather, these areas of primary focus indicate broad organizational purposes for generating information and connecting with public administrators in the information network.

About half the nonprofit organizations in the information network were primarily membership organizations. Members were generally individuals affiliated with a specific profession involved in criminal justice administration or drug treatment. Some organizations limited membership to those with specific government responsibilities. For example, members of the National Association of State Alcohol and Drug Abuse Directors were the executive officers responsible for the state-level alcohol and drug agencies in their states. In other organizations, such as the American Correctional Association, the American Probation and Parole Association, and the International Community Corrections Association, membership was open to professionals in the field as well as individuals and organizations with an interest in the mission of the organization. Table 2.3 summarizes the primary membership constituencies of the organizations in the information network that have a professional membership focus. The range of membership is quite broad, from more than twenty thousand individuals to the fifty states, which includes individuals, agencies, and private programs. Along with financial resources, membership size suggested the extensive reach of these organizations and, by extension, the reach and potential influence of the information network.

Another group of organizations in the information network focused primarily on research, technical assistance, and/or education within a profession or policy area. Some groups targeted specific state or local institutions. For example, the National Center for State Courts provided technical assistance, research, and a variety of programs and services to support state courts. The National Judicial College conducted continuing education courses and other special programming for judges. Others, such as the Justice Policy Center of the Urban Institute and the Vera Institute of Justice, were independent think tanks. Some of these organizations were affiliated with professional membership organizations. For example, the American Prosecutor's Research Institute was the research arm of the National District Attorneys Association, which is the professional membership organization for criminal prosecutors. The National Drug Court Institute was established as the research arm of the National Association of Drug Court Professionals to provide research specifically about drug court programs.

Across the organizations in the information network that existed primarily to provide research, technical assistance, and/or education, the topics spanned a broad range. Table 2.4 presents the topical orientations of the organizations in the information network that focused primarily on research, technical assistance, and/or education. The National Drug Court Institute was the only research organization devoted entirely to drug courts. But this group was not the only source of information about drug court performance. For instance, the National Center for State Courts examined drug court performance measurement systems and published the results in statewide technical assistance bulletins to assist local courts and state programs establish benchmarks and measure results (National Center for State Courts 2008). The Justice Policy Center published a large-scale analysis of drug court program effectiveness in a study that called for a significant expansion of the drug court model across the country (Bhati, Roman, and Chalfin 2008). The Vera Institute of Justice conducted extensive state-level studies of criminal justice systems and options for reform that consider the drug court approach. And the National Judicial College

Table 2.3 Network Organizations with a Professional Membership Focus

Name	Primary Constituency	No. Of Members
American Correctional Association	Corrections professionals	More than 20,000 individual members
American Probation and Parole Association	Professionals in probation, parole, and community-based corrections at all levels and branches of government	More than 3,000 individual members; 165 agencies and 9 affiliates
International Community Corrections Association	Community corrections professionals	More than 250 private agencies operating more than 1,500 residential and community alternative programs; and >1,000 individual members nationally and abroad
National Association of Drug Court Professionals[a]	Drug court and other specialty court professionals; justice system; alcohol and drug treatment, and mental health treatment professionals	Judges, prosecutors, defense lawyers, probation and parole agents, law enforcement officers, case managers, child protective services, case workers, therapists, treatment professionals, and court administrators associated with more than 3,000 drug courts and other specialty courts
National Association of Probation Executives	Chief executive officers of local, county, and state probation agencies	250 individual members; 25 organizational members
National Association of State Alcohol and Drug Abuse Directors	State agency directors of alcoholism and drug abuse agencies	Represents the single-state agencies that administer and manage public substance abuse and treatment programs
National Association of State Sentencing Commissions	State sentencing commissions; others responsible for or interested in sentencing policy	—[b]
National Council of Juvenile and Family Court Judges	Juvenile and family court judges and staff	More than 1,900 judges, referees, commissioners, masters, and other juvenile and family law professionals
National Legal Defender Association	Public defense attorneys	1,200 individuals in civil legal aid and public defender services; and 700 programs representing 14,000 public defense attorneys

[a] The National Association of Drug Court Professionals also established the National Drug Court Institute as a research arm.
[b] Membership in this organization could not be determined; individuals can become members by attending an annual conference and remain members for a year.

Table 2.4 Network Organizations with a Research, Technical Assistance, or Education Focus

Name	Purpose	Areas of Concentration
American Prosecutors Research Institute	Research and technical assistance for state and local prosecutors; research arm of National District Attorneys Association, the professional association for criminal prosecutors	Child abuse Community prosecution DNA forensics Gang response model Gun violence prosecution Homeland security Identity / white-collar crime Traffic law Violence against women
Justice Policy Center	Research center of the Urban Institute devoted to criminal justice policy	Federal Justice Statistics Resource Center Reentry and transition from jail to community Multisite drug court evaluation Public housing safety Jail sexual assault prevention Evaluations of crime policy initiatives
National Center for State Courts[a]	Court improvement organization	Information clearinghouse Research publications and library National Court Statistics Project Technical assistance publications Technical assistance services
National Judicial College	Judicial education	Continuing education for judges Master's and PhD in judicial studies National Tribal Judicial Center

Table 2.4   (Continued)

Name	Purpose	Areas of Concentration
Vera Institute of Justice	Research and resource center	Project-based research and demonstration projects in partnership with state and local governments and agencies Sentencing and corrections Cost/benefit analysis Substance abuse and mental health Court system analysis

[a] The National Center for State Courts has a formal collaborative relationship with the Conference of Chief Justices and Conference of State Court Administrators and serves as the executive secretariat for twelve other national court associations.

incorporated the drug court concept into its continuing professional education and graduate programs for judges around the country.

Finally, some organizations existed primarily to advocate for change. The thread of sentencing reform ran through all these groups and provided common ground for understanding drug courts and their role in systemic reform. Advocacy efforts included issues specifically connected to drug use, such as safe needle exchange practices, and also broader policy changes, such as the legalization of medical marijuana and decriminalization of drug use. These organizations favored alternatives to incarceration and sentencing reforms but did not favor drug courts as the best policy solution. Table 2.5 presents the organizations in the information network that were devoted primarily to advocacy for policy change. The information from these organizations provided administrators with yet another perspective on the policy options for addressing drug use and criminal activity.

It is important to note that the advocacy efforts of the majority of the nonprofit organizations in the information network were directed primarily at educating the public and government officials about their missions and their work rather than influencing legislative or executive policy through traditional lobbying efforts. All of the nonprofits in the information network were chartered as public charities, as are the majority of American nonprofits (Hodgkinson and Weitzman 1996).[5] The public charity charter signaled that the organizations demonstrated that their activities were broadly supported by the general public.[6] This classification also signaled

Table 2.5   Network Organizations with an Advocacy Focus

Name	Primary Focus	Areas of Concentration
Drug Policy Alliance	Advocacy and research for drug policy reform	Legalization of medical marijuana Dismantling the drug war Marijuana policy reform Nonprescription pharmacy syringe sales Mandatory minimum sentence reform
Justice Policy Institute	Advocacy and research in support of treatment and community-based alternatives to jail and prison	Adult corrections Drug policy Gangs Juvenile justice Public safety Racial disparity
National Center for Institutions and Alternatives[a]	Public policy research about alternatives to incarceration and technical assistance including expert services in sentencing mitigation and reform	Sentencing reform Sentencing guidelines expertise Death penalty mitigation Prison advocacy and consultation Jail suicide prevention and risk reduction
Open Society Institute[b]	Private operating and grantmaking foundation dedicated to social justice and human rights in the United States and around the world	Freedom and democracy Human rights Public health and access to care Transparency and access to information
Sentencing Project	Sentencing law and policy reform to address inequities in criminal justice system	Sentencing policy Drug policy Felony disenfranchisement Racial disparity Incarceration Collateral consequences Women in the justice system

[a] NCIA also operates adult and youth residential and clinical mental health programs.
[b] The Open Society Institute participates in numerous projects around the world through its affiliation with the Soros Foundations Network; this information is limited to U.S. programming.

that these organizations were restricted in their ability to lobby the legislative or executive branches. Thus, they advocated for their particular causes primarily through public education campaigns, member services, and the use of volunteers. These distinctions are held very dear by nonprofit organizations chartered in this way. To further separate legislative and regulatory advocacy from the work of publicizing their missions and urging the general public to support them, some organizations established separate nonprofit organizations chartered specifically to lobby legislators and other government officials.

Getting the Word Out

Across the information network, organizations used a variety of methods to make information connections with public administrators and policymakers. There was a strong collaborative tone to the information exchanges. Table 2.6 displays the various information methods used by national nonprofit organizations in the broad area of drugs and crime.

The results illustrated a rich field of opportunity for the cross-fertilization of ideas among organizations and between organizations and administrators. Ninety percent of the organizations participated jointly in sponsoring membership events or other group meetings, in forming working groups to study common questions, and in setting up the professional committees of their organizations. Advisory committees, annual conferences, seminars, and other types of training sessions were also common

Table 2.6   Information Connections in the Information Network

Method of Information Connection	Organizations Reporting (%)
Newsletters	95
Coordinated professional activities	90
Production of manuals/handbooks	90
Shared resources	84
Annual conferences	68
Surveys	63
Advisory boards	58
Seminars and training sessions	53
Certification	42
Formal exchange of personnel	21

Source: Author's interviews with key informants in national nonprofit organizations.

among a majority of the organizations. Organizations reported that these types of events provided time for meeting with the members of other organizations in the network as well as for providing information to state administrators. These events provided administrators with opportunities to meet with one another and exchange information.[7] About half the organizations developed manuals and handbooks. Each organization had an Internet presence and utilized its website as a method of communicating with state administrators. Personal contacts through group events, committee meetings, and annual conferences were more popular with the majority of organizations than less personal, more institutional procedures such as certification.

These information exchanges provided organizations with opportunities to support each others' efforts and further define their respective views. A further cross-fertilization of ideas occurred through conference programs that highlighted speakers from other groups in panel presentations and as award recipients. This cross-fertilization reinforced the expertise of various organizations and provided the opportunity to air opposing views. These connections spurred participation and interest among administrators. Members came to rely on these forums as a standard aspect of their work. Administrators commented that conferences and annual meetings provided a forum that "helps us bring new people along." New staff, or staff with new responsibilities, were exposed to a broad dose of information and opinions and have the opportunity to establish relationships that bring value to their agencies. As one administrator commented about annual conferences, "These meetings help us establish new relationships, and our programs have more continuity because of it."

The relationships between these organizations were also highly integrated with state, county, and local executive branch agencies and courts. The members of the professional membership organizations in the information network were, by and large, public officials and public administrators. Across the board, organization representatives noted the importance of maintaining regular contact with other groups through annual conferences and organization committee meetings. Face-to-face exchanges also seemed to foster trust and sustain relationships among different organizations: "It is so important to be at [organization's] national conference. . . . The information sessions are important even with all the information on the Internet. It is just as critical to be able to share issues face to face. Over the years, we have grown to know each other and shared so many ideas and problems." And: "Meetings give us a chance to catch up and discuss issues in detail. No matter how intense it gets back in the office, we know that we will have some time to share experiences and learn from each other."

Information Positions in the Information Network

Nonprofit organizations in the information network embraced the drug court concept to varying degrees and in different ways. The concept of an "information position" is an organizing principle that is used in this book to reflect the degree to which the idea of drug courts aligned with the mission of the organization and whether the idea of drug courts represented an opportunity for action. Essentially, the concept of an information position reflects the extent to which an organization embraced the drug court concept and was committed to its success. In figure 2.3 the organizations in the national information network are arranged according to their dominant information position. As this information position typology illustrates, individual organizations assumed specific positions about drug court policy. All recognized drug courts as one of a number of diversion options available to offenders and as a program that operated within a larger framework of alternatives to prison or jail. However, organizations engaged in drug court policy to a greater or lesser degree, depending on the salience of the issue to their missions and ideological orientations. Organizational perspectives also reflected the views of various professions engaged in the treatment of drug addiction, law enforcement, the criminal justice system, and judicial administration. These professional views were shaped, in turn, by shifting theoretical approaches to criminal justice problems and shifting public opinion regarding drug use and drug crime.

The diverse composition of the information network has implications for the quality and diversity of information that is disseminated by constituent organizations to state policymakers. Diversity of background and expertise could promote diversity in the viewpoints that were communicated to state policy makers and administrators. Mission diversity could also promote a mix of motivations for disseminating information. Professional associations and research groups develop and disseminate information that presents multiple points of view to inform their members. Professional associations and research groups present evidence-based information that contains critical evaluations of policy, as opposed to information from advocacy groups, which can be expected to focus primarily on the political implications for various policy choices. Research groups in

Figure 2.3 Information Positions of Organizations in the National Information Network

	Supporters	**Champions**
	American Probation and Parole Association	National Association of Drug Court Professionals
	American Prosecutors Research Institute	
	Justice Policy Center / Urban Institute	
	Justice Policy Institute	
	National Association of Probation Executives	
	National Center for State Courts	
	National Judicial College	
	National Center for Juvenile and Family Court Judges	
	Sentencing Project	
	Vera Institute of Justice	
	Bystanders	**Challengers**
	American Correctional Association	Drug Policy Alliance
	International Community Corrections Association	National Center for Institutions and Alternatives
	National Association of State Sentencing Commissions	Open Society Institute
	National Legal Aid and Defender Association	
	National Association of State Alcohol and Drug Abuse Directors	
	Low engagement to high engagement	

Low preference to high preference (vertical axis label)

particular provide critical evaluations of policy designs, effects, and outcomes. At the same time, the relationship between research and advocacy can influence the content of information disseminated by organizations and the perception of that content. Analysis and advocacy can become intertwined to the extent that information loses an objective foundation and can be viewed as the "rationalization for particular positions" (Radin 2000, 102).

Champions

Champion organizations were highly engaged in and highly supportive of drug courts as a policy solution. For champion organizations, the concept of drug courts essentially equates with the organizational mission and is the reason that the organization exists. As the seminal professional association for the field, the National Association of Drug Court Professionals (NADCP) was the catalyst for many facets of the drug court movement, and was the obvious example of a champion organization that was both highly supportive and highly engaged. Highlights of the work of the NADCP included training for drug court teams, national conferences for drug court professionals, and advocacy for the cause.

In addition to participating in this information network of national organizations, the NADCP was active in creating an infrastructure of drug court organizations that support drug courts within state and local government. The guiding principles promulgated by the NADCP in 1997 served as the basis for replicating the drug court philosophy across the country and internationally (NADCP 1997, 2004). The NADCP established a Drug Court Congress of professionals engaged in the drug court movement; the congress has two delegate representatives in each of the fifty states. In addition, the NADCP encouraged states to establish state associations of drug court professionals modeled after the national association and its guiding principles of the drug court philosophy. The state associations were established independently of the NADCP but appeared to follow these guiding principles established by the national organization. The NADCP also formed an ancillary organization, the National Drug Court Institute, as a research arm. Champion organizations can be expected to provide information that reinforces the need for action to address a specific policy problem, and that demonstrates the merits of a particular solution. The value of drug court programs was demonstrated, for example, through examples of best practices and model programs, and also by program evaluation data. Through such a research arm, the NADCP established a journal and provided numerous outlets for the presentation of research at national conferences and in other forums.

Challengers

Challenger organizations were equally involved alongside champions at the intersection of drug use and crime. Challengers, however, did not necessarily define policy problems in the same way or support the drug court concept as the appropriate solution. In fact the challengers defined the policy situation quite differently from the other organizations in the information network. The challengers favored decriminalizing certain conduct related to illegal drugs and supported treatment in lieu of conviction for a wide variety of current drug-related crimes.

The challengers saw drug courts as positive developments to the extent that drug court programs incorporate treatment. Consistent with their organizational missions, however, the challenger groups viewed drug courts as potential impediments to achieving a broader consensus on decriminalization as the most appropriate policy strategy. In this respect the Open Society Institute, the Drug Policy Alliance, and the National Center for Institutions and Alternatives were examples of challenger organizations. Each of these organizations was, and continues to be, an active advocate for various alternatives to incarceration for certain drug crimes and support for decriminalizing some drugs under some circumstances. The Open Society Institute and the Drug Policy Alliance in particular were active advocates in this regard. As challengers, they found opportunities to advance their positions by drawing distinctions between their approach and that of the champions.

In the case of drug courts, challenger organizations pushed other organizations—champions in particular—to clarify the value of drug courts relative to other options. Challengers discussed the idea of drug courts in the broader terms of the need for social justice and criminal justice reform. As one representative of a challenger organization noted, "We are not convinced that drug courts are the best way, but we *are* convinced that drug courts are not the *only* way."

Supporters

Supporter organizations were broadly in favor of the drug court program as one policy solution among other options. For supporters, the spread of drug courts provided an opportunity to provide their core services in research, technical assistance, or education with a fresh perspective. Organizations such as the American Probation and Parole Association and the National Association of Probation Executives report that their members are very supportive of the drug court concept, although the organizations themselves have taken no formal position on drug court policy. These groups formed links to drug courts through educational programs for their members such as attendance at conference panels on the topic.

Drug courts also represented an opportunity for supporters to advance their own missions by aligning their work alongside the drug court program. Supporters were directed toward other priorities by their organizational missions, but they became more involved with drug court policy as the program expanded across the states. The National Center for State Courts (NCSC) was particularly influential as a supporter as state court administrative offices became more involved. The NCSC was always a leader in assisting state court administrators with recommendations about organizational arrangements; the rise of drug court programs presented a new opportunity to provide assistance to state courts that wanted to incorporate drug courts and specialty court principles more broadly into the state court system. The NCSC provided technical assistance in building a consensus for new administrative practices and was actively involved in organizational reviews in many states.

Similarly, other supporter organizations aligned services with the drug court concept. For example, the National Judicial College designed judicial education courses about drug courts and other specialty courts, and the National Conference of Juvenile and Family Court Judges designed "micro-trainings" on drug courts for its members. The Justice Policy Center of the Urban Institute conducted evaluation studies of drug court programs, which were widely shared across the information network and with state and local administrators. The Vera Institute of Justice and the Justice Policy Institute conducted assessments of state criminal justice systems and included the drug court concept in their findings. The American Prosecutor's Research Institute of the National District Attorneys Association provided summaries of drug court programs for its members. This cross-fertilization among supporter organizations in relation to the drug court program formed the basis for other information exchanges and development of other collaborations, which in turn built capacity within public programs.

Bystanders

Bystander organizations did not devote significant effort to promote or defeat a policy initiative and did not express particular preferences about the policy. For bystanders, drug court programs were not part of the mission of the organization, although these programs were seen as part of the broader policy environment. Moreover, the organization did not perceive any present need or interest in acting in that arena. Organizations such as the American Correctional Association, the International Community Corrections Association, and the National Legal Defenders Association were bystanders. Each organization operated with a comprehensive view of the corrections system and alternatives to incarceration. Although the work of these bystander organizations encompassed alternatives to incarceration broadly defined, none were active advocates for drug courts per se. Bystanders were highly informed about drug court programs but relatively detached from them. As one representative of a bystander organization noted, "This is their [the NADCP's] territory; we understand what drug courts do, and we don't necessarily oppose them, but we don't develop information about them. We rely on the NADCP; that's their thing."

Information Positions and Shifting Interests

Organizations were well aware of their information positions and how they were different from, or similar to, the information positions of other organizations in the information network. Representatives from all organizations reported that they tracked information from organizations across the network and were aware of the approaches taken by other organizations. Generally, organizations in the information network observed that drug courts were related to their current missions but were also sufficiently distinct to warrant a separate focus. Many respondents noted some level of "friendly but serious competition" among organizations in the network, in terms of gaining recognition for a particular initiative or position on policy. All organizations in the information network consistently recognized the central leadership position of the NADCP. Across the network, organization representatives indicated that it was common for a single organization to take the lead on a particular issue or policy question, and for others in the network to rely on that organization for the most current information about that issue.

It bears repeating that information positions were not static or fixed; over time, organizations changed roles and moved among categories in the typology. In the early 1990s, when only a handful of drug courts had been established and the NADCP was formed, most if not all the organizations in the network were best considered bystanders. Over time, as the drug court concept permeated state court operations, other organizations began to incorporate the drug court philosophy into their own work. For example, the National Center for Juvenile and Family Court Judges and the National Judicial College developed courses of study that educated their members about the differences in philosophy and practice that are involved in choosing to operate a drug court. Organizations such as the Vera Institute of Justice became involved with drug courts and their relationship with other state criminal justice issues as they conducted statewide research projects in states like Alabama. For professional membership groups such as the American Probation and Parole Association, the National Association of Probation Executives, and the National Association of Drug and Alcohol Abuse Counselors, drug courts represented one of many competing possible placements for offenders outside traditional incarceration.

Supporter organizations looked more like champions as they conducted research or provided technical services that address drug court issues. As drug courts diffused broadly across many local jurisdictions, state court offices became involved as local courts looked for support. As drug courts became more popular, those states that elected to establish state drug court administration within the judiciary looked to the NCSC for guidance. The NCSC provided assistance to many states in incorporating drug courts into their state criminal court portfolios. One example of this assistance was the tool kit for problem-solving courts developed by the NCSC (Casey, Rottman, and Bromage 2007). The tool kit provided a "blueprint for using the problem-solving approach" as a case management strategy for offenders that continue to have contact with the criminal justice system. State offices in many states found the NCSC tool kit to be useful; it included assessment questions for courts considering this approach and outlined steps to take in implementing a drug court or other similar problem-solving court programs, such as a mental health court or a community court.

The NCSC also provided technical assistance in helping states develop statewide plans for drug courts and in conducting organizational reviews of state court systems and state administrative offices of the courts (AOCs). In Alabama, for example, the NCSC conducted an organizational review of the Alabama AOC, which, among its many other functions, administers the drug court program through its court referral officers. The Alabama AOC considered the recommendations of the NCSC as the state moved forward to expand the drug court program across the state.

Several states worked extensively with the NCSC to facilitate the process of customizing the NADCP's guiding principles by developing state-specific benchmarks and data elements that are central to their statewide programs. States called upon the NCSC to broker collaborative decisions among stakeholder groups. Within state court systems, the NCSC was instrumental in providing guidance in organizational arrangements, and professional judicial associations have many members who are drug court judges. Well-known and well-established supporter organizations provided credibility and stability during the diffusion process, helping the drug court idea move from a relatively radical notion to a more mainstream aspect of criminal justice administration.

The information network of national nonprofit organizations surrounding the drug court concept generated a rich information environment for state and local administrators. The information positions of organizations in the network indicated that public administrators had access to a robust range of competing opinions and policy perspectives about drugs and crime. Champions provided constant energy and commitment to a particular policy approach. Here, the NADCP provided unflagging support for the drug court movement. At the other end of the spectrum, challengers kept the champions "honest" about their programs. The Drug Policy Alliance, Open Society Institute, and other similar organizations continued to advocate for alternatives to criminal penalties for drug use and challenged the NADCP to demonstrate the successes of the drug court program. Supporter organizations provided assistance to champions but could not over-reach or stray from their central missions without losing credibility and support from their core constituencies. Supporters like the National Center for State Courts became engaged when the drug court concept became a matter of organizational concern for state court systems. Bystanders mobilized to provide assistance when their interests were implicated, or even to become challengers if their missions were threatened. For public administrators, this competition suggested a rich information environment that allowed them to examine competing facts and arguments across a range of policy options.

Conclusion

This chapter has focused on the national nonprofit information network that surrounded the drug court innovation from its inception as a few local programs through its growth into a national policy movement. Within a rich environment of ideas and values, the missions of these organizations reflected an ongoing ideological debate about drug use and criminal punishment in the criminal justice system. The perspectives of these organizations evolved over time from different perspectives about how to define the problems of drug use and how to address those problems within the criminal justice system. Organizations had different levels of affinity for the drug court concept and engaged with the concept in different ways, as reflected by the various missions and information positions of each organization. During the past two decades, the information positions of organizations as champions, challengers, bystanders, and supporters have shaped the diffusion of drug courts across the country. The concept of an information position provides a framework for organizing the information and activities of the national nonprofit organizations in the information network; this framework suggests interaction among organizations as well as multiple information flows between the information network and public administrators (box 2.2).

BOX 2.2

At the Conference of the
National Center for State Courts

At the National Center for State Courts conference, Judge Norwood tapped into a rich environment of information about criminal justice policy surrounding drugs and crime. In his informal discussions around lunch and dinner, he learned that many communities were struggling to find something new. The panel discussion exceeded his expectations and illustrated a range of views about the new idea known as drug courts. He heard about the drug court concept from many sources, from professionals that he knew and respected, and from national research organizations and professional groups that served judges and the court community.

Judge Norwood's experience illustrates the way that organizations in the information network interact with one another, with their members and with other groups around a new policy idea. Supporter organizations in the national information network took the opportunity to advance their own organizational missions by generating new information about the innovative concept of drug courts. The National Center for State Courts took an active role in presenting information about drug court programs by showcasing the concept at their conference. This information included presentations from the representatives of the champion group National Association of Drug Court Professionals and the challenger group Drug Policy Alliance. The National Judicial Conference would become a supporter organization and go on to develop judicial education programs about the drug court concept. The memberships of many of the organizations in the information network overlap and reinforce one another; this overlap provides legitimacy to new ideas as they are shared. The competing missions of these national organizations also generate a rich mix of ideas that members and participants take back to their communities.

Following the conference, Judge Norwood was ready to assemble a packet of materials to take to his colleagues at his first task force meeting. He had an outline of the drug court idea. He had a list of key objections to the approach, including concerns raised by other judges and national organizations. He had examples of the positions of many other national organizations about the revolving door between drug use and crime. These organizations were well known to the judges in his state, which would help him convey a national picture of the issue as well as how his Midwestern state could benefit from these new ideas.

Notes

1. The DCPO was subsumed into the U.S. Department of Justice's Bureau of Justice Assistance under U.S. attorney general John Ashcroft in 2002.

2. Therapeutic jurisprudence is defined as the "study of the extent to which substantive rules, legal procedures, and the roles of lawyers and judges produce therapeutic or anti-therapeutic consequences in the legal process" (Hora, Schma, and Rosenthal 1999).

3. Interviews with key informants were conducted from March 2004 through July 2004.

4. Several organizations were contacted as key informants but were not included in the information network for one or more of the following reasons: the mission and purpose of the group did not intersect with the drug court program in any way; the group had insufficient resources to exchange information with public administrators in any regular or structured way; or the primary purpose of the organization did not include contact with state or local officials. These organizations include Families against Mandatory Minimums, Family and Corrections Network, the Fortune Society, the National Association of Alcoholism and Drug Abuse Counselors, the National Association of Blacks in Criminal Justice, and National CURE (Citizens United for the Rehabilitation of Errants).

5. Public charities are defined under Internal Revenue Code Section 501(c)(3) (Hodgkinson and Weitzman 1996, 25).

6. Requirements for public support are defined in Internal Revenue Code Section 509; essentially, public support exists if a significant portion of the revenue of the organization flows from private donations and/or government grants.

7. This research did not systematically collect data on the information exchanges between drug court programs and federal government agencies. The majority of state administrators volunteered a variety of formal and informal connections with the National Institute of Corrections, the Bureau of Justice Assistance, the Department of Justice generally, the National Office of Drug Control Policy, and state departments of corrections.

3

Network Relationships, Implementation, and Policy Success

A NATIONAL INFLUENCE

This chapter focuses on the influence of sustained information connections between the national information network and public administrators as an independent explanation for policy change (box 3.1). As the illustrations and analyses in this chapter demonstrate, more extensive engagement with information led to more extensive state and local implementation, which was linked in turn to greater policy success.

For approximately the first decade of the drug court movement, the effort was essentially limited to the establishment of local programs. State-level support increased as local court programs looked for ways to institutionalize the drug court concept within state government and build a state platform for sustaining local efforts. For local programs, state-level institutional support provided increased stability, accountability, and funding support for local programs (Fox and Wolf 2004; Heck and Roussell 2007; Reilly and Pierre-Lawson 2008). By 2004, all states had initiated some type of state-level activity to support the drug court effort. These efforts ran the gamut from allocating state staff and funding support to passing enabling legislation to establishing collaborative working groups and advisory councils.

The national information network was instrumental in the spread of drug courts and their institutionalization across the states starting in 1989. The diffusion of drug courts and the growth of state support were driven by information connections between administrators and organizations in

BOX 3.1

Megan Pendleton's Experience

Megan Pendleton was excited about her new assignment as the treatment case manager on her county's new drug court planning team. She was very pleased to open the e-mail from her supervisor at the county's Alcohol, Drug, and Mental Health Services Board, which indicated that her travel request to attend a meeting of the National Association of Drug Court Professionals had been approved. The rest of her drug court planning team was attending, as were many other treatment and court professionals from around the state. Megan had met a few times with her drug court team to work on an application for a planning grant that they hoped to submit later in the year. As a case manager for alcohol and drug dependency cases, she was interested in learning from the other professionals on her team and also from people around the state who were exploring ways to begin a drug court in their community.

Megan looked forward to meeting informally with several of her treatment colleagues from other states while at the conference. She wanted to get their ideas about how to expand the network of collaborators within her state, and she had heard that a state drug court association was one way to develop more programs and generate support for the drug court concept in state government. She also looked forward to learning more about the broader administrative environment of the court system in which drug court programs operated. A keynote address was to be delivered by a board member of the National Center for State Courts, and the conference featured several sessions on court administrative issues. One of Megan's treatment colleagues had been named to the board of the National Association of Drug Court Professionals, and Megan planned to meet her for lunch to learn more about her colleague's national experiences. Judge Norwood, the judge on Megan's drug court planning team, had also invited everyone in the state to an informal session at the conference, where they could meet one another and share ideas. The e-mail announcement for the state meeting noted that the National Association of Drug Court Professionals had recently formed a national delegate body representing all fifty states and now called for states to nominate their delegates.

the information networks. These information connections included administrative contact with a wide range of nonprofit organizations in the network, long-term patterns of information exchange with champion and supporter organizations, and the development of new state professional associations centering on the drug court concept. Collectively, these information connections were enduring and wide-ranging and brought administrators in touch with useful types of information and decision processes that supported implementation and helped institutionalize the drug court concept within the state bureaucracy.

Over time, states that were extensively engaged with the information network also became highly involved in implementing drug court programs. These high-implementation states had more local drug courts per capita and more state support for drug court programs. In turn, high-implementation states were more likely to be states that saw, over time, improvement in standard, large-scale measures of crime and arrest rates. This indication of sustained influence over time reinforces the conclusion that the information network made a difference in the diffusion of this innovation and in the outcomes that have resulted from it.

The relationships among information, implementation, and outcomes were examined systematically based on the concepts illustrated in figure 3.1. Information, implementation, and outcomes were linked theoretically through the lens of information diffusion as a foundation for understanding the way that nonprofits and networked arrangements with the public sector have influenced the spread of new ideas and the development of institutional support for policy innovation. Information diffusion concepts suggested that greater information would support more extensive implementation, and in turn, policy success. The results illustrate the influence of the national information network and related networks of state and local officials on the diffusion of drug court policy and the growth of state institutional support on a national scale. This influence endured over time and in the face of rival explanations for widespread changes in drug court implementation and criminal justice policy outcomes.

This chapter begins with a discussion of information, implementation, and outcomes as the conceptual building blocks of the analysis. The chapter next presents the influence of the information network on implementation, followed by the influence of information on policy outcomes. The data used in these analyses were collected through the national survey of state administrators described in chapter 2, from published research and public records, and from the U.S. Census. States were used as the unit of analysis in multivariate models that compare the relative differences in the

Figure 3.1 Relationships between the Information Network, Intergovernmental Implementation, and Public Policy Outcomes

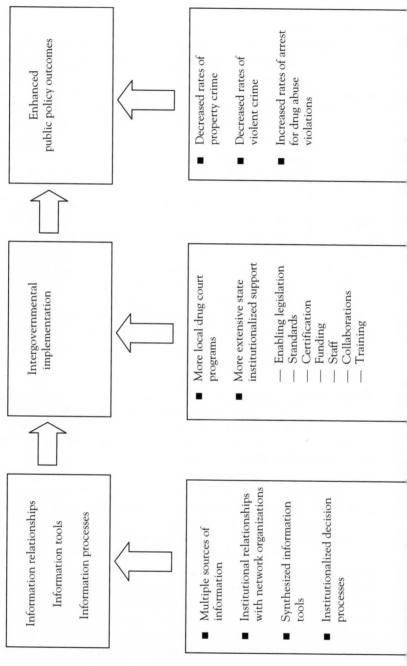

diffusion of drug courts at the local and state levels and changes in policy outcomes. Additional information about the variables, the survey, and the method of analysis is included in the appendix.

Intersectoral Information Connections

The concept of information encompassed the intersectoral information connections between state and local administrators and nonprofits in the national information network. The information connections examined here extended beyond information contacts. Information contacts alone do not guarantee information exchange between organizations in a network (Agranoff 2007). Here, information relationships and opportunities for information exchange were captured in several ways that reflect the breadth and depth of the relationship between the information network and public administrators. Contacts across the information network, relationships with key organizations, and engagement with useful types of information and decision processes were enduring and wide-ranging. These dimensions of information in the network included the number of information sources that state administrators used and the frequency of contact between administrators and organizations in the information network. Information relationships were also reflected through institutional arrangements between states and national nonprofits through governing board memberships and state professional associations. The variety, scope, and enduring nature of these information connections suggest that administrators found continuing benefit in their information connections and drew extensively upon nonprofits in the information network to advance the implementation of the drug court program. These information connections spanned the range of intergovernmental administration.

It is also important to note that these information connections were used as proxies for a strong body of information tools and processes that were generated by the information network. Embedded in these relationships were information exchanges of best practices, model programs, research reports, and the growth of a new drug court profession. Information exchanges within local governments and within states relied on collaborative decision-making processes that were derived from the information network. Taken as a whole, these intertwined relationships, forms of information, and collaborative decision-making practices provide a basis for concluding that the information connections examined here provided multiple opportunities for information exchange and that information exchanges have occurred.

Organization Contacts

States sought information about drug courts from a wide number and variety of organizations. All state administrators reported contact with at least one organization in the national nonprofit information network about drug court programs, and most had contact with a wide range of organizations about this topic. Table 3.1 displays the range of nonprofit organizations that administrators reported as sources of information about drug court programs.

Administrators cited an average of at least seven different organizations as sources of information (mean = 7.4; mode = 5) out of the nineteen nonprofits in the network. For a little more than half the states (about 60 percent), information sources were concentrated within a group of up to six organizations. The remainder of the states (about 40 percent) reported information contacts with a wider range of information sources, ranging from seven organizations to all nineteen organizations in the information network. At the extremes of the range, one state (Virginia) reported information contact with all nineteen organizations; three states (Arkansas, Iowa, and Wyoming) reported contact with only one organization. Every nonprofit organization in the information network was mentioned by at least one state as a source of information about drug court programs.

Most commonly, administrators looked to professional associations and research organizations for information. Professional associations that were promoters or supporters of the drug court concept were mentioned most often. Administrators were extensively engaged with the National Association of Drug Court Professionals (NADCP) in the implementation of local

Table 3.1   The Distribution of Nonprofit Organizations as Information Sources

No. of Observation (States)	No. of Nonprofit Information Sources						
	1–3	4–6	7–9	10–12	13–15	16–18	19
50	13	16	6	4	6	4	1

Author's survey of the fifty states.

drug court programs and in building state office support. Nearly every state cited the NADCP as an information source, and two-thirds of state administrators felt that the NADCP was their most important nongovernmental source of information about drug courts. Three-quarters of the states also identified the National Center for State Courts (NCSC) as an information source. The NCSC is a well-established organization dedicated to state court performance and management. State offices called upon the NCSC to provide assistance in organizational development and state court administration issues concerned with drug court operations. This relationship became more extensive as drug court programs became a more common feature of state court systems. Together, the NADCP and the NCSC were cited by administrators as the most important sources of information for building and sustaining drug court programs. Information contacts extended well beyond these two organizations to other organizations that were supporters, bystanders, and challengers of the drug court idea. Professional associations for state court judges, such as the National Judicial College and the National Council of Juvenile and Family Court Judges, were cited by about half the states as important sources of information about drug courts. Research organizations such as the Urban Institute, the Vera Institute of Justice, and the Justice Policy Institute were used by about one-third of the states. Professional associations for other professional groups, such as the National Association of State Alcohol and Drug Abuse Directors and the American Probation and Parole Association, were noted as information contacts for about one-quarter of the states. Challenger organizations such as the Drug Policy Alliance were noted in about one-fifth of the states. The groups represented the full spectrum of champions, supporters, bystanders, and challengers with regard to the drug court concept. Not surprisingly, champion and supporter organizations were the most common sources of information about the implementation of the innovation.

The number of organizational contacts was measured with a simple count of the organizations that administrators reported as sources of information. Frequency of contact was assessed in terms of how often administrators looked for or received information from organizations in the network. Frequency of contact was measured using a scale of frequency ranges described in the appendix. The number of organizational contacts and the frequency of contact were measured without regard to the type of information.

Board Memberships

State officials and representatives of local drug court programs were also involved in extensive and enduring relationships with the NADCP and the NCSC through service on the governing boards of these organizations. Board membership provided numerous and continued opportunities for information exchanges among board members and the various constituencies of the organization. Service as a volunteer board member of a nonprofit organization indicated a sustained commitment over time to the ideals and goals of the organization. Here, the boards of directors of these organizations included judges and other state and local officials from various states as well as professionals with expertise related to the mission of the organization.

The NADCP was founded in 1994 by representatives of the first twelve drug courts across the country. The NADCP's board of directors has counted among its members many of the judges involved in the early drug courts, including Jeffrey Tauber (California), Harlan Haas (Oregon), and Susan Bolton (Arizona). NADCP board members played a central role in presenting testimony before Congress in support of federal funding and in advocating across the country for the drug court mission. During the period of this study (1989–2004), local drug court judges and other public officials from twenty-four different states served terms on the NADCP's board of directors.

Table 3.2 gives the states with representatives that have served on the NADCP board. It also illustrates the average number of terms (three years) that an official from each state served on the board during the period of this study. Some states had multiple representatives, and some representatives served more than one term. California and Maryland had the greatest representation; both states had representation for an aggregate of eleven years of service.

The NCSC was formed in 1971, and its governing board comprises state court judges and court administrators. The array of board service on the NCSC is presented in table 3.3. California was strongly involved in this organization during the time of this study; the NCSC's board had representation from somewhere in California every year from 1989 through 2004. Thirty-nine states were represented on the NCSC's board of directors during this period; many states were represented for multiple terms and by different representatives, as was the case with the NADCP's board of directors.

State office staffs and local drug court programs found it advantageous to have local drug court judges serve on these boards. In the words of one

Table 3.2 National Association of Drug Court Professionals Board Membership by State, 1994–2004

					Years of Board Membership						
	1	*2*	*3*	*4*	*5*	*6*	*7*	*8*	*9*	*10*	*11*
Names of states	MI SC	—	NJ RI VA	AL DE NM NC PA	OK OR	AZ IL	CO LA TX	KY MO NV NY	—	FL	CA MD
No. of states	2	0	3	5	2	2	3	4	0	1	2

Source: The data were collected from newsletters of the National Association of Drug Court Professionals and Internal Revenue Service Form 990, 1994–2005.

Table 3.3 National Center for State Courts Board Membership by State, 1989–2004

	Years of Board Membership											
	1	2	3	4	5	6	7	8	9	10	11	>15
Names of states	AR	AK	LA	CT	PA	AL	MO	OK	AZ	FL	IL	CA
	IN	NJ	MD	DE		CO	OH		IA	GA	MI	
			MT	ID		KS	OR		UT	MN	WA	
			NE	ND		ME	TX			NC		
			NH	TN		NY						
			WI			VA						
			WY									
No. of states	2	2	7	5	1	6	4	1	3	4	3	1

Source: Data collected from National Center for State Courts Annual Reports, 1989–2004.

state administrator, "We were thrilled to learn that our drug court judge had been nominated to the [NADCP] national board. This will give us access to the big picture. The information that [he] will bring back will be key to our plans going forward."

NADCP board membership provided access to a broad, national perspective about the drug court program and state court operations. It provided early access to information about current trends and issues with drug court programs and in court management more broadly. By learning about these issues at a national level, judges may have been more inclined to initiate and support programs at home. Drug court personnel also viewed service on the national board as a way of establishing credibility for the drug court program. As one state administrator expressed it, "Board members bring visibility to the state and its programs. Some of our judges have been doing this [operating drug courts] for a long time now. Being on the national board says to everyone that their work is important. Having a national board member in our state brings prestige to our state conferences; 'national board member' makes a great headline."

The information relationship worked both ways. Board membership also provided opportunities for state and local officials to influence the decisions of these national associations and shape policy. In general, nonprofit organizations frequently encourage board members to meet with their congressional representatives and other government officials to make the case on a particular issue; board members can make the case to their representatives as volunteer constituents rather than as employees of an organization that is advocating for change or asking for money. Here, state and local administrators were encouraged by the idea that local judges from their drug court circles would have the opportunity to lobby Congress for program support. State and local administrators felt that the experience would generate additional enthusiasm for the work of local programs and encourage understanding of the need for financial and policy support at the state level. One administrator commented: "This helps them [board members] see how hard it is to find funds. We have to look beyond money from federal grants, and so it is really important to build support at the statehouse. When they see how much work it is in Washington, they are even more supportive with the legislature back home."

Board membership suggests an extensive information relationship that endures over time, before, during, and after a board member's term. Because board positions are voluntary and take time away from other professional responsibilities, board membership suggests a strong level of interest in the mission of the organization. For the NADCP, board membership also implied a strong connection to the drug court concept and positive motivation to advance the drug court idea. NCSC board membership implied a more general commitment to advancing the professionalism and operation of individual courts and state court systems. Board membership brought a degree of formality to the information connections between administrators and nonprofits and between states and national organizations. A typical board member was named for service of a term of three years or more, and frequently these terms were renewed at least once. Meetings of the board occurred regularly, and board service typically involved work on one or more committees. Information connections between members of the NADCP and NCSC boards helped cross-fertilize ideas and paved the way for the NCSC's involvement in the adaptation of state court administrations to accommodate drug court programs.

The extensive information connections represented by board service were difficult to quantify precisely. The magnitude of the relationship between the national boards, local programs, and state offices was reflected in the total number of years of service on the board over time. The accumulated board-years of service provided by all the state and local officials who served on the NADCP board from 1994 to 2004 totaled approximately 140 years of volunteer effort, or an annual effort of 12.5 volunteer years; for the NCSC this effort from 1989 to 2004 was approximately 240 years of service, or 15 volunteer years per year.

This dimension of the information relationship between states and the national nonprofit information network was captured through separate, annual counts of the board members from each state serving on the governing board of the NADCP and NCSC from 1989 to 2004. The relative formality of board relationships and their endurance over time strengthened the conclusions that can be drawn here about the influence of information based in part on these relationships.

State Professional Associations

State associations of drug court professionals were also an important dimension of the information flow from the national information network to administrators and across programs within states. Drug court professionals across the country formed their own state associations to advance the idea of drug court policy, to learn from each other, and to share information. These state groups supported and fostered professionalization through regular state drug court conferences for local drug court team members. These state groups also sponsored professional conferences for state court judges and appeared as speakers and panelists at state conferences of judges and other professional groups represented in the national information network. State drug court associations began in the early days of local drug court programs. The first state drug court associations were formed shortly after the formation of the NADCP. The earliest formal recording of a state association is that of the California Association of Drug Court Professionals, which was formed in 1996.[1] Table 3.4 shows the spread of state drug court associations by year of incorporation.

Between 1996 and 2004, a total of twenty-nine states established associations for drug court professionals modeled after the NADCP. Single-state associations were formed in twenty-three states. Also, a regional arrangement, the New England Association of Drug Court Professionals, was established by six states: Connecticut, Maine, Massachusetts, New Hampshire, Rhode Island, and Vermont.

The process of building a state association mirrored the drug court team concept and brought together diverse constituencies of law enforcement, treatment, and court professionals. As with the national professional association, the NADCP, state drug court associations were broadly representative of the cross-professional, interjurisdictional drug court team concept. In Missouri, for example, the members of the Missouri Association of Drug Court Professionals included drug court administrators, drug court commissioners, treatment providers, prosecuting attorneys, and defense counsel, including representation from the federal public defender office, the Missouri Department of Social Services Treatment Section, and the Missouri State Highway Patrol (Missouri Association of Drug Court Professionals 2008).

Some state drug court associations had specific responsibilities in addition to the education associated with professional groups. These additional responsibilities typically emanated from state statutes that established drug court programs. For example, Florida's drug court enabling legislation gave the Florida Association of Drug Court Professionals statutory responsibility for soliciting recommendations from its members regarding the "expansion, operation and institutionalization" of drug court programs. The Tennessee Association of Drug Court Professionals was involved in drafting the state's enabling legislation and is consulted about appointments to the state's Drug Court Advisory Council (Tennessee Office of Criminal Justice Programs 2007). This aspect of the information relationship between administrators and the information network was indicated by whether a state had formally established an incorporated association for

Table 3.4 State Drug Court Professional Associations by Year of Incorporation, 1996–2004

Distribution and Totals	1996	1997	1998	1999	2000	2001	2002	2003	2004
Distribution									
8							CT		
7							ME		
6			GA				MA		
5			LA		AZ		NV		
4			IN		CO		NH		
3		MI	NY		IL		OR		
2		MO	TX	NM	UT	FL	RI		IA
1	CA	OK	WA	OH	VA	PA	VT		MS
Annual total	1	3	6	2	5	2	8	0	2
Cumulative total	1	4	10	12	17	19	27	27	29

Note: Connecticut, Maine, Massachusetts, New Hampshire, Rhode Island, and Vermont formed the New England Association of Drug Court Professionals.

Sources: State incorporation records and Internal Revenue Service annual information returns for nonprofit organizations.

drug court professionals based on the NADCP model; incorporation suggested a measure of permanence and durability in the information exchanges associated with these groups.

These state associations expanded the reach of the NADCP and established another path for communication between the national organization and state and local administrators. These state associations also provided a forum for meeting and exchanging information across local programs within states. State associations intertwined with other state or local groups, and they acted as a part of a larger network of organizations that spanned state, local, and national boundaries.

Two examples from the states illustrate the layered connections and interrelationships among state drug court associations, local drug court programs, and national nonprofit organizations and their influence on the diffusion of the drug court concept in that state. The first example centers on the formation of the Missouri Association of Drug Court Professionals. One of the earliest connections to the drug court program in Missouri came in 1995, when Ann Wilson, then an alcohol and drug abuse coordinator from the Missouri Administrative Office of the Courts (AOC), attended the first annual conference of the NADCP in 1995. Her interest was piqued because of her familiarity with Missouri's court-ordered, community-based education and treatment for offenders arrested on drug- and alcohol-related traffic offenses.

Following the NADCP's annual conference, Missouri convened a statewide judicial conference on the topic of addiction in February 1996. The speakers included Judge Harlan Haas, who established one of the first drug courts in the country (in Portland), representatives from the office of U.S. attorney general Janet Reno and Claire McCaskill, then the prosecutor for the Jackson County drug court in Kansas City.[2] Continuing the momentum, Missouri sent more than thirty representatives to a subsequent NADCP conference, where they determined to form the Missouri Association of Drug Court Professionals (MADCP). The position of alcohol and drug abuse coordinator within the Missouri AOC was established as the organizer for this effort. As became the case in many other states, the Missouri state association was established as a nonprofit public charity and governed by a volunteer board. Members were drug court practitioners drawn from all areas of the state and represented the range of professions within the drug court team. Current members include drug court administrators, drug court commissioners, treatment providers, prosecuting attorneys, and defense counsel, including representation from the federal public defender office, the Missouri Department of Social Services Treatment

Section, and the Missouri State Highway Patrol (Missouri Association of Drug Court Professionals 2008).

Today, the primary responsibility for state-level administration of drug court programs in Missouri rests with the Missouri Drug Courts Coordinating Commission. The efforts of this coordinating commission were coordinated by the same state alcohol and drug abuse coordinator (Ann Wilson) in the Division of Court Programs and Research within the Missouri AOC from the group's inception until her retirement in late 2008. These relationships flow full circle back to the national information network. For example, Wilson was inducted into the Stanley M. Goldstein Drug Court Hall of Fame on May 31, 2008, during the NADCP's Fourteenth Annual Training Conference held in Saint Louis. In another example, in 2009, Chief Justice William Ray Price Jr. of the Missouri Supreme Court was named the chair of the coordinating commission and also became the chair of the board of the NADCP. Price followed a line of strong representation on the NADCP board from Missouri; current U.S. senator Claire McCaskill served as an NADCP board member from 1994 to 1998 and as its chair from 1995 to 1997.[3] Price received the Claire McCaskill Award from the Missouri Association of Drug Court Professionals in 2006.

The MADCP example illustrates the range of information relationships that preceded a state association of drug court professionals as well as those that flowed from the group after it was established. These interrelationships included new collaborations, such as the coordinating commission, that were established specifically to facilitate the drug court initiative. These interrelationships also included institutional connections with state executive agencies and formal bodies within the judiciary, such as the Judicial Conference Task Force. Not all these information relationships were formal, but all involved awareness of the work of other groups on the drug court topic. Overall, these relationships sustained the influence of information by providing multiple channels for the further diffusion of ideas from national organizations and by reinforcing ideas across groups within the state.

The relationships centering on the Tennessee Association of Drug Court Professionals (TADCP) also illustrate the multiple layers of connections and interrelationships surrounding the drug court program. The TADCP began relatively informally as a small group of drug court practitioners, including the drug court administrator of the Rutherford County drug court (Murfreesboro), one of Tennessee's earliest drug courts. This group was instrumental in the drafting and passage of Tennessee's drug court statute and its enactment in 2003. The drug court statute established a statewide Drug Court Advisory Committee (DCAC), which was modeled after the interdisciplinary drug court team concept. One of the members of the DCAC in 2008 was the Rutherford County drug court administrator, who coauthored the state drug court statute.

The DCAC was constituted as a relatively small group of five members, but it maintained connections across state government through a group of ex-officio members from the state judiciary and other executive branch agencies. These ex officio members included a drug court judge, a district court prosecutor, and representatives of the Department of Alcohol and Drug Abuse Services in the Tennessee Department of Mental Health and Developmental Disabilities, the Administrative Office of the Courts, and the Tennessee Commission on Children and Youth (Tennessee Office of Criminal Justice Programs 2008). The experience of these ex officio members provided the DCAC with broad access to a wide range of constituencies. As an example, one of the ex officio members of the DCAC in 2008 was Judge Don Ash of the Sixteenth Judicial District Circuit Court; at that time, Ash was also the presiding judge of the Rutherford County drug court. Ash served as the president of the Tennessee Judicial Conference, comprising the state's 178 appellate and trial court judges. In 2007, Ash was elected to a second term as presiding judge of the Tennessee Court of the Judiciary, the body responsible for adjudicating the state's Code of Judicial Conduct. In addition, Ash served as a faculty member in the National Judicial College graduate program.

The DCAC also maintained a formal connection with the Tennessee Office of Criminal Justice Programs (TOCJP). The state's enabling legislation established the TOCJP as the state agency responsible for statewide drug court efforts. This work included defining, developing, and gathering outcome measures for drug court treatment programs; collecting, reporting, and disseminating drug court treatment data; supporting a state drug treatment court "mentor" program; sponsoring and coordinating state drug court treatment and training; and awarding, administering, and evaluating state drug court treatment grants (Tennessee Office of Criminal Justice Programs 2005). The DCAC was given responsibility for reviewing the drug court program criteria established by the TOCJP for conformity with the NADCP's guiding principles and for advising the state office on grants to local programs.

The TADCP was formally incorporated in 2005. The state drug court association played a vital role in monitoring and adapting legislation to support and sustain Tennessee's drug court programs (Tennessee Office of Criminal Justice Programs 2005). The TADCP and the TOCJP worked together, while receiving advice from the DCAC, to sponsor statewide conference opportunities, and many meetings of the two groups are scheduled to follow one another. The Tennessee drug court statute also required consultation with the TADCP about appointments to the DCAC (Tennessee Office of Criminal Justice Programs 2007).

The self-reported opinions of state administrators about their voluntary relationships with other members of the drug court community at the state, local, and national levels demonstrated that the information connections with boards and state associations also depicted layers of exchange across the intergovernmental spectrum. This breadth demonstrates the reach of the information network and illustrates several of the multiple possibilities of information flow observed in earlier studies of information diffusion in intergovernmental systems (Mossberger 2000; Mossberger and Hale 2002). These organizational contacts and institutional relationships only scratch the surface of the myriad and fluid information connections among state administrators and national nonprofits. If anything, these concepts understate the richness of information that flowed from these organizations to state administrators.

The Implementation of Drug Court Programs

The concept of implementation reflects the spread of local programs and the growth of state support mechanisms. Local implementation was assessed as the annual number of local programs that became operational in a state, adjusted for the state's population. By 2004, all states had initiated some type of state-level activity to support local drug courts. In this analysis, state implementation activities included categories of support reported through the national survey and from published reports of state drug court activities (Huddleston, Freeman-Wilson, and Boone 2004; Office of Justice Programs 2003, 2004a). These included general enabling legislation in support of drug courts, appropriation legislation, the establishment of state advisory boards, state administrative rules and orders for the operation of drug courts, drug court coordinator positions, state-sponsored training conferences, state standards for drug court performance, other dedicated state staff, informal collaborative working groups, and drug court management information systems. The various state activities that supported and institutionalized the drug court concept are presented in table 3.5.

Table 3.5   Range of State Activities to Support Drug Court
Implementation

State Activity	Respondents (%)
Statewide informal collaborations or working groups	86
Legislation in support of the drug court concept	80
State drug court coordinators	66
State-sponsored training	60
State standards	42
Legislation appropriating funds	40
State management information systems	40
State department or office	32
Legislation establishing a commission or advisory group	26
State rules or administrative orders	8

Sources: Compiled by the author from a fifty-state survey of state drug court
administrators ($N = 50$); Office of Justice Programs 2001a, 2001b, 2003, 2004a.

By far the most common steps taken to develop a state-level drug court
effort were to establish informal statewide collaboration or working groups
and to enact state enabling legislation that formally authorized the drug
court program. Most states passed some form of enabling legislation in
support of drug courts; however, fewer than half actually appropriated state
funds specifically for drug court operations. Another aspect of state institutionalization was the allocation of dedicated staff support at the state level.
Two-thirds of states utilized some form of drug court coordinator position
in a state office. A majority of states conduct state-sponsored training
events. All these activities supported information exchanges among local
drug courts, state offices, and national organizations.

The data about local programs were provided in electronic format from
the Drug Court Clearinghouse maintained by the Office of Justice Programs at American University in conjunction with the Bureau of Justice
Assistance in the U.S. Department of Justice. State activities were
reported by state administrators through the national survey and to the
Office of Justice Programs' Drug Court Clearinghouse.

Outcomes and Change

In addition to links between information and implementation, this study
analyzed links between information from the national information network and policy outcomes. Generally, drug courts have been considered to

be an effective public policy initiative. Drug court programs are successful when measured by programmatic standards such as program graduation rates and also in breaking the cycle of additional criminal behavior (Belenko 1999b; Berman and Feinblatt 2005; Cissner and Rempel 2005; Deschenes et al. 2000; Goldkamp 2003; Guydish et al. 2001; Harrell, Roman, and Sack 2001; King and Pasquarella 2009; Latimer, Morton-Bourgon, and Chrétien 2006; Marlowe, DeMatteo, and Festinger 2003; Marlowe, Heck, et al. 2006; Peters and Murrin 2000; Roman, Townsend, and Bhati 2003). Evidence suggests that drug court programs are associated with reductions in recidivism that endure significantly beyond the duration of an individual's program participation (Marlowe, Heck, et al. 2006; U.S. Government Accountability Office 2005). Research suggests that different client populations may fare differently within programs and may warrant different approaches to judicial supervision or other program components (Marlowe, Festinger, et al. 2006; Shaffer et al. 2008).

Comparisons across programs or against national norms, however, have been a continuing challenge. National impact evaluations of drug court programs did not develop as the program spread across the country. This was due in part to wide differences in the way that programs were designed and in the data that they chose to collect about program operations (Bhati, Roman, and Chalfin 2008; King and Pasquarella 2009). Local programs developed their program content and measures of success according to particular community needs and individual community interpretations of the NADCP's guiding principles for drug court operation. By 2008, initiatives to establish unified standards for performance were under way in many states; however, the individual nature of each state's effort essentially undercuts a systematic comparison across states.

The evaluative picture of drug court programs also included a culture of storytelling embedded within the drug court philosophy; Nolan (2001) observed that this philosophy fostered evaluations based primarily on qualitative data. As part of the therapeutic process, participants talked about their experiences as drug users and about how the program changed their lives. Program participants were encouraged to tell their stories to the drug court judge, to other members of the drug court team, and to each other as part of the process of behavioral change. Drug court judges used these stories as a part of their community public relations for the drug court concept. Drug court alumni told their personal stories as a part of the training process for drug court personnel. This philosophy was reflected in the use of qualitative data for evaluating success. Qualitative methods have been a prominent aspect of drug court evaluation from the beginning of the program; anecdotes of individual accomplishments are buttressed by data collected through focus groups, participant surveys, and personal narratives (e.g., Belenko 1998; Goldkamp 1999; Terry 1999). On the whole, the drug court movement had supported the use of qualitative narratives as measures of success; moreover, as a matter of philosophy, the drug court movement holds these measures to be equally as appropriate as quantitative measures for assessing the success of behavioral change (Nolan 2001).

The lag in the development of widespread empirical measures that could be used for comparative cross-state evaluation was also an artifact of the lack of sufficient postprogram outcome data developed by drug court programs. The early federal grants to support drug court planning and operation required local courts to collect data as a condition of funding; however, data collection on a variety of possible program outcomes was officially discontinued in 2002 (U.S. General Accounting Office 1997, 2002). This lack of data was significant given the large number of local drug court programs that received federal grant support from the federal Drug Court Program Office (U.S. Government Accountability Office 2005).

As a consequence, large-scale measures of change in the criminal justice system were used as a proxy for program-specific measures of success in order to make comparisons across states and over time. In the absence of more finely tuned measures, state policy administrators must consider large-scale measures of change, such as reduced crime rates and increased arrest rates, when making policy decisions about programs that are intended to reduce crime (Meier 1994; Welsh and Farrington 2000). Increased arrest rates were expected to accompany the increased use of drug court programs and the increased attention and resources that they brought to bear on drug use issues (Boyum and Kleiman 2002; Sherman 2002). Increased arrest rates were also expected in part because relapses are common among drug court program participants (U.S. Government Accountability Office 2005). Crime and arrest data were drawn from U.S. Census reports and the U.S. Department of Justice's Uniform Crime Reporting System (UCRS) published for the states. Property crime and violent crime rates were the aggregate rates for UCRS index offenses; index offenses were used as benchmarks and to facilitate comparisons across states. For property crime, these offenses were burglary, larceny/theft, and motor vehicle theft; for violent crime, the index offenses were murder and nonnegligent homicide, forcible rape, robbery, and aggravated assault. Drug abuse arrests data included all arrests classified as drug abuse violations under the UCRS; these are the sale, manufacture, or possession

of narcotics, marijuana, synthetic narcotics, and other dangerous nonnarcotic drugs.

Other Influences on Innovation

Comparative studies of policy diffusion across the American states have
identified various conditions as determinants of the adoption of innovation or new policy ideas (Gray 1973; Savage 1985; Walker 1969). These
determinants suggest a greater likelihood that states will adopt an innovation. Determinants can be grouped into categories of factors associated
with political context, resources, and pressures for change (Mooney 2001;
Mooney and Lee 1995). These influences can be internal or external to
the states themselves (Berry and Berry 1990, 1999). Internal factors
include the relative political, economic, and demographic characteristics
of states; analysis of internal determinants suggests that states adopt new
policies when their political, economic, or sociodemographic environments are favorable. Similarly, in a federal, intergovernmental environment, state policy choices can be facilitated or hindered by national policy
initiatives, external actors and relationships, and the choices made by
neighboring states (Berry and Berry 1990, 1999; Mintrom 2000). These
conditions contribute to the spread of innovation in general and are rival
explanations that could explain the proliferation of drug courts and state
support for drug court programs, and the links between drug courts and
policy success.

The State Political Context

Political factors are essential to any consideration of the reasons that states
make decisions about policy innovation; after all, state policy decisions are
made through political institutions. The idea of state political context has
evolved from various measures of party control over government institutions and measures of political participation to encompass the ideologies
of political leaders and citizens (Berry et al. 1998). Ideology is a useful
concept for explaining the spread of drug courts for several reasons. First,
the idea of drug courts is grounded in a philosophical shift about policies
that address drugs and crime. Also, support for drug courts does not fall
neatly along party lines such that Democrats strongly favor the program
and Republicans strongly oppose it. Instead, state administrators proudly

noted that support for drug courts has been broadly bipartisan. In discussions with administrators about the extent of support for drug courts among state court judges, the consensus was that judicial support or opposition stemmed from individual beliefs and values rather than political party membership.

In the states, a conservative tone dominated the ideological debate about drug use and crime from the 1970s forward. This influence has played out through increasing criminalization and increased penalties for drug use. Drug treatment (and other alternatives to incarceration generally) were viewed as more liberal approaches, with decriminalization seen as perhaps the ultimate liberal stance. In a few states, citizens mobilized to propose shifts in state policy toward alternatives to incarceration that provided drug treatment, or that reduced or eliminated penalties for some types of drug use. For example, interested citizens attempted to establish mandatory drug treatment through the initiative process. In 1996 Arizona voters approved Proposition 200 (also known as the Drug Medicalization, Prevention, and Control Act) to require treatment instead of incarceration for convictions for simple possession or use on the first two offenses. In 2000 voters approved California Proposition 36, which mandated drug treatment in lieu of incarceration for low-level, nonviolent drug offenders convicted solely of possession for personal use. In 2002, however, Ohio voters turned down ballot initiative Issue 1, which reflected essentially the same approaches as the Arizona and California initiatives. Citizen opinions were not an obvious, widespread independent influence on state policy, and so consideration was limited to the ideologies of government officials and political leaders. Government ideology was measured using the index of Berry and her colleagues (1998), which is constructed from annual measures of roll call voting scores of state legislatures, the party of the governor, and assumptions about political elites.

Racial and ethnic diversity also affected the political context of state policy decisions and were important considerations for evaluating the spread of drug courts and policy success. Increased minority diversity in the population has been associated with higher rates of incarceration during the period of this study (Hero 2003). The disproportionate criminal justice impact on African Americans expanded during the last three decades of the twentieth century through the enactment of various crack cocaine laws and sentencing requirements (Hero 2003; King and Mauer 2002; Mauer 1999). Varying levels of racial and ethnic homogeneity within state populations have also been linked to a broad range of state policy outcomes (Hero 2003; Hero and Tolbert 1996). States with homogeneous white populations that do not identify with particular ethnic groups (i.e., Vermont) appear more generous on a wide range of health, education, and welfare policies in comparison with states with higher percentages of racial and ethnic groups (i.e., Mississippi). These studies suggest that states with greater diversity would adopt a less generous range of alternatives to incarceration, if those alternatives were seen as providing benefits for particular minority groups.

Resources

Regardless of political factors that favor or oppose a particular policy initiative, states need resources to pursue new ideas and to bring policy decisions to life. States with abundant resources have slack resources available to pursue innovation and new policy opportunities; in contrast, states that experience strains on resources are expected to be limited in their ability to initiate new ideas (Downs and Mohr 1976; Walker 1969). State resources are fundamentally measures of state economic strength. Typical examples include measures of state and resident income, education, wealth, industrialization, and urbanization. Affluent states have been generally associated with innovation or earlier policy adoption. Wealthier states were earlier adopters of civil rights, education, and welfare policies (Gray 1973); state lottery policies (Berry and Berry 1990); and abortion reform regulations (Mooney and Lee 1995). Professionalized legislatures are also strongly associated with greater levels of available state resources; state legislatures that have higher levels of legislative compensation, time in session, and staff are considered to be more professional (Squire 1992). Legislative professionalism has been linked to early adoption and state spending in various policy areas, including public assistance (e.g., Derthick 1970) and juvenile corrections innovation (e.g., Downs 1976). Legislative professionalism has also been linked to more extensive implementation in policy that is associated with administrative changes that support technological advances, such as e-government (Tolbert, Mossberger, and McNeal 2008). Because drug courts directly affected judicial administration, judicial or court professionalism could also have accounted for some portion of the diffusion of drug court programs. The concept of available resources was measured in various ways. Gross state product, educational attainment, and median income were drawn from the U.S. Census over time. Professionalism was measured through established indexes (e.g., Glick 1981; Squire 1992).

Pressures for Change

Policy diffusion and innovation are also influenced by pressure for change—in other words, the severity of a problem or the degree of need for a solution. States in which a problem is particularly severe will be more likely to adopt policies to address that problem than will other states. Greater need (demand) for change increases the likelihood that proposals for change will reach the policy agenda (Mintrom 2000). Increases in policy-specific measures of need are positively related to the adoption of more stringent state policies (Lester et al. 1983; Meier 1994).

Throughout the evolution of the drug court program, states experienced pressure on resources as a result of increased incarceration, drug crime, and drug use. The criminal activity connected to drug use is associated with the relative proportion of youth in the population. Criminal activity is most common for persons in their later teen years and early twenties and declines sharply by the midtwenties as a consequence of maturation and familial factors (Sampson and Laub 2005; Tittle and Ward 1993).[4] Drug-related crimes are also associated with the relative concentration of the population living in urban areas. The density and complexity of cities, as well as the anonymity that cities provide, present lower probabilities of arrest and recognition for offenders, and also lower costs of transporting criminal tools and the products of crime (Glaeser and Sacerdote 1999). Increases in criminal activity also have a historic association with joblessness; an inverse relationship between lawful work and criminal activity is especially strong in younger age groups (Votey and Philips 2003). Need or demand can also be gleaned from the amount of money that states spend on particular policy areas. States with higher correctional system expenditures may have felt pressure to look for alternatives to incarceration, including drug courts, for potential cost savings. Need was measured in various ways, including the presence of the younger age group eighteen to twenty-four, correctional system expenses, the rate of unemployment, and the concentration of population in urban centers. All data were drawn from the U.S. Census.

From Information to Implementation

Decisions about whether to begin a drug court and how to support that effort were shaped by political factors, available resources, and pressures for policy change. Decisions were also influenced by the information network, which spurred states to begin more programs and develop more extensive methods of institutionalizing support for local drug court programs. To understand the simultaneous influence of these factors, and to understand whether the information network was influential, a form of multivariate time series analysis was used to test the influence of information on drug court diffusion across the states over time. This method uses annual data from the fifty states over the period of the study and controls for competing factors that may also explain the growth of state and local programs or changes in policy outcomes. Multivariate analysis improves the generalizability of the findings. The use of control variables minimizes the influence of competing explanations for the findings and accounts for the demographic variation and policy-specific conditions in the states. Additional information about the method and model specifications is included in the appendix. The influence of the information network is highlighted through several analyses.

First, the number of information sources had a significant influence on state support for drug courts. States that sought information about drugs and crime from a broader range of national nonprofit organizations in the information network took more steps to institutionalize drug courts at the state level. As table 3.6 illustrates, state administrative support for the drug court initiative was fostered by a more extensive array of nonprofit information sources in the information network. The information network was a significant influence alongside two other factors. One important factor is the growth of local programs; as the illustrations given above indicate, local programs looked to state offices for support in many ways—for example, funding, staff assistance with grant writing, and data collection. As the number of local programs grew, state offices became more common and legislatures began to pass statutes in support of drug court programs. State offices began to collaborate with local drug court personnel through advisory boards and informal working groups. The greater the proportion of local drug courts in a state, the more extensive the array of state supports. The second factor that influenced the growth of state support was the ideology of political leaders; in 2004, states in which state political officials and party leaders were more liberal were more likely to support drug courts at the state level.

The frequency of contact with national organizations was not a significant factor in the growth of state support. This lack of significance may be due to the extensive contact reported by administrators; virtually all state administrators reported that they were in contact with multiple organizations at multiple times throughout the year and through various means.

Table 3.6   Influence of the National Nonprofit Information Network on the Extent of State Support for Drug Court Programs, 2004

Independent Variable	Regression Coefficient, Scope of State Drug Court Implementation
Information sources	.034***
Local drug courts	.428***
Liberal ideology of state political leaders	.005*
Constant	1.123
Pseudo R^2	.121
Wald chi^2	66.87
Number of observations	50

***$p < .001$; **$p < .01$; *$p < .05$; two-tailed.

Note: Unstandardized Poisson regression coefficients. Variables are defined in the text and appendix. Controls included state-level measures of frequency of contact with the national information network, education, wealth, correctional expenditures, racial diversity (Hero and Tolbert 1996), legislative professionalism (Squire 1992), and judicial professionalism (Glick 1981); none were significant.

Neither legislative nor judicial professionalism was influential in the growth of state support for drug courts. With regard to legislative professionalism, this finding is not particularly surprising given the incremental nature of changes in legislative salaries and staff levels and the fact that state supports are a relatively recent development. The potential influence of judicial professionalism remains an open question in terms of its relationship to the spread of drug courts; the overall administration of state court systems has changed considerably during the past several decades, and these changes may be reflected in more contemporary measures of operation. Correctional system expenditures were also not predictors of the scope of local implementation. This lack of influence of correctional expenditures may reflect a relative lack of comprehensive information about the costs of drug courts in comparison with other alternatives to incarceration.

Although this snapshot using survey data established a link between information from the national network and the expansion of the drug court program, it captured just a single slice in time and uses a single, relatively crude measure of the relationship between the nonprofit network and state administrators. The significance of the information network came into sharper focus through a broader analysis over time. A broader view of the influence of the information network is presented in table 3.7, which illustrates the relative influence of several key information connections throughout the history of the drug court program.

Over time, the enduring links between states and the boards of directors of the National Association of Drug Court Professionals and the National Center for State Courts were associated with more extensive drug court implementation. States that had officials who served as members of the board of directors of the NADCP were more likely to have a more extensive local implementation of drug court programs, and they were more likely to have more extensive state supports in place. States where associations of drug court professionals had been established in replication of the national NADCP model were also more likely to have more extensive state and local drug court operations. The influence of the NCSC was felt at the state level; however, there was no link between NCSC board membership and the spread of local drug courts in a state. These results are consistent with the champion role of the NADCP in fostering local programs

Table 3.7   Influence of the National Nonprofit Information Network on Drug Court Implementation, 1989–2004

	Regression Coefficient	
Independent Variable $_{i,t}$	State Implementation	Local Implementation
Nonprofit information network		
NADCP board of directors	.525***	.134***
NCSC board of directors	.127*	−.010
State drug court associations	1.360***	.188***
Education	.019*	.008**
Income	.000*	.000*
Liberal ideology of state political leaders	−.001	−.002***
Constant	−2.144*	−.700***
R^2	.384***	.201***
Wald chi^2	411.45***	272.70***
Number of panels (i)	50	50
Number of observations	800	800

***$p < .001$; **$p < .01$; *$p < .10$; two-tailed.

Note: Time-series cross-sectional data for the fifty states. Unstandardized regression coefficients. The subscript i contains the unit to which the observations belong, in this case the state, and controls for variation between states. The subscript t represents the time intervals at which the variable was measured, in this case each year from 1989 to 2004. Variables are defined in the text and in the appendix. Controls that lacked significance for either state or local implementation include state unemployment rate and racial diversity.

and state support systems. These results are also consistent with the state-level focus of the NCSC and its role in fostering the professional operation of state court systems and as a supporter organization for the drug court concept within state court systems.

The significance of these information relationships over time attests to the sustained commitment of both organizations in pursuit of their respective missions. The findings here suggest a synergy within the information network and highlight the distinction between champion and supporter organizations. Both the NADCP and NCSC facilitated the growth of state and local drug court programs, but each did so in ways that corresponded to its organizational mission. The NADCP championed the growth of local programs and the institutionalization of state support systems. The NCSC supported that growth by pursuing its mission to assist state court systems with organizational and operational issues.

These relationships illustrated the multiple paths of influence between administrators and the information network and a synergy resulting from the interaction of local drug court teams, the NADCP, state associations of drug court professionals, and emerging state offices with responsibility for drug court programs. Relationships with the information network were self-reinforcing; the network influenced the growth of local programs and state offices, which in turn expanded the network of information connections and possibilities for information exchange. Members of these groups attended conferences together, served jointly on committees and task forces, and formed working groups to address common concerns. The growth of local programs created pressure for action within state court systems and in some cases within the state executive office for criminal justice services; in turn, this generated more information exchanges with the national information network.

Other Explanations for Program Expansion

The influence of the information network endured over time, even when other explanations were considered. State resources encouraged the expansion of drug court programs and promoted efforts to institutionalize innovation. States that had greater relative wealth were more likely to have more local programs per capita and more forms of state support for local drug court programs, which suggests that slack resources were important for the spread of this innovation. This result is consistent with the broad body of research on policy diffusion at the state level, which predicts that wealthier states are more likely to adopt policy innovations. Here, information connections were influential in addition to other resources.

Over time, the proliferation of local drug court programs was associated with conservative ideological views. Although a liberal ideology was an influential factor in 2004, the scope of the analysis over time supports the conclusion that a conservative ideology was in fact the more significant influence. States with more conservative political leadership among elected officials and party leaders were more likely to have more local drug courts when adjusted for differences in population. During this period, when states were legislating new crimes, harsher penalties overall, and stringent penalties for drug crime, the conservative view appeared to have encouraged local support for drug courts as an innovation that was perhaps "tough enough" on crime. It also reflected the influence of the conservative ideology regarding criminal justice policy that dominated the states and promoted incarceration generally. Even as states adopted alternatives to jail or prison and drug courts spread across the country, states continued to lock up offenders in traditional criminal justice programs. The influence of the conservative ideology also reflected to some extent the political appeal of coercive treatment, where drug treatment was imposed under threat of judicial action for noncompliance, as compared with the notion of therapeutic treatment. As more time passed, political leaders may have viewed drug courts as a more conservative policy option in comparison with other alternatives to incarceration.

Interestingly, minority diversity was not linked to the expansion of the drug court concept in the way that it has been linked to state decisions to expand the provision of social welfare benefits and other social policy decisions. Increased minority diversity was not significantly related to the number of local programs or to increased state support for institutionalizing the drug court concept. This suggests that drug courts were not viewed as providing benefits to any specific racial or ethnic group. When local communities considered establishing a drug court or states considered supporting the concept, decision makers saw the drug court program in terms of the benefits of the program for communities as a whole.

An important observation about this portion of the analysis is that the influence of information persisted over time and in the face of rival explanations for policy change. Contact with more organizations in the national information network and greater numbers of local programs significantly increased state support. A snapshot of the relative effect of greater levels of information on the growth of state support for drug courts is given in table 3.8. The level of influence is the variation in the number

Table 3.8 Effect of the National Information Network and Local Drug Court Programs on State Drug Court Support, 2004

Level of Influence		Estimated Acts[a]		Effect[b]		Effect[c] (%)	
Level	Standard Deviation	National Network[d]	Local Programs[e]	National Network[d]	Local Programs[e]	National Network[d]	Local Programs[e]
Very high	+ 2	7.05 (.73)	8.04 (.97)	2.08	3.08	+ 20.8	+ 30.7
High	+ 1	5.91 (.37)	6.31 (.41)	0.94	1.33	+ 9.4	+ 13.3
Mean	—	4.97 (.27)	4.97 (.27)	—	—	—	—
Low	− 1	4.19 (.38)	3.84 (.43)	.78	1.13	− 7.8	− 11.3
Very low	− 2	3.95 (.43)	3.08 (.53)	1.07	1.89	− 10.1	− 9.0

[a] Estimated acts of state implementation are calculated as expected values with standard errors in parentheses. Estimations were produced using Clarify Software for Interpreting and Presenting Statistical Results (King, Tomz, and Wittenberg 2000). Simulations began with a baseline established by setting all regression coefficients from table 3.5 at their mean values. Two separate simulations were performed by varying the number of sources of information in the national information network and proportion of local drug court programs per 100,000 state population around their means while holding all other values at their mean values.

[b] Effect is the difference between the estimated number of acts of state implementation and the mean.

[c] Effect is the difference between the estimated number of acts of state implementation and the mean expressed as a percentage of the total acts.

[d] National network is the number of different nonprofit organizations in the national information network identified as sources of information for individual states in the national survey of state administrators. Levels of influence are calculated by varying the number of sources around the mean.

[e] Local programs is the number of local drug court programs per 100,000 state population.

of organizations reported by states as their information contacts for information about drug courts.

As the number of organizations in the mix increased above the mean to higher levels of information contact, states increased their array of support measures. An increase in the number of organizations by 1 standard deviation above the mean increased state activity by almost 10 percent. Similarly, as the number of local drug courts per capita increased above the mean, states increased their array of state support measures as well, and by an even greater margin. An increase in local drug courts per capita of 1 standard deviation above the mean increased state support activity by more than 13 percent. It should be noted that, as information contacts decreased and as the ratio of drug courts dropped, state support declined but did not disappear. However, the clear effect of contact with more organizations in the information network was to increase state activity to support drug court programs. Similarly, the clear effect of establishing more drug courts was to increase state activity. Information is provided in the appendix about the calculation of these effects as expected values.

The chapter thus far has illustrated the influence of the national nonprofit information network on the implementation of policy change, as seen in the expansion of local programs and the growth of state institutional support for the drug court concept. The concluding portion of the chapter completes the link between information, implementation, and policy outcomes to demonstrate the links between the information network and policy change.

Beyond Implementation to Positive Policy Outcomes

Throughout the history of the drug court program, a more extensive implementation of local programs and state institutional supports for drug courts were related to changes in property crime and violent crime rates. This section of the chapter illustrates the influence of implementation—and by extension, information—on crime and arrest rates while controlling for rival explanations. To assess the influence of the extent of implementation on state rates of crime and arrest, rival explanations were considered. The multivariate method of analysis employed annual data from the fifty states over the period of the study and controlled for competing factors that could explain changes in state-level policy outcomes; this approach followed the form of the previous analysis. A two-stage model was used to control for the endogenous nature of information and to increase the theoretical significance of the results. Additional discussion of the method is included in the appendix. Because the extent of local drug court implementation influenced the level of state institutional support, the influence of state implementation on outcomes was considered separately from the influence of local implementation.

As indicated in table 3.9, a more extensive implementation of drug courts at the state and local levels was linked to declines in property crime and violent crime. In states with more local drug courts per capita, and a more extensive approach to state institutional support, rates of property crime and rates of violent crime declined. Moreover, an extensive implementation of drug courts at the state and local levels was linked to increased rates of arrest for drug abuse crimes. These influences endured over time and were significant relative to other large-scale factors that should also influence crime and arrest rates.

The potential effects of an increased implementation of state and local programs are illustrated in table 3.10, which summarizes the predicted effects if state and local implementations of drug courts are higher than average. These predicted effects are illustrated by varying the level of implementation around the mean and holding the values of the other variables constant. High implementation was represented by 1 standard deviation from the mean, and very high implementation was represented by 2 standard deviations. Controlling for other factors, high state implementation was associated with a 6 percent decrease in the state rate of property crime, a 20 percent increase in the state drug abuse arrest rate, and an 8 percent decrease in the state rate of violent crime, holding all other variables constant at their means.[5] Very high state implementation was associated with a decrease of 11 percent in the rate of property crime, an increase of 40 percent in the state rate of drug abuse arrests, and a 17 percent decrease in the rate of violent crime, again holding all other variables constant at their means.

The effect of more extensive local implementation was similar. High local implementation was associated with an 8 percent decrease in the state rate of property crime, a 13 percent increase in the state drug abuse arrest rate, and a 5 percent decrease in the state rate of violent crime, holding all other variables constant at their means. Very high local implementation was associated with a decrease of 15 percent in the rate of property crime, an increase of 28 percent in the state rate of drug abuse arrests, and a decrease of 11 percent in the rate of violent crime, again holding all other variables constant at their means.

Table 3.9 Influence of Drug Court Implementation on Criminal Justice Policy Outcomes, 1989–2004

	Outcome					
	Property Crime		Drug Abuse Arrests		Violent Crime	
Independent Variable$_{i,t}$	State	Local	State	Local	State	Local
Implementation[a]	−292.594***	−2,030.896***	57.967***	371.554***	−30.924*	−175.921**
Education	47.600***	60.993***	−11.755***	−14.135***	−9.885***	8.814***
Income	−.071***	−.070***	.005***	.005***	−.005***	.005***
Unemployment	6.813	14.284	−19.396***	−20.667***	−19.844***	20.33***
Racial diversity	3,124.246***	3,126.153***	314.088***	317.805***	632.500***	627.552***
Urban population	27.433***	27.356***	2.811***	2.836***	5.821***	5.800***
Age 18–24	67.076*	70.857*	−26.441***	−26.968***	−25.709***	−25.588***
Constant	−630.901***	−1,708.059*	1,220.234***	1,401.715	1,039.167***	965.315***
R^2	.546***	.560***	.478***	.488***	.593***	.593***
Wald chi^2	1,702.44***	1,573.50***	1,238.36***	1,467.54***	1,237.79***	1,271.28***
Number of panels (i)	50	50	50	50	50	50
Number of observations	800	800	800	800	800	800

***p < .001; **p < .01; *p < .05, two-tailed.

Note: Time-series cross-sectional data for the fifty states. Unstandardized regression coefficients. The subscript *i* contains the unit to which the observations belong, in this case the state, and controls for variation between states. The subscript *t* represents the time intervals at which the variable was measured, in this case each year from 1989 through 2004. Tolerance statistics indicate no multicollinearity.

[a] State implementation and local implementation are constructed as measures of predicted probability as explained in the appendix; remaining variables are defined in the text and described further in the appendix.

Table 3.10   Effect of More Extensive Drug Court Implementation on Criminal Justice Policy Outcomes, 1989–2004 (percent)

	Outcome		
Implementation	Property Crime	Drug Abuse Arrests	Violent Crime
State			
Very high[a]	−11	+40	−17
High[b]	−6	+20	−8
Local			
Very high[a]	−15	+28	−11
High[b]	−8	+13	−5

Note: Effects represent calculated as expected values using coefficients presented in table 3.8 and expressed in percent; estimation of expected values is explained in the text and appendix.

[a] Very high implementation is calculated at 2 standard deviations above the mean.

[b] High implementation is calculated at 1 standard deviation above the mean.

Several policy-specific indicators were also linked to changes in these large-scale outcomes over time. Greater racial diversity was associated with increased rates of both property crime and violent crime, and with increased rates of arrest for drug abuse crimes. Similarly, rates of property crime, violent crime, and arrests for drug abuse crimes were linked to urban populations. During this period, as the proportion of a state's urban population increased, the rates of property crime, violent crime, and arrests for drug abuse crimes also increased. Other demographic factors were significant as well, but they did not demonstrate consistent relationships across all outcomes.

On balance, these links between the extent of implementation and positive or desirable policy outcomes suggest that a more extensive diffusion of drug court programs at the state and local levels was significantly associated with the same state context that experienced reductions in crime rates and increases in arrests for drug abuse crimes. This analysis is tempered in part by the fact that drug court programs were not designed to be available for all offenders; drug court programs were not typically open to all criminal defendants, for example. Further, the drug court concept had not been extended to reach all those within the criminal justice population at potential risk of drug dependency or drug abuse (Bhati, Roman, and Chalfin 2008).

Conclusion

This chapter has examined the influence of the national information network through information relationships that have endured over time. Extensive information relationships between national organizations, state offices, and local programs developed through board memberships with key national organizations that championed and supported the drug court movement. These enduring information connections between state offices, local programs, and organizations in the national network made a significant difference in expanding the program across localities within states and in expanding the institutionalized support from state offices. State associations and board memberships with national organizations provided stability to an information infrastructure that was valuable to public administrators in designing, implementing, and sustaining their efforts. State associations that mirrored the drug court team framework provided support for the growth of statewide offices. National board memberships provided state offices and local programs with personal access to the national views of opinion leaders about the role of drug courts in relation to policy problems concerning drugs and crime. Through these relationships, drug court personnel accessed diverse views and opinions about drug courts. State and local administrators became aware of other approaches to drug use and criminal justice reform. The influence of these national information relationships was sustained over time and was significant in the face of rival explanations for policy change. Through these information connections, administrators translated information into implementation and, in turn, to improved state policy outcomes on a national scale (box 3.2).

BOX 3.2

After the Conference

Megan left the conference with a full to-do list. At the informal meeting of the state's delegation, she was asked by Judge Norwood to chair a steering committee to form a state drug court association. During conference sessions, she talked extensively with the members of the other drug court teams and with her treatment colleagues. These teams had a vast array of experience in different aspects of the problems with drug use, crime, and state court systems. Megan learned that state associations had formed in a few states and were quite active in drafting legislation and working on ideas to strengthen state government involvement. Some people at the conference had suggested that state associations encouraged the formation of more local

drug courts and led to more state support and, ultimately, better outcomes. State associations were hosting meetings to share information
between team members and across their states. Megan was also
pleased to learn that Judge Norwood had been asked to present the
findings of his state supreme court task force to the National Association of Drug Court Professionals governing board. She was also
pleased to learn that her supervisor at the county's Alcohol, Drug, and
Mental Health Services Board had been asked to serve as a state delegate to the Congress of Drug Court Professionals.

Megan's experiences illustrate the framework of relationships that
were developed and promoted within the national information network
by the new champion organization National Association of Drug Court
Professionals and the well-known National Center for State Courts as
a supporter organization. Champion organizations can be expected to
establish a variety of forums that encourage broad participation and
representation that will present their ideas to a national audience. The
formation of the professional organization itself is one of those forums,
as are ancillary groups such as the Congress of Drug Court Professionals. State professional associations that were modeled after the
national professional group provided further institutionalization of the
linkages between the champion national organization and the work of
public administrators in local communities and state offices. Supporters such as the National Center for State Courts continued to demonstrate their support for the new idea through their presence at national
conferences; as the idea took hold across the states, this organization
assisted state judicial offices and state court systems in their efforts to
incorporate the innovation into existing systems.

On the plane ride home, Megan sketched an agenda for the steering committee over the coming year. Her goal would be to formally
establish a statewide drug court organization that could showcase the
program by hosting a statewide conference on drug courts. She would
ask her local prosecutor to pull together a panel of speakers on the
role of attorneys in the process. The county's Alcohol, Drug, and Mental Health Services Board could assemble a panel of treatment
experts. She would invite Judge Norwood to talk about the work of
their local team in forming their local drug court, and she would ask
someone from the National Association of Drug Court Professionals
to speak about the history and goals of the drug court movement. She
would ask Judge Norwood about contacting the National Center for
State Courts for a presentation about what other states were doing to
bring the drug court idea to scale within their state court systems.
Megan also wanted to include a panel of representatives from other
supporter groups that represented legal and judicial professionals and
other groups of public administrators such as probation and law
enforcement.

Notes

1. The date of corporate formation for each state association was determined by a search of state records of incorporation in the fifty states and Internal Revenue Service filings for this type of nonprofit organization.

2. Claire McCaskill was elected Jackson County (Kansas City) prosecutor in 1992. She previously served in the Missouri legislature and in the Jackson County legislature. In 1999, she was elected Missouri state auditor; in 2006 she was elected to represent Missouri in the U.S. Senate.

3. In a somewhat ironic twist of circumstances, Price was appointed to the Missouri Supreme Court in 1992 by Missouri governor John Ashcroft and has held that office by election since 1994. Ashcroft went on to become U.S. attorney general under President George W. Bush and was responsible for eliminating the Office of Drug Control Policy during his tenure.

4. See Sampson and Laub (2005) for a discussion of the contribution of Sheldon and Eleanor Glueck and others to this body of work.

5. The simulation of expected values is described further in the appendix, along with other information about the method and approach.

4

Using Strategic Information to Build Programs

TEMPLATES, MENTORS, AND RESEARCH

A **central value** of the national nonprofit information network is the synthesized information that nonprofits generate. Typical examples include best practices, model programs, and evaluation research. Synthesized information is useful for public administrators because it combines multiple perspectives and the experiences of multiple actors and cuts the costs of seeking information (Mossberger and Hale 2002; Yin and Andranovich 1986, 1987). Synthesized information is an especially strategic type of information that acts as information "software," which administrators find more useful than other types of information when designing and implementing public policy changes (box 4.1). This information software is not electronic information per se but rather the information that helps administrators interpret the relatively inflexible parameters of the legal requirements or grant applications that frame the outline of policy changes. Information software has been linked to states that acquire more information and experience more extensive policy implementation (Mossberger and Hale 2002).

In the case of drug courts, nonprofit organizations in the information network generated several specific forms of synthesized information that administrators found to be important. Administrators were particularly interested in learning about examples of successful programs, implementation tools, and program evaluation information. Administrators were drawn to information that synthesized experiences and multiple perspectives about how to start up local programs and how to begin to develop state institutional support. In the words of one respondent, administrators were looking for information that would indicate "what works." More

BOX 4.1

County Court Administrator Caroline Overhill

County court administrator Caroline Overhill was pleasantly surprised to find a large box of materials waiting for her in the courthouse mailroom. The box contained information about a new program called a drug court that had several community leaders talking. Caroline first heard about the idea last night from Zoey Evanski at a campaign fundraising event for the presiding judge of the countywide trial court. Zoey was a well-known community philanthropist who had raised a significant amount of money to support progressive causes including new methods of drug and alcohol rehabilitation. During the course of their conversation, Zoey introduced Caroline to Bruce Mendoza, the director of New Directions for Families, which provided transitional housing in the county for nonviolent offenders reentering the community from prison. Zoey and Bruce were excited about the idea of starting a drug court within the county, and they wanted to share with Caroline a wealth of information that they had garnered from visiting a drug court in another state.

Caroline was interested but skeptical. Her county alone had nineteen judges and some were already part of a long-standing statewide task force on criminal justice reform. She wondered how a new initiative could fit into the bigger picture in her state. She also wondered whether any of the judges in her county would be interested in another new idea. The presiding judge in her county had always been supportive of programs like New Directions for Families, but the statewide reform task force was politically charged and, at times, seemed to have a monopoly on "new" ideas. Zoey and Bruce had solid reputations for their community service and follow through; Caroline knew that if they seemed enthusiastic, she should find out more about their idea. Caroline asked Zoey and Bruce to send along some information that she could review with the presiding judge. Inside the box was a list of its contents. Two DVDs catalogued a series of drug court sessions that Zoey and Bruce and others had observed in other states. Caroline noticed that Judge Norwood's court was featured; she knew that her presiding judge had served with Judge Norwood on a national committee on court reorganization for the National Center for State Courts. A policy template for drug courts written by the National Association of Drug Court Professionals was in the box, along with a best practices manual written by a local drug court team and stack of research supporting the drug court philosophy. She flipped through the best practices manual and saw a list of organizing principles and an outline of a collaborative process for bringing a community together around this new idea. Caroline placed a couple of calls to her counterparts in other counties in the state and asked them to send her anything they had on drug courts.

drug court administrators reported that information on best practices, program evaluation, and model programs was much more useful than other types of information. These three types of information transmitted detailed interpretations of the issues that were addressed in implementing drug court programs and thus helped administrators assess the relative merits of various approaches. Nearly 80 percent of state administrators identified these types of information when asked to identify the single type of information that was most important for their efforts. In comparison, information such as that on state and federal legislative trends and funding was useful, but to a lesser degree.

These findings suggest that synthesized information contributed to the diffusion of drug courts as an innovation. These findings also reflect emerging research regarding the role of nonprofit organizations in developing evaluative information and in supporting local policy initiatives (Brooks 2004; Carman 2001, 2007). By developing and distributing these types of strategic information, the national nonprofit information network made an important contribution toward building capacity in the public sector.

State administrators preferred information on best practices, model programs, and program evaluation in part because they found that these types of information were helpful in developing program standards and, in turn, demonstrating program effectiveness. One respondent noted that best practices information itself "reflects a sense of standards." Administrators commented that best practices and program evaluations typically contained statistics that could be used for many purposes. Many administrators were seeking research-based practices supported by statistics that helped demonstrate program effectiveness. The staff in one state looked for "a model that offers the best recidivism rates on the law enforcement side." An administrator in another state noted that performance measurement information was particularly important for drug courts because "drug courts have been criticized for patting themselves on the back without using performance measures."

Further, states that preferred information on best practices, program evaluation, and model programs were more likely to have in place greater numbers of state administrative practices in support of local drug court programs. Administrators believed that these forms of information were linked to their ability to secure funding support. Several states noted that these types of information were useful in making presentations to state legislatures and were necessary in order to seek government funding. Synthesized information, including information about what other states have done, provided a type of strategic shorthand for administrators, which, as we would expect, helped them cut the costs of seeking information. Administrators commented that this type of information was "practical and easy to implement with minor adjustments" and made it "easy to locate good ideas." One administrator noted that specific examples of practices and programs were "easier to see and read about than information that may or may not apply." Similarly, evaluation research "provides a variety of ideas for improving programs and for institutionalizing drug courts." Another noted that "with little direct experience in setting up a drug court, we were able to look at [an example] and fit it to our resources."

These types of synthesized and interpretive information helped foster the states' implementation of drug court policy. Administrators preferred information that increased their ability to implement programs efficiently and to implement ideas "that work." Throughout their responses, state administrators reflected a collective sense that simply knowing about funding sources was not enough. To convince state legislatures, for example, to provide additional financial support, other information about examples of success, performance, and effectiveness must be marshaled. Information that helped state administrators "make the case" was a valuable asset in those efforts. Synthesized information was used strategically to demonstrate performance, illustrate similarities, and "light the path" about how to begin local programs and how to accomplish state-level implementation of institutional supports for local drug court efforts.

This chapter focuses on three types of synthesized information from the information network that were important in shaping programs as drug court policy took hold across the country—best practices, model programs, and research studies. Some types of information will be more likely to evolve from champions as opposed to supporters, challengers, or bystanders. As their information position suggests, the champion organization the National Association of Drug Court Professionals (NADCP) took the lead in developing and disseminating a significant body of program-specific information, including the important elements of the drug court approach and suggestions about how to go about establishing a drug court program. However, champions were not alone in developing synthesized information. Supporters and challengers were also engaged in providing this type of information; these organizations contributed significantly to the overall information mix that supported drug courts as a viable policy option.

A Policy Template of Best Practices

Best practices can help administrators answer important questions about policy implementation and program performance. Best practices are generally considered to be examples of effective strategies and exemplary program elements (Camp 1995; Letts, Ryan, and Grossman 1999). By examining best practices, administrators can learn about the traits of successful performance in a given area. Administrators can use best practices as a point of comparison or benchmark to understand how their work compares with successful performance. These comparisons can provide administrators with a road map for adjusting their operations to become more similar to successful practices. Best practices and benchmarking can be used to compare organizations or programs with one another, and can also reflect an assessment of internal characteristics that are linked to success.

Best practices may be supported by rigorous research; however, in practice the concept is less formal. Often, best practices are compilations of practitioner wisdom endorsed by those with considerable experience with the topic. Best practices reflect views that have gained wide acceptance in the practitioner community. These views are often reflected in the issues that appear on organizational conference agendas, in the topics selected for training sessions across professions, and in the awards given to particular programs or practices. In talking about best practices, administrators acknowledged that the concept was somewhat idealistic; no practice was automatically best or even necessarily effective. In the words of one administrator, "It's like a search for the holy grail."

The concept of best practices is also complicated by the assumption of an empirical link between specific practices and some enhanced level of effectiveness. Effectiveness is not a singular concept and, in the case of local programs, is often defined within local constituencies. Thus, what may be a best practice in one community may be simply unworkable in another. Best practices can provide a framework for measuring program accomplishments against those of peers; however, peer selection must be done with care. Drug court administrators remarked that the selection of comparable peers was "tricky" and was likely to be complicated by local differences. For instance: "It does us no good to compare ourselves to programs that we know have more resources or a different political mix. We have to look inside the ideas at the details to know what might translate well in our jurisdiction." With these caveats, however, examples of practices used by other programs provided a jumping-off place for the spread of ideas, program implementation, and further analysis of the drug court concept.

The idea of best practices for drug court programs has taken on multiple meanings during the past twenty years. At first, when the drug court idea was new, the early programs were widely considered to be examples of best practices in reforming the criminal justice system response to nonviolent drug offenses (Belenko 1998; Peters and Murrin 2000; Tauber 1998; Terry 1999). These early programs illustrated a new model of judicial administration that also remained highly localized and tailored to local needs and preferences. Examples from California, Oregon, and Arizona illustrate some of the earliest innovations in the field. In 1991, in Alameda County, California, the Oakland-Piedmont-Emeryville Municipal Court began its operation as a drug court under the leadership of Judge Jeffery Tauber. Tauber initiated the drug court concept through a drug diversion program named FIRST (Fast, Intensive, Report, Supervision, and Treatment Diversion Program), which was notable for its "reality" basis and its use of a contractual system of rewards and sanctions. "Reality" meant accepting that participants would relapse into drug-seeking or drug-using behaviors, and that relapse would not be a basis for termination from the program. The Oakland court also addressed systemic delays in case administration that delayed offenders' entry into treatment. In working with the probation department, the court instituted a process of overnight diversion eligibility screening to more quickly connect eligible offenders with a probation officer and a supportive treatment regimen (Bedrick and Skolnick 1999).

In the same year, the program known formally as the STOP (Sanctions, Treatment, Opportunity, Progress) began in Multnomah County, Oregon (Portland). This initiative began as a drug treatment track within an expedited drug case management program. Multnomah County had already initiated several drug offender initiatives before beginning a drug court program. Among these were an intensive supervised probation program with dedicated drug treatment resources, a random drug testing and evaluation program, and substance abuse services for pregnant drug-abusing women. However, pressures in the criminal justice system created a need for additional policy intervention. Treatment capacity was frequently limited, treatment was frequently delayed by as much as four or five months, and the presumptive sentence for offenders charged with first-time possession did not include a standing court order for drug treatment (Belenko 1999a).

In Maricopa County, Arizona (Phoenix), the use of alternatives to incarceration for probationers such as shock incarceration, intensive probation supervision, and community punishment programs had not affected the growth of the prison population. The First-Time Drug Offender Program was established as an intensive, supervised drug treatment program for first-time felony drug offenders sentenced to probation (Deschenes and Peterson 1999). As multiple courts began to establish drug court programs, differences in operating practices became apparent, although programs appeared to embrace a core set of values and approaches.

With the advent of the NADCP as a national professional organization dedicated to drug courts, the idea of best practices in drug court administration took another step. The champion organization NADCP established a set of principles to frame the drug court concept. Through its Drug Court Standards Committee, the NADCP developed a set of tenets that reflected the drug court concept and that distinguished drug courts from other court-based treatment strategies. *Defining Drug Courts: The Key Components* was published by the NADCP in 1997 and contained ten key components or guiding principles that expressed the philosophy, organization, and operation of drug courts (NADCP 1997).

These guiding principles served as a template of best practices that was used to replicate the drug court concept across the country. These guiding principles moved the drug court concept from a collection of a few innovative programs to a cohesive philosophical framework that shaped the spread of the program in its modern form. Administrators used these principles as the basic architecture for constructing drug courts and in making decisions about how to implement their programs. The drug court philosophy and these key tenets were considered to be best practices in the area of judicial administration and criminal justice reform. Drug courts were hailed as best practices or examples of "what works" in numerous panel presentations at professional conferences sponsored by the NADCP and many other organizations in the information network. Adoption of the drug court philosophy as one form of best practice was urged as a method of judicial reform in some states.

As a champion organization, the NADCP reinforced the guiding principles framework in several ways, each of which also fostered new information links and methods of information exchange. The NADCP conducted informational and training programs for prospective federal grantees, and its representatives discussed the guiding principles at national and state drug court conferences around the country, posted extensive information about them on its website, and recognized particular court operations as exemplary. In conjunction with the Office of Justice Programs within the U.S. Department of Justice, a national clearinghouse was established at American University to catalog publications and collect data about federal drug court grants. As local programs began to seek state support, the NADCP drafted model drug legislation that contained the guiding principles and encouraged states to choose this model when adopting enabling legislation. *Key Components* was reissued in 2004 through a publication prepared by the NADCP under a grant from the Drug Court Program Office of the Office of Justice Programs (NADCP 2004).

Administrators followed the NADCP guiding principles framework as a package of best practices on the basis of evaluative research that found several early programs to have positive effects (Belenko 1998; Deschenes et al. 2000; Guydish et al. 2001; Harrell, Roman, and Sack 2001; Peters and Murrin 2000). This package approach was useful in communicating the concepts to state and local administrators. The framework was a powerful method of transmitting a host of information about values and ideas as well as specific dimensions for designing and organizing a drug court program. The guiding principles essentially became an information tool or vehicle for replicating the values, ideals, and content of the drug court concept. Across the board, administrators mentioned the guiding principles as the central element in the development of their local programs and state offices. As one administrator put it, the guiding principles "are the road map that got us started in the same direction as other drug courts."

Local interpretations of the guiding principles varied widely as communities interpreted them and applied them within the specific context of their own local criminal justice systems. Local customization was an important aspect of the NADCP's contribution as a champion organization and an important contribution from the information network. Variations in local interpretations demonstrated local control over the program's content and method of operation. Across the framework of the guiding principles developed by the NADCP, administrators consistently remarked that they were interested in the interpretations of other local programs and state offices: "Let's see who else is doing what we do" and "Let's see how other courts are interpreting this." These interpretations were useful for administrators as they looked at their own programs. These interpretations were also useful in building support for the drug court concept and for demonstrating that it could be successful. Administrators felt that it was important to be able to have a range of examples to use in discussions with local leaders; examples helped tell the story of the program and build a sense of legitimacy about the innovation. Examples and interpretations from other communities illustrated how changes could be implemented and were helpful in overcoming potential resistance or skepticism about drug courts. As one administrator commented, community leaders who were positively impressed with options and possibilities for making policy changes might also be likely to resist programs that seemed to depend on many requirements. Here, "showing them *how* it can be done is a big part of convincing them that it *can* be done."

Local variations also demonstrated flexibility in policy design and implementation as opposed to a one-size-fits-all, top-down approach. Table 4.1 presents the NADCP's guiding principles and gives examples some of the interpretations of the guiding principles developed within different drug court programs. These examples illustrate just a few of the approaches that local programs have used to define various aspects of the drug court concept.

Local interpretations of the drug court tenets ranged from the general to the specific. For example, one element of the guiding principles (GPs) is the concept of an array of alcohol and other drug treatment services integrated with the judicial process of case administration (GP 1). The precise role of treatment providers is not prescribed. Integration was interpreted by some local programs to mean the inclusion of treatment representatives on local drug court teams or state steering committees. It was also interpreted as an imperative for treatment representatives to participate in all drug court team meetings, or for courts to incorporate treatment reports into case files in some specific way.

Another key element of the drug court approach is the nonadversarial approach of the court process that occurs in tandem with protecting public safety and the due process rights of participants (GP 2). This was understood by some courts to mean that the drug court team had identified a protocol or script for prosecutors and defense counsel to follow so that they never disagreed with one another in front of participants. It was also used to describe the target population of the program, meaning that the court was open to using the drug court concept for a wide range of offenses in the interest of public safety.

The idea of a continuum of services (GP 4) was interpreted to mean that drug court programs rely on treatment administered through a series of progressive phases. In other courts, the interpretation expanded to mean a continuum of services that included treatment along with education and employment services, or participation in specific twelve-step self-help programs such as Alcoholics Anonymous or Narcotics Anonymous. Drug court teams and state administrators shared different interpretations of

Table 4.1   Interpreting the NADCP's Guiding Principles as Best Practices

Guiding Principle	Examples of Local Interpretations
1. Integrated alcohol and drug treatment with judicial case processing	• Treatment provider representatives are members of the drug court team or other collaboration • Drug courts receive written reports from treatment providers
2. Nonadversarial approach to promote public safety and due process rights	• Defense attorneys and/or prosecutors attend all drug court hearings and/or all drug court team meetings • Prosecution and defense present united front in court
3. Early identification and prompt placement	• The time within which placement must occur is specified • Eligibility requirements are specified
4. Access to a continuum of services	• Treatment occurs in phases along a continuum • Treatment is one of a range of additional services including mental health, social work, education, and/or employment
5. Frequent drug/alcohol testing	• Various frequencies are specified and linked to program requirements. • Various methods and procedures are specified
6. Coordinated strategy for court responses	• Various sanctions and rewards are specified including incarceration and decreased frequency of drug testing • Protocols are established for various situations
7. Ongoing judicial interaction with each participant	• Frequency of participant contact with judge is specified • Participation of judge in staff and policy meetings as well as court hearings
8. Monitoring and evaluation against program goals	• Program statistics are collected and reported • Independent evaluations are conducted
9. Continuing interdisciplinary education of program staff	• The drug court team attends national and state drug court conferences • Training focuses on drug court coordinators and case managers
10. Partnerships with community agencies and community-based organizations	• The drug court team is interdisciplinary • A steering committee exists with broad representation from the community as well as drug court disciplines

Sources: Guiding principles from National Association of Drug Court Professionals (1997); adaptations provided by local and state administrators.

drug testing protocols—how the process was conducted, including who conducted the tests; how frequently tests were administered; procedures for randomizing samples; various turnaround times for samples; and the length of time that participants were required to test drug free before graduation (GP 5). Drug court teams also learned about different types of sanctions and rewards that were used in programs as their coordinated strategy to respond to participants' behavior (GP 6). Some programs utilized incarceration as a sanction, others used gift certificates and other small items as rewards, and some concentrated all the authority for rewards and sanctions with the drug court judge.

One of the central innovations of the drug court approach was the role of the judge. Administrators turned to the NADCP for information about their options and to make connections with other programs to get ideas about how to structure that role. GP 7 states that "ongoing judicial interaction with each participant is essential." As a baseline, the idea of judicial interaction was interpreted to mean that drug court judges attend every drug court session. In addition, programs established protocols that required the drug court judge to attend every team meeting to discuss participants' progress and every meeting of every collaborative or working group concerning drug courts. The idea of ongoing interaction was also interpreted as a measure of frequency or continuity of drug court participants' interactions with the drug court judge—for example, every two weeks, every month, or at some other interval.

Administrators also mentioned other examples of best practices that centered on management techniques. These tended toward strategies to be used with collaborative, interdisciplinary teams and the essentials of monitoring the performance of the program. These included the use of written guidelines about program content that were shared with program participants; these guidelines covered a wide variety of topics, including the frequency of drug testing, the frequency of treatment, the frequency of court appearances, the potential sanctions and rewards that were possible, and the circumstances that would trigger any of these events. Other best practices centered on the guiding principle that pertains to monitoring and evaluating programs against goals (GP 8). In this area, as with the other guiding principles, program-level examples of best practices were diverse, and they included the use of electronic records for overall court case management or specifically for drug court programs and various reporting frequencies. Examples of these best practices for managing drug court operations are given in table 4.2. As with the guiding principles, these concepts were defined within local communities.

Table 4.2 Illustrations of Best Practices in Drug Court Implementation

Concept	Best Practice Strategies
Teams	• Develop and maintain an interdisciplinary, nonadversarial team that includes law enforcement and treatment. • Include the drug court judge, drug court coordinator, prosecutor, public defender, and/or private defense counsel, case manager, treatment provider, law enforcement officer. • Meet regularly to discuss general program issues outside the discussion of specific cases.
Collaboration	• Create forums for stakeholders to coordinate an approach to set goals, design the ten key components for their community, and set standards based on the ten key components. • Create an environment where team members can represent their agencies or programs but can also be flexible about boundaries in order to reach a group decision.
Monitoring and evaluation	• Clearly define target populations, eligibility criteria, and goals. • Develop measurement systems to demonstrate progress toward goals.
Continuity	• Create a charter or memorandum of understanding to memorialize how the team operates. • Include the roles and responsibilities of each team member and how decisions are made in the group. • Use this to train new team members.

The NADCP's guiding principles remain the fundamental framework for drug court program content and have been relatively institutionalized within the information network. Many supporter organizations in the information network provided information about the guiding principles through links on their organization websites or other publications; examples include the National Center for State Courts, the National Council for Juvenile and Family Court Judges, and the National Judicial College. The NADCP's guiding principles were broadly considered to be examples of best practices derived from evidence-based research that supports the concept of coerced treatment. Administrators spoke of maintaining "fidelity to the NADCP model" and "protecting the drug court brand." Despite the localized implementation of particular parameters, local interpretations of the guiding principles were considered to be best practices precisely because they reflected local practices. Administrators observed the need to continue to operate drug court programs in the manner developed by the NADCP. Administrators noted the difficulty in establishing incontrovertible evidence about how best to remedy an entrenched problem within the offender population, and they were strongly inclined to continue to apply the NADCP's guiding principles in the absence of evidence to the contrary.

The examples of best practices given in this section illustrate the issues that local programs faced in interpreting the essential elements of the drug court concept. The guiding principles provided a framework for communication across the information network and for customization. These best practice examples also illustrate a path from initial implementation to performance measurement and comparative assessment. As these and other examples were shared across local programs and state offices, administrators learned from one another about specific practices that helped other programs solve problems and accomplish goals. Administrators had the opportunity to assess the potential of these ideas for use in their home jurisdictions.

This process of self-examination and comparison is linked to superior organizational performance. Camp (1995) suggests that this process leads organizations to be proactive in seeking solutions and solving actual problems. The process also aligns programs with a common set of principles and a consistent practice of local interpretation. As the process continues, organizations gain an improved understanding of their outputs and of their strengths and weaknesses.

On the whole, the process reflected a pattern of bottom–up implementation. Before the formation of a national professional organization dedicated to drug courts, local programs drew upon practices used in the newly established drug courts. Following the formation of the NADCP in 1994, local programs became engaged in the drug court concept through the guiding principles framework as a best practice; the guiding principles themselves drew upon practitioner experiences and emerging research that supported a new concept. Finally, local programs engaged in the process of working out the details of particular practices and attempted to tie practices to measurable results. Building on past efforts, additional systematic analyses of the guiding principles sought to link particular operating practices to varying levels of program results. Significantly, these efforts also occurred in relation to the NADCP's guiding principles. One study tracked the interpretations of the principles in eighteen adult drug courts and assessed the significance of those interpretations against graduation rates and program costs (Carey, Finigan, and Pukstas 2008); the study identified practices that were substantially similar across these programs and those that were substantially different, and it assessed whether these practices influenced certain program outcomes and costs. This report represented another step in the evolution of performance measurement of the drug court concept. State offices and local programs can be expected to examine their operations against the practices identified in this report and to make adjustments toward those practices that demonstrate improvements in the areas that align with their program goals. The results of this study should provide the basis for further analysis of linkages between specific interpretations and desirable outcomes at the program level. The results of this study should also provide a basis for refining the development of statewide standards that are under way in many states.

Providing a Policy Experience

"Have you seen our drug court yet?" "Have you been to a drug court graduation?" It is something of an understatement to report that drug court personnel were excited to share the experiences of their programs through observation. Invitations to observe drug court proceedings were extended in nearly every face-to-face conversation that occurred during the collection of data on this project. In addition, frequent invitations to observe were extended during the many telephone and electronic conversations that took place.

Observations are a part of the drug court culture and have been promoted by the champion organization NADCP in several ways. Nolan (2001) noted that observations and mentoring processes are part of an intentional strategy to help newcomers learn to craft messages about the drug court program. The NADCP played a central role in facilitating the observation of drug court proceedings through role-playing demonstrations and live feeds of drug court operations at annual conferences. Demonstrations and observations were followed by discussion and provided conference participants with the opportunity to ask questions and interact with their peers about what they saw and what it meant to them. In addition, the NADCP established a mentor court network program in 1996 that began with a mentor court site in each of seven states (California, Florida, Kentucky, Missouri, Oklahoma, Nevada, and New York; Nolan 2001).

The mentor court program institutionalized a method for direct observation of existing drug courts and dialogue with drug court practitioners. Mentor courts also institutionalized a measure of power at the community level and in local courts. The mentor drug court concept was based on the premise that local drug courts were the most logical venues in which to educate and train court practitioners. This process promoted local engagement and local control over program decisions; the local focus on resources was particularly important for sustainability because the majority of program support was local (Cooper 1997). Mentor court visits were highly popular from their inception. The mentor court network expanded to include at least twenty-five experienced drug courts and provided experience and referrals that matched interested local communities with mentor opportunities in operational drug courts. In 1999 more than 2,500 individuals visited a mentor drug court, and 1,900 of those visits occurred in conjunction with drug court training programs (Office of Justice Programs 2000).

The network of mentor drug courts transmitted information as a policy experience—a form of information synergy coupled with the synthesized information of a typical model program. As a policy experience, mentor courts provided much more than simple discussion sessions. Mentor courts provided technical expertise and expert assistance on a regional basis, and they agreed to host visiting jurisdictions and training sessions in their area. In the mentor court program, newly formed drug court teams visited mentor court sites and watched court sessions. Team members met with the local drug court team and discussed the process. During their attendance, prosecutors, defense attorneys, judges, treatment professionals, and probation personnel were typically encouraged to ask questions about the court's operations. Mentor courts also provided a forum for sharing problems. Administrators observed that mentor court visits gave them the opportunity to talk with people who understood the issues that drug courts encountered and provided opportunities for mutual support. In this way, potential drug court professionals and community leaders gained new knowledge about the drug court concept.

Observation was a key element of the mentor court process and a central information tool that facilitated program replication and institutionalization. Administrators believed that observations of other programs were an essential part of learning how to start and sustain a drug court program and how to improve their own programs. Administrators remarked about the importance of having local judges see the process in action and the dramatic change of opinion that can occur through observation and the mentoring process. Observations of the nation's first drug court in Miami-Dade, Florida, were common. A report from the Join Together Project of the Boston University School of Public Health illustrates the experience of one Massachusetts judge. Robert Zieman is now the presiding judge of the Dorchester Drug Court in South Boston and a leader in promoting drug courts. He was initially opposed to the idea but reported a significant change of opinion following a visit to the Miami-Dade court: "I went to a workshop about it at a bar association meeting, and I thought the guy was out of his mind. . . . For those familiar with court proceedings, drug courts are very different. . . . You really have to go, watch what happens, talk about it afterwards. But once you've seen it in action, it all makes sense" (quoted by E. Edwards 2004).

Judges were not the only members of the potential drug court team who had enlightening experiences while observing mentor courts in action. A public defender attending the Miami-Dade drug court as a participant in the mentor court exchange process had a similarly strong reaction upon observing the drug court proceeding and its nontraditional courtroom atmosphere, which included periodic applause from a jury box full of program participants and informal interaction with the judge: "One of the women in the program stood up and told the judge that she wanted to give him a present. 'I'm thinking, what kind of court is this where they give judges presents?' [she] said. 'Then, [the woman] starts singing, "You Can't Hurry God," and the guys in the jury box are singing harmony. Everybody in the room, all these lawyers and judges from all over the country, were crying. . . . If I could get that for my clients, I'd be willing to put up with a lot'" (Conroy 2002).

Designation as a mentor court brought recognition and status for local programs and local drug court judges through various avenues. One example was the recognition given the Philadelphia Treatment Court for its designation as a mentor court. Court representatives publicized the selection of the Philadelphia Treatment Court as a mentor drug court site in a monthly judicial publication: "While the demands on the Philadelphia Treatment Court resources will increase with this designation, training various jurisdictions and becoming a host city for future drug court conferences sponsored by the United States Department of Justice and NADCP is viewed as a monumental accomplishment for our court, the City of Philadelphia, and the Commonwealth of Pennsylvania" (First Judicial District of Pennsylvania 2001).

The Philadelphia Treatment Court was recognized by the Philadelphia City Council in a resolution that established May 2006 as "National Drug Court Treatment Month" in the city and also recognized the court's status as a mentor court:

Whereas, The judges, prosecutors, defense attorneys, treatment professionals, law enforcement and corrections personnel, researchers and educators,
national and community leaders and other dedicated to the movement have
had a profound impact through hard work and commitment to their communities; and . . . we support the monumental accomplishments of the Philadelphia Treatment Court, the first established in the Commonwealth of
Pennsylvania in 1997, . . . and we recognize that the Philadelphia Treatment
Court has received national distinction as a mentor court from the U.S.
Department of Justice and the National Association of Drug Court Professionals (NADCP), one of only 30 mentor courts in the country. (Philadelphia 2006)

This type of recognition spread information and provided stakeholders in
the drug court concept with an opportunity to reiterate collaborative relationships across professional communities and reinforced links to national
organizations such as the NADCP.

The Covington District of the Louisiana Department of Public Safety
and Corrections noted the mentor court status of its drug court program
on its website: "[Our] Drug Court Program is recognized as one of the best
in the country, and has been named as a 'mentor program' for other drug
courts to emulate. We have recently begun participation in the state's first
felony DWI Court Program, modeled after the highly successful Drug
Court Model (2009)."

Selection as a mentor court knitted together other aspects of the
NADCP template. Mentor courts successfully completed a national-level
orientation through the NADCP's Drug Court Planning Initiative or
received a federal drug court planning grant from the Office of Justice
Programs. Mentor courts also documented the manner in which their
operating policies and procedures reflected the implementation of the
NADCP's guiding principles. States leveraged the idea of mentor court
status to support state efforts to collect data. In Tennessee, for example,
mentor courts agreed to implement and report the Tennessee statewide
drug court performance measures to the state office that administers all
federal criminal justice grants and agreed to use the state office as a
clearinghouse for information (Tennessee Office of Criminal Justice Programs 2004).

The mentor court concept was also familiar to supporter organizations
in the information network. Supporter organizations in the network used
the concept of model courts to provide mentorship opportunities in the
judicial administration of various types of programs. As one example, the

National Council of Juvenile and Family Court Judges (NCJFCJ) developed an extensive model court program to improve the systemic response and outcomes in child abuse and neglect cases in juvenile and family court systems. Collaborative projects connected child welfare and protective services agencies, attorneys, the foster care administration, and officers of the court to improve outcomes for children and families. A national network of thirty-one model courts under the NCJFCJ's Child Victims Act Model Courts Project served as models and mentors to jurisdictions nationwide. This project linked with the Juvenile Drug Court Training and Technical Assistance Project, sponsored by the U.S. Department of Justice's Bureau of Justice Assistance, to help juvenile drug courts implement or enhance their programs (National Council of Juvenile and Family Court Judges 2009).

The mentor court provided a synergistic policy experience in its own right. In addition, the idea of mentor courts and the concept of court observation as a method of transmitting information spurred synergy between champion organizations and supporters in the information network. Consider the example of Judge Leonard P. Edwards of the Superior Court of California for Santa Clara County. In 2004, Edwards received the Rehnquist Award for Judicial Excellence conferred annually by the National Center for State Courts. Rehnquist Award winners are state court judges who exemplify the highest level of judicial excellence, integrity, fairness, and professional ethics. Edwards was the first juvenile court judge to receive the award, which was presented at a ceremony held at the U.S. Supreme Court. Among Judge Edwards's credentials for this award were his efforts in establishing two mentor courts. One of these mentor courts was among the country's first dependency drug treatment courts, which was also named a mentor court by the NADCP. Another was a juvenile dependency court, which was designated a national model court by the National Council of Juvenile and Family Court Judges. An account of the award and these mentor courts was given in the *Journal of the Center for Families, Children & the Courts*, along with the text of Judge Edwards's speech. The introduction observed that Edwards's current court was one of the most visited courts in the country; hundreds of legal professionals traveled there to observe and learn the model practices that he implemented (L. Edwards 2004).

Mentor courts also provided an opportunity for further collaboration within stakeholder communities. As one example, the NADCP named the Fayette, Kentucky, drug court as a mentor training site for drug courts and Community Oriented Policing Services (known as COPS), a widely recognized local law enforcement initiative. This joint designation acknowledged the importance of collaboration between these two policy communities. These collaborations reinforced the common ground between law enforcement organizations and drug court advocates in the national information network. And the collaborations suggested that law enforcement was a supporter of the drug court concept in this local community. The local police force had been nationally recognized as an outstanding force and supported the local drug court by assigning a liaison officer, making home visits with case specialists, hosting mentor trainees from various states, aiding with alcohol testing, and performing many other functions (Noble and Reed 1999). As another example, the National District Attorneys Association supported the idea of mentor court programs and distributed information about a wide range of mentor courts across the information network (National District Attorneys Association 2005). Recognition conferred legitimacy to the mentor court programs and bridged the professional gap between prosecutors and defense attorneys as well as with other professional groups. Recognition suggested the credibility of these programs as alternatives to traditional court processes and criminal justice practices.

Research across the Information Network

Champion organizations such as the NADCP were at the forefront in developing and disseminating information about best practices and model programs that pertain specifically to the drug court concept. As the examples given above illustrate, supporter organizations also played a role in lending credibility to initiatives that meshed with their own objectives. In the area of research and evaluation, the broader influence of the information network became even more apparent. Not surprisingly, early research and evaluative information about drug courts was promoted by the NADCP and published through its research arm, the National Drug Court Institute. Other organizations in the information network also provided a rich mix of research, evaluation, and technical assistance. Supporter organizations were active in providing information that addressed particular management challenges as the program was diffused to the state level. Challengers were active in providing other points of view about other options and in questioning whether the drug court program was the appropriate road to take. Sustained information relationships between administrators and a variety of information positions have intertwined and reinforced one another as this policy has been diffused and as implementation and evaluation have begun.

As an example of the influence of research information from various organizations in the information network, consider the evolution of drug courts in Alabama. The Alabama experience integrated research from multiple sources into an initiative for statewide reform across the criminal justice system. The expansion of local drug court programs was integrated with the overall process of sentencing review that was guided by work with national research organizations in the information network. Studies from supporters and challengers flowed among a variety of commissions, boards, and task forces charged with studying criminal justice issues and making recommendations for reform. The information in some of these studies supported the position of the champion NADCP, which has also been quite productive in generating research about drug court programs. The information in other studies challenged the concept of drug courts. Together, these studies guided the development of a comprehensive approach to policy reform that includes the drug court program. The implications of these studies spurred the creation of new task forces and working groups to consider new policy alternatives. This integration was not unique to Alabama, and it illustrates the variety of intersectoral information relationships that surrounded policy research and technical assistance to administrators.

In the early 1990s, Alabama adopted a variety of reforms to address an increasing prison population and to incorporate drug treatment and alternatives to incarceration into the state justice system. State reforms included a mandatory alcohol and drug abuse treatment programs for certain drug offenses and a local community corrections framework for nonviolent offenders. Several local jurisdictions embarked upon drug court operations during the early years of the drug court movement; four drug courts were established in major urban areas—including Mobile, Tuscaloosa, Birmingham, and Jefferson County—between 1993 and 1997 (Office of Justice Programs 2000).

In spite of these attempts to address increases in the criminal justice population, the Alabama prison population increased dramatically relative to the nation as a whole (Green and Pranis 2005). In response to this pressure, a judicial study commission was established in 1998 by the executive branch and the judiciary to identify the strengths and weaknesses of the Alabama criminal justice system. On the recommendations of this commission, the Alabama legislature created the Alabama Sentencing Commission (ASC) as a state agency reporting to the Alabama Supreme

Court. The ASC was established as the research arm of the criminal justice system with responsibilities for collecting, analyzing, and reporting information and making recommendations to the governor, legislature, attorney general, and judicial study commission. The ASC was also charged with reviewing and making recommendations about the continuing crisis of state prison crowding (ASC 2002, 2003, 2004, 2007, 2008).

From its inception, the ASC collaborated with the Vera Institute of Justice and sought information about criminal justice reform options from a wide range of sources. As early as 2000, the Vera Institute had published reports on drug court performance (Fluellen and Trone 2000). These reports challenged the record of existing research about drug courts, particularly in terms of the limited number of studies and the limitations inherent in attempts to generalize findings across programs that were very different from one another. Of particular importance, Vera also reported the cost savings associated with use of drug courts as an alternative to traditional incarceration and supported the drug court approach as one of several potential cost reduction strategies (Wool and Stemen 2004). In its first annual report, the ASC featured its continuing relationship with Vera. The ASC also noted the relationships between commission members and a wide range of contacts in the national information network. ASC members participated in and attended national seminars on sentencing policies, community corrections, reentry programs, and probation and parole issues. Crucial technical assistance was provided by Vera through briefings with executive board members and staff on key policy issues, sentencing practices in other states, and national sentencing trends. Vera also connected ASC members with others serving on sentencing commissions and active in criminal justice reform efforts in other states (ASC 2002).

The result in Alabama was a holistic approach to the criminal justice system and an effort to incorporate drug courts within a larger reform framework. Starting in 2000, a central aspect of the relationship with the Vera Institute focused on collecting data to capture various dimensions of the Alabama criminal justice system. Vera actively promoted the creation of a statewide database, and this recommendation was adopted by the ASC (2002, 2003, 2004, 2007, 2008). Vera also recommended an increase in community-based alternatives to incarceration. From 2000 forward, the ASC's recommendations also consistently reflected the need for additional sentencing options for nonviolent felony offenders and opportunities for diversion from state prison rather than incarceration.

The Alabama criminal justice database itself became a springboard for further recommendations that pertain to drug courts and other alternatives to incarceration. The Alabama Administrative Office of the Courts (AOC) has collected data through its case management system since the adoption of mandatory treatment in 1990, and it has used this case management system to collect and distribute information about Alabama drug courts and other treatment referral programs in an effort to promote consistency in case management services across the state's courts (ASC 2002, 2008; Alabama Administrative Office of the Courts 2008). The case management system revolved around a network of court referral officers deployed throughout the state courts and centralized in the Alabama AOC. These court referral officers became the case managers on drug court teams in courts that have implemented drug court programs.

The Alabama AOC designed and implemented a Web-based case management system for use by court referral officers working with offenders convicted of driving under the influence of alcohol in the state. The system, called the Model Integrated Defendant Access System (MIDAS), was implemented for offenses for driving under the influence of alcohol under the guidance of Michael Gregory, who now serves as the drug court project manager within the Alabama AOC. MIDAS was facilitated through a grant from the National Highway Transportation Safety Administration (NHTSA). Alabama was one of only four states awarded this NHTSA grant, which was intended to produce case management systems that can be replicated by other states. MIDAS was a collaborative project between NHTSA, the Alabama AOC, the Alabama Department of Economic and Community Affairs and Department of Public Safety, and the University of Alabama (University of Alabama 2008). This infrastructure serves as a platform for further design to suit the state's drug court efforts; the ASC and the Alabama AOC will continue to work together on this effort (ASC 2008). Today, Alabama's drug courts are considered to be part of a larger group of accountability courts administered with assistance from the Alabama AOC. The term reflects a more comprehensive perspective that encompasses other local court programs.

Challenger organizations also focused attention on Alabama's reform efforts and the dynamics of the Alabama criminal justice system. In 2005, the Drug Policy Alliance commissioned and released a policy report titled *Alabama Prison Crisis* (Green and Pranis 2005). This report analyzed the disproportionate rise in Alabama's incarceration rate during the past twenty-five years from a relatively average ranking among other states to one of the top five in 2005. The report offered various explanations for the current situation; contributory factors include sentencing practices that incarcerate nonviolent and low-level offenders and the lack of a viable community corrections system with a continuum of alternatives to incarceration (Green and Pranis 2005).

Against this backdrop, local drug court programs were heavily promoted as a result of support from Supreme Court Chief Justice Sue Bell Cobb (D), who was elected to the Alabama Supreme Court in 2007. Cobb made statewide expansion of the drug court program a major focus of her office following her election; her objective was to establish one drug court in each of Alabama's sixty-seven counties by 2010. Her initiative produced dramatic growth in the number of local courts; in February 2008 thirty-eight adult drug courts were operational in thirty-six different counties, encompassing twenty-six of the state's forty-one judicial circuits. Expansion had bipartisan support from Governor Bob Riley (R), who committed $250,000 in state funds as seed money toward the effort (ASC 2008).

Chief Justice Cobb also appointed a Drug Court Task Force within her office. The group of twenty-seven community leaders and representatives from all three branches of government was chaired by retired district court judge Pete Johnson, a longtime leader of the state's drug court efforts. In 1995, Judge Johnson initiated the Drug Court in the District Court of Jefferson County (Birmingham Division), funded by a grant awarded to the University of Alabama at Birmingham under the Treatment Alternatives to Street Crime program. The Drug Court Task Force was charged with mapping the method to establish an effective drug court in each county in the state. The task force was also responsible for establishing uniform standards for the drug court programs and seek the necessary support and funding to sustain a model statewide drug court system within the broad framework of the NADCP's guiding principles (ASC 2008). The task force planned to revive the Alabama Association of Drug Court Professionals. As early as 1997, a group convened to support drug courts in Alabama through an association of drug courts; however, the literature does not reflect that this group made a formal transition to professional association (Alabama Administrative Office of the Courts 1998, 2008). The Alabama AOC planned to utilize the assistance of the NADCP in helping the task force establish the state association. Alongside the drug court initiative and the work of the Alabama AOC and the task force, the ASC continued to work with the Vera Institute to develop a continuum of comprehensive alternatives to incarceration, including the statewide expansion of drug courts and training and evaluation initiatives as well as other community corrections options as part of the state's overall effort to reduce its prison population and control costs.

The focus on data-driven reforms led to additional research support and collaboration with other organizations. The Vera Institute provided technical assistance to the ASC, the Alabama Supreme Court, and other state and local stakeholders through the Cooperative Community Alternative Sentencing Project. This work was funded by the Pew Center on the States as part of its Public Safety Performance Project, which was launched in 2006 to provide expertise and technical assistance to thirteen states that want a better return on their public safety investments. The project selected Alabama to receive intensive and nonpartisan research, analysis, and expertise. Alabama's focus on collaboration and data-driven research was central in its selection for this additional support. Among other factors, Alabama's leaders demonstrated both a bipartisan commitment to explore meaningful policy change and a dedication to collecting and using criminal justice data as a basis for sound reform (Pew Center on the States 2008).

Alabama's involvement with these organizations expanded the information base as new research reports were released. Through its Public Safety Performance Project, Pew focused new attention on corrections policy in the states. The findings of Pew research publications—such as *One in 100: Behind Bars in America 2008* and *One in 31: The Long Reach of American Corrections* (Pew Center on the States 2008, 2009)—percolated through the Alabama criminal justice system as a direct result of these collaborative relationships. The Alabama AOC also focused on research published by the Justice Policy Institute in 2007. *The Vortex: The Concentrated Racial Impact of Drug Imprisonment and the Characteristics of Punitive Counties* (Beatty, Petteruti, and Ziedenberg 2007) presented evidence of racial disparity in conceptualizing drug crime.

The National Center for State Courts (NCSC) continued to play a strong role as a supporter of processes that help state court administrative offices incorporate drug court program concepts into their state court systems. With the NCSC's guidance and technical assistance, the Alabama AOC conducted an internal assessment of how best to serve the Alabama court system in light of the implementation of sentencing reforms and a more extensive network of community-based alternatives to incarceration, including drug court programs. The NCSC published numerous research studies and technical assistance reports that synthesized the experience of drug court programs across the states. These reports provided information on models and trends in drug court administration and operation around the country (e.g., Casey and Rottman 2003; Casey, Rottman, and Bromage 2007). As the drug courts program expanded, the NCSC's reports reflected the emerging issues facing local programs and state initiatives to institutionalize support for drug courts.

As is the case in every state, the specific projects, offices, and task forces illustrated in the Alabama example were unique to the state's political context and the institutional structures of its criminal justice system. The Alabama experience illustrates the general case, which is that research relationships provided a strong pathway for information exchange and synergy among organizations that led to additional information and relationships. These research relationships shaped the evolution of the Alabama drug court program into one component of a data-driven initiative that is supported by the state as well as through local programs. These research relationships were also common to other states. Among the states examined closely in this study, many had some level of formal interaction with the NCSC in the form of technical assistance or planned to investigate such an approach in the near future.

The dissemination of these research studies was not limited to Alabama. Research reports and comparative compilations of program information were widely available from the NCSC through the publications section of its website. Current research publications—such as the Justice Policy Institute's *The Vortex* (2007) and Pew Center on the States' *1 in 31* (2008) and *1 in 100* (2009)—were mentioned frequently by state administrators. These and other studies were on the radar within judicial professional circles and sentencing commissions across the information network. The Vera Institute and other national research organizations publicized their efforts in state-specific projects, such as the one under way in Alabama. General information links to these studies were incorporated into organization websites and made it easy for administrators to examine projects in other jurisdictions. The influence of research information has been to transmit to administrators a series of different information sets about drug courts and about the larger picture of drugs, crime, and state policy choices. Studies compared states to one another and illustrated the successes and failures of policy choices across a series of states, or across the country as a whole. This form of synthesized information provided a basis for administrators to compare their policy choices across jurisdictions. This information was also integrated by administrators into the process of making policy decisions specifically about drug courts and more broadly about the direction of state criminal justice policy.

Conclusion

In this chapter the experiences of administrators have illustrated the value they found in the information tools that were created by the organizations in the national information network and that were fostered and supported by interactions across the information network. Through best practices, model programs, and research information about drugs and crime, public administrators were able to access multiple experiences, values, and ideals from the network and from each other. Administrators used these synthesized forms of information as a strategy for developing local programs and state institutions. The policy template acted as a form of best practices, both for the drug court concept and for the development of state and local programs. Mentor courts reinforced the philosophy of the drug court experience and fostered new connections across programs and states. These information tools flourished in an environment of research about national trends, state issues, and different policy approaches. Together, these information tools put administrators in touch with the experiences of other programs. Administrators had access to a wealth of comparative information and examples that they customized to fit their circumstances and preferences.

These information tools also illustrate the influence of information positions within the national information network. Administrators looked to champions and supporters for tools that could be used to replicate a general set of ideas across jurisdictions. Administrators looked to champions and supporters to see what should be done, and how to proceed with implementation at the local and state levels. Administrators looked across the network for research that would validate the drug court concept as a policy solution. At the state level in particular, administrators looked for a wide range of research information to understand how the drug court program could be integrated into their state's systems for judicial administration and criminal justice. Through the process of using these information tools, administrators continued to interact with the national information network and with one another; as a result of the sustained interaction based on these information tools, the drug court program steadily advanced toward institutionalization in state offices (box 4.2).

BOX 4.2

Caroline's Mentor Drug Court Visit

Caroline found a host of information shortcuts in that box of mail. The best practices information from the National Association of Drug Court Professionals and the local drug court manual provided a template for organizing a local drug court around the preferences of her community. The DVDs showed mentor drug court sessions that illustrated the unique drug court approach and that allowed those interested in the concept to ask questions of their professional counterparts in other jurisdictions. Caroline compiled a summary of the research reports and presented this information to the presiding judge. Along with Zoey and Bruce, Caroline and her presiding judge assembled a team of stakeholders and scheduled a mentor drug court visit to Judge Norwood's drug court.

Caroline's team visit was the beginning of the drug court concept in her state; from that box of information tools, the idea spread widely and garnered attention and interest from state officials. From that mentor court visit, a drug court was established in Caroline's county court and interest grew around the state. State officials became interested in learning about how they could become involved in this policy change. Along the way, Caroline and others became acquainted with research studies that showed that other states had tackled sentencing issues alongside reforms in drug treatment.

These experiences highlight the extensive array of information tools that champions and supporters developed around the drug court innovation. Champions can be expected to develop information tools that help administrators plan, design, and implement a new idea. Here, these tools included the program guidelines and manuals that could be customized to fit local preferences. These tools also helped promote the drug court experience through site visits and mentor court programs. The information tools that evolved were familiar to supporter organizations; this familiarity facilitated acceptance across professional groups and helped bring about institutionalization at the local and state levels. Research from a host of organizations including supporters and challengers helped hone the drug court concept. From these studies, administrators gained a systematic, structured understanding of the challenges to the idea and to its implementation. Research studies gave administrators a practical basis for analysis and comparison of the conditions under which this policy innovation appeared to take hold and thrive and the conditions that prevailed within their individual jurisdictions. In total, these synthesized forms of information provided administrators with a comprehensive information package that could be used to determine whether and how to begin local drug court programs and establish institutional support for the idea within state government.

5

Information and Systemic Change

NEW PROFESSIONALS AND NEW INSTITUTIONS

Synthesized information tools such as a policy template, the mentor court policy experience, and research studies illustrated one aspect of the influence of the national information network in building capacity for public agencies as they seek to implement new programs. Enduring institutional relationships with organizations in the network through board memberships and state professional associations illustrated another aspect. In the story of the diffusion of drug court programs, there was yet another layer of influence from the network that extended beyond the types of information that were exchanged and the relatively informal collection of organizations. This additional layer of influence was found in a process of collaboration and decision making that coalesced on the basis of specific information tools from the network. This combination of tools and process influenced the intergovernmental relationships surrounding drug courts. New formal relationships developed based on the concept of a drug court professional and a drug court team. New local collaborations formed to design drug court operations by using the guiding principles of the National Association of Drug Court Professionals (NADCP) as a policy template. New state collaborations formed on the basis of this same template to design state programs and develop performance standards. Task forces and working groups emerged across the states at both the state and local levels (boxes 5.1 and 5.2).

Within these new groups, interactions between administrators and organizations in the information network surrounding drug court policy were repeatedly facilitated by information tools that incorporated processes that fostered collaboration among diverse groups. Those collaborative

---

BOX 5.1

The Experiences of a
State Court Administrator

Dolores Groleaux is a state court administrator responsible for supervising court referral officers. In her southern state, court referral officers have been involved for many years in making connections between drug offenders and treatment services as a condition of probation. Although a few local judges have embraced the drug court concept, drug courts are not widespread across her state. This will now change, because Governor David Vitale's campaign to fund drug courts to combat the rapid spread of methamphetamine use in the state has just been enacted by the state legislature. A key aspect of Governor Vitale's campaign focused on the findings of a judicial task force in a neighboring state chaired by Judge James Norwood, a long-standing friend of the governor. Dolores wonders how best to introduce her court referral officers to the drug court concept and to engage them effectively in this new approach. She knows that not all court referral officers embraced the drug court concept; the state's previous treatment programs were administered through contract arrangements and referral officers were not directly involved. Dolores knows that drug courts are supported by the National Association of Drug Court Professionals; she turns to their website to learn more.

---

efforts resulted in decision making about state and local programs and created platforms for further collaboration. The result was a fluid exchange of information across a series of interactive relationships that *institutionalized* information and collaborative processes in relation to this particular policy change. This institutionalization expanded the capacity of state and local governments to pursue the drug court program.

This chapter examines two examples of information concepts that prompted further collaborative processes. The first is the professionalization of drug courts as a policy concept. The second is the use of a policy template to frame collaborations to develop standards and other performance metrics. These two examples illustrate the broader systemic efforts that evolved from the work of the NADCP as the champion organization within the national information network over the life of the drug court initiative. Of particular importance, however, the influence of these collaborative information processes was not limited to champion organizations.

BOX 5.2

The Program Director's Experiences

As the program director for treatment court services in the state administrative office of the courts, Alex Scherer faced a significant new challenge. All the state's treatment courts followed the model established by the drug court program more than twenty years ago. The state administrative office of the courts had always been supportive of the drug court idea, but it had never offered much in the way of resources. Well-established local programs had served as models for other programs around the country, and their team members were influential with the national drug court community and with newer teams in the state.

Before taking the helm as state program officer, Alex headed up a small grant program in the state administrative office of the courts that provided funding to all sorts of drug treatment services across the criminal justice system. Now local drug court leaders wanted to find dedicated state funding for their unique form of programming. Interest in state funding was running high among local drug court teams, given the publicity that had followed the efforts of next-door neighbor Governor Vitale to establish a state funding initiative for local drug courts in his state. Alex felt confident that the chief justice would entertain a proposal to provide state funds for local drug court programs, but Alex needed to collect data to show that his drug court programs worked and that the local teams were consistently pulling in the same direction.

As Alex concluded his exploratory meeting with local drug court administrators from around the state, he sensed tension and uncertainty in the room about the relationship between his state office and local drug court teams. He could tell that local programs were not in favor of court-based treatment programs that diverged from the drug court model and were highly skeptical of introducing state control over local drug court operations. One of the handouts provided by a local drug court judge was the list of guiding principles for drug court operations; Alex recognized it as the template for the drug court model and something that was familiar to all the local representatives. As he looked over the meeting sign-in sheet, he was a bit surprised at the wide range of professional titles on the list—treatment professionals, attorneys, judges, administrators, probation officers, and more.

Alex wondered how he would be able to bring this diverse group together under one umbrella to establish a unified focus across the state. He also wondered how to begin organizing his staff within the state office and how to begin collecting the necessary data. The chief justice would probably want to seek legislative support for dedicated drug court funding, given the track record of Governor Vitale in his

> state. Alex envisioned convening a new statewide judicial task force
> that would develop state standards for drug court performance; the
> task force might also explore draft legislation that could connect state
> standards to funding for local drug court programs.

These information processes incorporated the efforts of champions, supporters, and challenger organizations over time. Champion organizations promoted the skills and various institutional arrangements that were necessary to support the policy initiatives that they favored. Supporter organizations provided ancillary information that assisted public offices with various aspects of implementation. And supporter organizations also became more engaged in providing assistance as state offices became interested in taking steps to institutionalize drug courts within their states. Meanwhile, challenger groups continued to press for different policy solutions through advocacy efforts and research publications.

Professionalization and the Twenty-First-Century Team

Professionalization is generally understood as a process of establishing a defined set of skills and a path of education and/or training to acquire them (Klinger and Nalbandian 2003). The fields of public administration and public policy have become increasingly professionalized through the growth of specialized areas of public service and new avenues of formal education in the discipline. As the public administration environment has become more complex, public organizations have increased the ranks of professional specialists—accountants, social workers, and environmental engineers—who possess the technical knowledge that is required to design and implement policy solutions. Increased professionalism is linked to more effective performance in both public and nonprofit organizations (Berman 2006; Cayer 2004; Rainey and Steinbauer 1999). This professionalization has contributed to the ability of public-sector organizations to perform work that requires greater specialization.

Across all fields of public service, professionalism is desirable because it provides a basis for the neutral administrative competence that is considered the hallmark of contemporary public administration. Professionalism generally provides a sense of unity and purpose and enhances the standing of the field. Professions are associated with core values and ideologies that contribute to a focus on the quality of work rather than simple efficiency (Friedson 2001; Radin 2006).[1] In addition, professionalism may forestall some measure of negative public perception that government either is inept or is a purely political enterprise. Despite the benefits, professionalization within public administration has been a bit of a double-edged sword. Professional specialization may contribute to additional fragmentation and turf battles within organizations based on the competing opinions of various professional groups of staff members (Cayer 2004). These battles of experts can also occur among public agencies and between public organizations and their nonprofit collaborators.

In today's environment, however, simple professionalization is no longer sufficient to address the complex, interdependent nature of the work. In interdependent environments, public organizations must not only develop technical expertise but must also develop capacity to bridge areas of technical expertise and resolve technical disputes by forging a consensus among experts. In collaborative settings, effective public administrators require diverse skills that cross boundaries between disciplines and policy areas and that synthesize experiences from multiple perspectives in order to reach decisions. Goldsmith and Eggers (2004, 159, 178) argue that public agencies need to foster a new skills portfolio for public service that focuses on interpersonal and political competence as well as technical skill across a range of functions that are performed both within and outside a government organization. These "advanced generalists" conceptualize networks and develop effective knowledge-sharing practices across them (Goldsmith and Eggers 2004, 184). In this way, these advanced generalists create information networks and act as network facilitators for their organizations by recognizing network opportunities, developing and maintaining network connections, and building skills for participating in them. Through these efforts, public organizations can develop the skills necessary to govern in the networked environment.

As a champion organization for the drug court concept, the NADCP has taken the lead in professionalizing both the idea of drug courts and the people who work within them. This professionalization has occurred through the interrelated concepts of a drug court team and a drug court professional. The drug court team was formed as an interdisciplinary collaborative group that drew upon the expertise of its constituent professions in order to make decisions. The drug court team concept included the traditional professions of law and medicine, including judges, lawyers (prosecutors and defense counsel), and medical and mental health treatment staff. The drug court team incorporated public administration functions that were professionalized more recently, including probation officers, law enforcement, and case managers.

The concept of a "drug court professional" did not exist before the drug court concept and was intertwined with the idea of the drug court team. The term "drug court professional" was used to refer to all members of the team. The concept blended knowledge across these professions and built a knowledge and skill base that drew on multiple professions and multiple government agencies and departments. The concept also established a professional identity for all team members. Within the drug court team, the idea of professionalization conferred a measure of status and legitimized the drug court administrative staff that interacted with traditional professional groups such as judges, prosecutors, public defenders and other defense counsel, social workers, and drug and alcohol treatment specialists. The interdisciplinary, interjurisdictional, and cross-functional concept of a drug court professional illustrates the type of skill set required to navigate a relatively more complex and interdependent administrative environment. Figure 5.1 illustrates the typical array of professional relationships found in a local drug court team.

The concept of a drug court professional has been diffused widely throughout the states as local programs have spread. The concept of a drug court professional helped advance the drug court concept by providing focus and stability. The concept provided common ground between diverse professional norms and promoted a sort of cross-disciplinary third way to resolve differences. Rather than forcing a choice between one approach and another, the interdisciplinary context of the drug court professional contributed to the formation of a new space for decisions that were not necessarily aligned with one professional view or another.

Professionalization also provided a ready-made basis for the act of networking itself. Professionalization provided a rationale for meeting and exchanging information within the professional community on a regular basis. Professionalization was also central to the culture of many of the organizations in the national information network, which are themselves professional membership associations. The NADCP sponsored annual conferences for drug court professionals and conducted countless training sessions for local drug court staffs. Administrators noted that NADCP staff members were "always available" to travel to the states, speak at state drug court conferences, and provide technical assistance. Local programs were

Figure 5.1 The Cross-Professional Arrangement of a Typical Local Drug Court Team

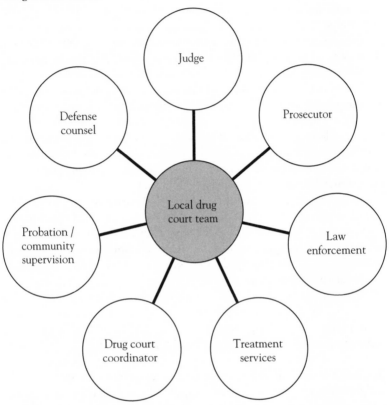

encouraged to participate in NADCP conferences and training as a drug court team, which further reinforced the cross-professional and cross-jurisdictional flavor of the drug court policy approach.

The team concept became part of the daily language of drug courts and was used as a sort of shorthand for information exchanges and learning. Administrators and drug court professionals commented frequently about the importance of "seeing what other teams are doing." Drug court administrators commented on the team as a common denominator across programs and jurisdictions because all teams work with the same complement of members. As one administrator put it, "We understand the difficulties. Even though everyone thinks their program is unique, we have so many things in common, maybe more in common than we have differences. We understand [each other's] problems." Administrators also noted the power of example. If "other teams are doing it" (meeting the challenge of the day), then administrators gained confidence that a solution could be developed for similar situations. "We know that there is a way to do it, and we can start to think about how to make their idea work for us back home."

The influence of professionalization extended beyond the national professional organization into state associations of drug court professionals and was reinforced by the NADCP through ancillary organizations such as its Congress of Drug Court Professionals. The drug court professional concept also extended information connections beyond those within the drug court team and with national and state drug court professional associations. As a team of professional members, the drug court team had ready-made connections to other national professional groups. Through the concepts of the drug court team and the drug court professional, local drug court programs gained instant access to a broad range of established professional associations. Many of these associations were part of the national information network and were identified by key informants as supporters of the drug court concept. Figure 5.2 illustrates the relationships between members of the typical drug court team and other professional associations in the national information network.

Fostering Collaboration through Policy Templates

The NADCP's policy template of guiding principles was widely used as a content framework that provided a vehicle for communication across programs and for local customization. This template had a broader role than content, however. It was also a vehicle for collaboration and decision making. The template's overarching role was to create and institutionalize a process of synthesis through collaboration concerning the guidelines. Through this process of collaboration, the guidelines came to life in local communities and, over time, in state offices as well. More broadly, the policy template was a catalyst in promoting a process for reaching agreement that grew beyond the drug court concept into new institutions and policy areas. The template unified the substance of the drug court approach by providing a common framework for discussion and decision making about participation, content, and program goals. This collaborative process was essentially a continuous, reiterative cycle. The cycle began in local drug courts, extended to the development of state-level programs,

Figure 5.2   Connections between a Local Drug Court Team and National Professional Associations

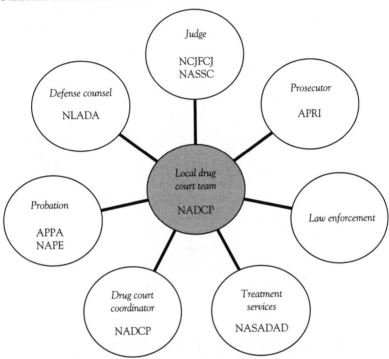

Note: APPA = American Probation and Parole Association; APRI = American Prosecutors Research Institute (National District Attorneys Association); NADCP = National Association of Drug Court Professionals; NAPE = National Association of Probation Executives; NASADAD = National Association of State Alcohol and Drug Abuse Directors; NASSC = National Association of State Sentencing Commissions; NCJFCJ = National Center for Juvenile and Family Court Judges; NLADA = National Legal Aid and Defender Association.

and returned again to influence local programs through the development of performance measurement standards and certification efforts. The basic elements of this cyclical framework are depicted in figure 5.3.

Within the broad parameters of the policy template, local communities and state programs were self-directed to determine what they intended to accomplish, who would be involved, and how they would measure success. Collaborative relationships developed concerning the guidelines in order

Figure 5.3   Intergovernmental Synthesis Based on the NADCP Policy Template

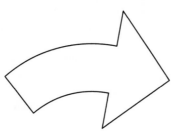

Local synthesis to
develop local program
content, process, and
evaluation measures

State synthesis of local
programs to develop
state program

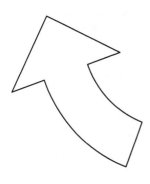

State and local
synthesis to develop
performance measures

to establish the drug court program and to determine program content, methods of support, and ways to evaluate success. These collaborations built capacity by creating arenas for collecting and sharing information within local programs and between local programs and state offices. These collaborations also expanded capacity by fostering new relationships and new institutions to address new concerns, such as funding support, standards, and measures of success. These relationships endured beyond the specifics of drug court programs and formed the basis for further collaboration, decision making, and policy change.

At the local level, the template provided a process for collaborative decision making. By working within the NADCP's guiding principles, local judges and other members of the drug court team defined drug court programs within the preferences and resources of the local community. After the decision was made to begin a drug court, the drug court team brought the drug court policy framework to life through collaboration concerning the guiding principles. These collaborative deliberations synthesized the multiple perspectives and values of different professional groups. Teams determined the actual goals of the program and how to measure success against those goals. These decisions became part of the larger pool of information that was considered by state administrators in designing state support and oversight. Decisions at the state level were influenced by participants from local drug courts and reflected a synthesis of the local decisions about content and process that were made in establishing local programs. State decisions were reflected back to local programs and continued to influence the way that local programs operated; and local operations continued to reflect information back to state offices that was used to refine state standards and evaluation measures.

The collaborative processes fostered by the policy template extended beyond local communities into a broad range of intergovernmental relationships. Through the implementation of the NADCP's guiding principles, new intergovernmental ties were forged between local programs, state judiciaries, and executive branch offices. These new relationships were promoted in many cases by state legislation that incorporated the policy template into state law.[2] This incorporation occurred either by explicit restatement of the guiding principles or by explicit reference to them. These relationships were also fostered by statutory requirements to develop statewide performance measures for drug court operations concerning the guiding principles. These strategies intertwined with one another during the diffusion of the drug court program across local jurisdictions and as local programs looked to their state governments for support.

As illustrations, consider the incorporation of the NADCP's guiding principles into state law and the evolution of state standards in Florida, Indiana, and Missouri. Each incorporated the principles into state law and into some form of state standards for drug court operations. The specific institutional arrangements and chronologies differ somewhat in the illustrations that follow; however, the overarching results were remarkably similar in demonstrating the significance of the guiding principles as a process template for collaboration and capacity building. Throughout, new relationships and new institutions were formed within each state, and these relationships and institutions created another layer in the intersectoral information network and fostered new information connections.

The Policy Template and the Florida Information Network

Florida's earliest drug court programs predate the existence of the NADCP and the information tools and processes that have evolved in the information network during the past twenty years. The state's first drug courts opened under an established umbrella of probation and intervention programs in its criminal justice system that included treatment components. The Florida Supreme Court Task Force on Treatment-Based Drug Courts was established to examine drug courts. The purpose of this task force was to make recommendations on the legal, policy, and procedural issues confronting drug courts. The task force was also authorized to propose amendments to procedural rules of court and to make recommendations about funding and allocation of resources.

The composition of the Florida Task Force illustrates the multidisciplinary and multijurisdictional reach of collaborative efforts that emerged surrounding the drug court program. The membership reflected the various stakeholder groups that made up the drug court team at the local level, including judges, magistrates, and drug court personnel, as well as representatives from several state executive branch agencies. The task force was also required to maintain liaison relationships with other stakeholders, including the state bar association and those responsible for the state trial court budget. The group's charge was wide ranging and included the long-term sustainability of drug courts and the development of statewide components, such as evaluation (Supreme Court of Florida 2006; Supreme Court Task Force on Treatment-Based Drug Courts 2004d).

During the 1990s the work of the Florida Task Force intertwined with an increasingly strident statewide focus on drug interdiction and the relationship between drug use and crime. In 1999 the task force formally adopted the NADCP's guiding principles as policy for drug court operations in the state court system. The task force tailored the principles and developed performance measurement recommendations for local drug court programs. These task force recommendations have been an integral aspect of Florida's state-level drug court administration since 1999 and represented a statewide consensus about how to measure drug court policy activity. The recommendations defined key concepts and provided local programs with a template for collecting information about their operations. The task force also recommended legislation to fund drug court coordinator positions in the state judicial circuits.

The Florida Task Force's recommendations prompted the state legislature to incorporate the NADCP's guiding principles into the state criminal code in 2001. Following the pattern of representation that was established for the composition of the task force, the enabling legislation encouraged participation from a broad range of state executive agencies, local government and law enforcement agencies, and other public or private groups. The recommendations of the task force continued to shape the Florida drug court program. Performance measures have been extended beyond adult programs to include other populations.[3] In 2006 state legislation established a drug court coordinator in each judicial circuit, contingent upon state funding (Supreme Court of Florida 2006; Supreme Court Task Force on Treatment-Based Drug Courts 2004a, 2004b, 2004c, 2004d).

Administrative assistance for the Florida Task Force was provided by the Florida Office of the State Courts Administrator (OSCA), which also provided technical support and assistance to all state courts. As part of its overall charge, the Florida OSCA office served as the central statewide information link between the task force and the drug court community. In the mid-1990s, drawing on the early drug court experiences in Dade and Broward counties, the Florida OSCA developed a reference manual for the judicial community and other stakeholders regarding the process of establishing a drug court. The office also facilitated and coordinated opportunities for circuit-level drug court coordinators to convene through the annual state drug court conference and other venues.

The Florida OSCA also spearheaded the collection of data from local drug courts on the performance measures established for the drug court initiative. Local courts participated voluntarily; as is typical of many administrative offices that support state court systems, the Florida OSCA has no formal oversight authority over local court operations (Supreme Court of Florida 2006). The Florida OSCA reported strong participation from the local courts even in the absence of a mandate, and its publications illustrated many local court activities and examples of progress. Through its reflection of local practices back to the state court community, the Florida OSCA promoted its interpretation of best practices—which its administrators termed "promising" practices—and facilitated information sharing about these practices across the state.

The Policy Template and the Indiana Information Network

In Indiana, the NADCP's policy template provided the platform for state, local, and intergovernmental decisions concerning state standards and the certification of drug court programs. As in Florida, enabling legislation was instrumental in incorporating the NADCP's guiding principles into a collaborative framework for decision making. The first Indiana drug courts began in 1996 in Vigo County (Terre Haute) and in Gary City Court (Office of Justice Programs 2003). At that time, the Indiana state courts also operated a court alcohol and drug referral service that had been established in the 1970s; this court referral program was certified through the state executive mental health and social services agency. Control over court referral programs shifted from the executive to the state judiciary in 1997; funding uncertainty within the executive branch had the potential to weaken the certification of these programs and their accountability. The oversight of court referral programs was transferred to the Judicial Conference of Indiana, the state judiciary institution that is composed of all state court judges. As local drug courts came online alongside the existing certified court referral program, the Judicial Conference fielded requests for a drug court certification program and established a subcommittee to conduct a pilot program to explore a certification process tailored to the drug court concept (Carey and Finigan 2007).

The Judicial Conference pilot project produced a framework for drug court legislation and administrative rules. The Indiana legislature enacted drug court enabling legislation in 2002 that explicitly defined a drug court as one that follows the NADCP's policy template. This legislation also established a drug court certification process administered by the Indiana Judicial Center (IJC). The IJC supported the Judicial Conference in the areas of research, judicial education, and administration of the drug court certification program. The IJC is a separate entity from the state administrative office of courts, although both serve as administrative support for the state judiciary. Drug court administrative rules that included the certification procedure were adopted by the Judicial Conference in 2003. These administrative rules were developed by adapting the earlier court referral program rules and regulations to reflect the actual practices of drug court programs. The NADCP's policy template was also explicitly incorporated into these administrative rules (Judicial Conference of Indiana 2008).

The NADCP's policy template formed the heart of Indiana's drug court certification effort. Drug courts submitted implementation plans that described how their court incorporated the NADCP's policy principles into its policies, procedures, and practices. The policy template also influenced the program evaluations of the Indiana drug courts. Program evaluations that were conducted by the Indiana Judicial Center of local programs focused on compliance with the guiding principles (IJC 2007a, 2007b, 2008).

Where Florida took a voluntary approach to local compliance with the NADCP's policy template, Indiana law gave the IJC explicit statutory authority to withhold certification from local drug courts or to withdraw it entirely. State administrators recognized that authority and reported that it was important to consider local customization and local capacity in the certification process. State staff viewed their mission as helping drug courts accomplish statutory and administrative requirements within the constraints of their local jurisdictions, and as working to create an atmosphere in which local courts and state staffs could work together to resolve certification issues or meet a challenge.

In practice, the Indiana certification approach was one of collaboration and partnership with local courts rather than enforcement. Indiana state performance measures also evolved based on the NADCP's policy template. In 2009, a process to develop performance measures for drug courts was under way under the auspices of another multidisciplinary and cross-jurisdictional task force of the Judicial Conference Committee on Problem Solving Courts. This task force drafted definitions and performance measures on concepts such as recidivism, retention, graduation, and sobriety. The task force approach included a survey of local courts, an investigation of approaches taken by other states, and a feasibility study for local courts to determine their capacity to collect particular data regarding performance measures.

As the drug courts have matured in Indiana, the state judiciary have begun to address drug courts within the broader concept of problem-solving courts. The concept of the problem-solving court office evolved in Indiana, in part based on suggestions from other states at a meeting of the National Congress of State Drug Court Administrators.[4] In 2006, the Judicial Conference established a Problem-Solving Courts Committee to guide drug court and other problem-solving court activities at the state level. This committee was constituted by the chief justice of the Indiana Supreme Court with broad representation across the courts and also included probation officers and drug court staff members. The state shift in focus toward the problem-solving label was indicated in a 2006 title change of the state-level position of drug court coordinator to problem-solving courts administrator within an Office of Problem-Solving Courts in the IJC. One impetus offered in Indiana for the shift toward the label of problem-solving courts was that the concept of problem-solving courts cast a wider net and facilitated the distribution of state resources across a wider range of court initiatives, including mental health and reentry programs. Indiana viewed the problem-solving court concept as an avenue for extrapolating the NADCP's guiding principles to other populations, and thus as a method of extending innovation to similar populations with the expectation of similar positive results in behavioral change. In Indiana, problem-solving courts were expanded in 2006 to include the idea of reentry courts; mental health courts and family dependency courts were on the legislative agenda in 2009.

The Policy Template and the Missouri Information Network

Similar themes were observed in the expansion of drug courts in Missouri, which occurred through a blend of collaborative processes that include the NADCP's policy template as well as organizational development support from supporter organizations and independent evaluative information. Missouri had early experience with the drug court innovation. The Jackson County (Kansas City) drug court was one of the first twelve local programs in the nation in 1993, and the Missouri Office of State Courts Administrator developed one of the early resource manuals for designing and implementing local drug court programs (Missouri Office of State Courts Administrator 1998; Office of Justice Programs 2000). Statewide enabling legislation was adopted in 1998. This legislation was the product of the deliberations of a bipartisan task force established by the Missouri Judicial Conference. As in Florida and Indiana, the Missouri Judicial Conference Task Force was broadly representative, and it included participation from legislators and judges as well as the executive branch.

The Missouri enabling legislation did not itemize the NADCP's policy template. Instead, the template was incorporated into a variety of administrative processes established by the Missouri Drug Courts Coordinating Commission, which was established in 2001 as a state executive–judiciary collaborative and charged with policy and resource decisions for the drug court initiative statewide. The Coordinating Commission was constituted with broad representation from state executive departments and members of the state judiciary. The commission built upon earlier state-level collaborative efforts across branches of government, including the work of a task force on drug courts.

In 2004, the Coordinating Commission issued statewide drug court performance measures derived from the NADCP's guiding principles (Missouri Drug Courts Coordinating Commission 2008). As is the case in other states, these measures were essentially the Missouri interpretation of the policy template as developed by local practitioners and synthesized through review by the Coordinating Commission. The process of developing these measures was facilitated by the National Center for State Courts (NCSC). The NCSC provided technical assistance on other statewide projects within the Missouri state court system and provided various forms of assistance to other states in implementing state processes and routines to support the drug court program effort.

The Coordinating Commission also implemented a statewide process to monitor compliance with the key components of the NADCP's guiding principles. The process and criteria were devised through input from local courts and a statewide study of established programs in 2001. A statewide drug court evaluation advisory commission of representatives of well-established Missouri drug courts assisted in constructing the evaluation criteria. The study reported the progress of the Missouri drug courts against the Missouri benchmarks established for each of the NADCP components (University of Missouri at Columbia School of Social Work 2001). This study provided a statewide baseline for assessing consistency and variation in drug court activities according to Missouri protocols; more broadly, the data provided a snapshot of the ways in which local courts were operating within the key policy tenets of the NADCP.

A statewide procedure to monitor compliance with the NADCP's guiding principles was developed from a field audit of drug court programs conducted by the Missouri Administrative Office of the Courts (AOC) drug court staff. Local option and local control are evident. The Missouri AOC makes recommendations and suggests practices to local drug courts but does not force compliance. In fact, staff noted that the Missouri AOC changed the initial language of the state audit report from "recommendations" to "comments" to avoid a perception that the state was prescribing local practices (Missouri Office of the State Courts Administrator 2008).

The Intergovernmental Balance between Customization and Consistency

As the illustrations from Florida, Indiana, and Missouri indicate, the policy template of the NADCP's guiding principles served not only as a content guide but also as a process guide for convening multiple stakeholders and arriving at a consensus across diverse professional orientations. Through the process of arriving at state standards based on the guiding principles, local programs and state offices fostered a process of intergovernmental synthesis. This synthesis contributed to the capacity of the drug court program and built collaborative institutions, relationships, and tools that could be used in future policy endeavors.

As these examples have illustrated, state institutions became involved in response to the pressure from the growth of local programs over time.

As the density of local drug court programs increased, states engaged in a wider range of activities to support and institutionalize the drug court concept. State standards had the obvious benefit of facilitating some sort of performance measurement; statewide standards brought greater uniformity to program operations within states. Standards and certification were used as the basis for eligibility for various state incentives such as grant programs, training opportunities, and funds. These metrics also had a dark side. Local programs were eager for state support but often did not want to relinquish local control over program operations. This feeling was particularly acute given the strong grassroots flavor of the drug court program and its genesis in local courtrooms.

From the local side of the equation, local programs looked to state offices for resources, legitimacy, and stability. More than one local program official commented about the importance of continued state interest and support. One administrator put it this way: "I hope state support continues to grow. Our state had drug courts for five years before any state implementation started. I hope that our AOC can put their label on this and support it to promote growth."

From the state side of the equation, states were faced with resource requests from a new, highly diverse collection of local programs. Throughout state–local deliberations about the nature and extent of state involvement, questions were posed about the degree of centralization and consistency that should be, or could be, imposed on these diverse local initiatives. State and local officials alike recognized that consistency could be achieved through the centralized administration of grant funds, or, for example, through state administrative rules and orders. Centralization or statewide consistency could also result from statewide advisory boards, or from funding streams. A state-level presence could also provide a common infrastructure to support data collection procedures across local programs and administrative support for evaluation processes. Capacity for data collection and evaluation were particularly costly aspects of state centralization efforts and were also significantly underdeveloped at the local level. The following comment from one state administrator reflected the views of many others: "The state office value is in administration rather than the specifics of local operation. State involvement helps promote consistency. State offices can be used to conduct program evaluations and comparative assessments within the state, and to bring in a perspective that local programs cannot have."

Notwithstanding the potential value of state administrative support for local programs, the process of setting standards was a continuous intergovernmental exercise in balancing local autonomy and state interests.

Within state offices, administrators viewed the concept of a statewide standards manual in different ways. Consider the following comment regarding a manual developed for structuring adult drug court programs: "While we consider the manual to be the framework from which all of the adult drug courts must structure their programs, we do see some differences between counties that reflect the diversity in our counties; . . . the differences that are found are expected as we are not looking for 'cookie-cutter' programs but rather an equitable process" (Office of Justice Programs 2006). Now compare the previous comment with another one from a state court administrator: "Courts all vary with the personality of the judges and whether they are liberal or conservative, so a one-size-fits-all is not realistic. As judges see the success in another court, they are motivated to try [drug court programs]. . . . Otherwise, it is like herding cats to get all our local judges on the same page. And they don't have to be."

The NADCP's policy template formed an essential aspect of this intergovernmental synthesis because it provided common ground for discussion between local programs and state offices. Local drug court personnel were intimately familiar with the guiding principles because local programs operated within the framework of these principles for many years before state involvement. That common ground was particularly important for programs grounded in the judiciary. Centralized administrative control within state judiciaries is actually quite limited, even among states that have established a unified state court system (Flango and Rottman 1992; Rottman and Hewitt 1996); tension typically exists between state supreme courts and local courts on matters of control over court operations. Although state supreme courts have a bully pulpit from which to promote particular policy choices, they do not dictate to lower courts. In short, local courts do not often view state centralization as a step in the right direction in any area of court operations, and yet some matter of centralization was seen as necessary for a unified approach. Within state AOCs, some administrators were concerned that "locals are all doing their own thing" and that some standardization was necessary to address cross-jurisdictional issues: "There are problems that local courts cannot address unless there is a state plan, for example, transfers of college students between local jurisdictions that have drug court programs that are not the same, or that have no drug court program at all."

State and local administrators commented about the difficulty that state offices had in gaining a measure of state oversight or influence after local programs had become established. Among some administrators, there is a feeling that federal grant support to plan and implement drug courts should not have gone directly to local programs but to a state agency: "They should have worked through the states and insisted on a state agency with capacity. Many local courts have very low numbers [of participants] and no capacity, but it is very difficult to develop state structure now that locals have had some success and have gained some territory."

Administrators discussed multiple benefits from collaborating on the basis of the NADCP's guiding principles to develop statewide standards and as a strategy for providing technical assistance to local drug courts. The common ground of the guiding principles provided a vehicle for collaboration that extended the perspective of local customization and local control into intergovernmental collaborations. The principles provided general guidance but required customization to take on concrete meaning in implementation. At the local level, this customization process was an opportunity to involve multiple stakeholders, including different branches of government, different levels of government, and different professions. As the examples given above illustrate, this was true as the process extended to include state offices. Numerous intergovernmental collaborations and task forces evolved to address state-level standards for drug court programs. Representatives of local programs were heavily involved in these collaborations and task forces. As a consequence, the different requirements of various local programs within a state were shared statewide. To arrive at a common state framework, local processes were aggregated and synthesized to reach common ground across localities and to arrive at common definitions, interpretations, and practices that would apply statewide.

By building state standards based on the NADCP's guiding principles, state administrators were essentially encouraging programs to demonstrate compliance with the principles. This approach provided local drug courts with a way to distinguish their operations from those of noncompliant courts. If states provided resources in exchange for compliance, standards then also became a way for local programs to distinguish themselves from competing programs. In that way, state standards developed based on the guiding principles provided a vehicle for preserving the integrity of the drug court concept as it was originally conceived by the NADCP. The process of developing a statewide interpretation of the guiding principles also helped build credibility for the state effort among local programs. State reliance on the guiding principles helped sidestep local perceptions of state programs as arbitrary or unresponsive to local needs.

Administrators in state offices and in local programs agreed that state funds targeted for drug court programs should be limited to those programs established under the NADCP model. Administrators in several states described a potential scenario in which local jurisdictions might seek to obtain state drug court funds by establishing treatment programs for offenders that were not as rigorous as a drug court. In Tennessee, for example, state and local administrators noted that, in the future, "real" drug courts would be those certified according to state standards and that only certified drug courts would be eligible to apply for state grant funds; however, "rogue" or "knock-off" drug courts would not. Similarly, Georgia's Judicial Council Standing Committee on Drug Courts was committed to maintaining the "drug court brand" as established by the NADCP's guiding principles. The Standing Committee took several steps to institutionalize the NADCP's principles through the services that the state office provided to Georgia courts. The Standing Committee's application for grant funding included a section for applicants to demonstrate the ways in which their drug court advances the NADCP's principles. The Georgia AOC provided grant applicant training that focused on how to complete the application and planned to require this application training for future grant applications (Judicial Council of Georgia Standing Committee on Drug Courts 2008a, 2008b).

Executive Oversight and the Tennessee Information Network

State endorsement of the NADCP's guiding principles also appealed to local jurisdictions as a way to foreclose additional state requirements on local programs. Local perceptions about state control were particularly pronounced where state oversight emanated from the executive branch rather than the state judiciary. Because the vast majority of state drug court offices were established within state court systems, executive branch oversight of the operation court programs was typically exercised from a distance, through large-scale checks and balances and blunt instruments such as the state budget or the power of judicial appointment.

Consider the development of state support for drug courts in Tennessee as an illustration of executive oversight of these court programs. In Tennessee the state's administration of drug court programs was coordinated by statute through the Tennessee Office of Criminal Justice Programs (OCJP), an executive branch office that provided strategic planning for the acquisition, distribution, and management of federal and state grant funds for local criminal justice efforts and the criminal justice system statewide. The Tennessee OCJP evolved as the state agency responsible for statewide drug court administration as a consequence of this expertise in federal and state grant procurement and administration, and the funding of early local drug court programs through federal grants that fell within the purview of the office. Early drug court programs in Tennessee were established in the late 1990s through federal funds granted directly to local governments under U.S. Department of Justice grant programs, including Byrne grants and the Residential Substance Abuse Treatment for State Prisoners programs.[5]

In 2003, Tennessee enacted drug court enabling legislation through the Drug Court Treatment Act, which sets the blueprint for state agency involvement today. The Treatment Act designates the Tennessee OCJP as the administrative agency with oversight responsibility for statewide drug court efforts. The act also establishes the NADCP's policy template as the foundation for the Tennessee drug court program, and thus the legislation outlines the NADCP tenets. Finally, the act establishes roles for a new statewide advisory committee and the state association of drug court professionals in state administrative oversight of local drug court programs.

Initial statewide efforts with respect to the Treatment Act were directed at demonstrating that local programs were complying with the act and, by implication, with the NADCP's guiding principles. The Tennessee OCJP sought the technical assistance of the National Center for State Courts to facilitate development of performance measures that demonstrated how the local programs were implementing the guiding principles and indicators or benchmarks of program success. These performance measures were developed with deliberate and extensive local input and became the basis for a state certification program. The drug court advisory committee and representatives of local drug court programs reviewed each NADCP principle and developed the certification benchmarks. The drug court advisory committee and representatives of local programs modified performance measures to reflect local conditions and resources, and they looked for ways in which the state office could develop statewide programs that would augment local needs for outcome evaluations and training. This collaboration produced performance measures and indicators tailored to state conditions; statewide training on these measures was provided to local drug courts that are intended to serve as mentors for emerging local programs (Cheesman and Rubio 2004). Data collection began on statewide performance measures in 2005; all drug courts that received state funds must participate, and other courts were encouraged to do so (Tennessee Office of Criminal Justice Programs 2005).

The Tennessee certification initiative began in 2008 and was administered by the Tennessee executive Office of Criminal Justice Programs (OCJP). Certification began with the oldest (and most-established) local drug court programs in the state. The objective of the certification process is to establish accountability for the expenditure of public funds and a measure of effectiveness and quality through the linkage of program operations to best practices. The certification process was simultaneously directed at two goals; as one state administrator describes it, certification in Tennessee was also the development of best practices and performance measures. Certification promoted a level of standardization and further institutionalized the drug court concept (Cheesman and Rubio 2004; Tennessee Office of Criminal Justice Programs 2008).

The Tennessee OCJP promoted the benefits of certification but had no authority to impose the process on local courts. Beginning in 2010 certification was a condition of federal grant awards and state funds administered through the Tennessee OCJP. This linkage between funding and practices seemed likely to encourage local court participation. Local courts recognized the benefit that comes from being able to demonstrate performance, but they were also invested in maintaining the integrity of the processes that they had developed locally and without state assistance. Local courts expressed a strong desire for local autonomy for drug courts as local programs with a history and identity grounded in individual communities. Some local courts had advocated for certification for some time and were excited about having a state-sanctioned process that legitimized the work that they had been doing for years; in other jurisdictions, local reaction to state certification remained mixed.

In Tennessee the state Drug Court Advisory Committee used the NADCP's guiding principles as a framework for developing best practices to be applied in the state's certification process. Local drug court teams were reassured significantly by this use of the guiding principles. Local drug courts saw the principles as a protective backstop against state control. By using the template of the principles, local drug courts had a measure of confidence that the state executive office was not dictating to local courts or otherwise usurping local functions. Local programs were "worried about the direction that this [certification] would take" until it was made clear that the guiding principles would provide the framework for content and for the involvement of multiple stakeholders representative of the drug court team concept.

Local programs also felt that the NADCP's guiding principles kept the Tennessee OCJP from trying to expand the requirements for drug court programs into foreign territory that, while well intentioned, could make it impossible for the programs to succeed. This observation underscores the different conceptualizations of certification across professions as much as it underscores the need for local programs to have significant control over their operations. During the discussion of certification requirements, the proposal was made to certify drug courts as alcohol and drug treatment facilities according to well-established principles that were already codified in state law. The state Drug Court Advisory Committee rejected this approach because such facilities were outside the operational mandate of local courts and the consensus was that standards would impose a significant burden on local courts and local jurisdictions.

State administrators noted that local challenges represent opportunities to further enhance the drug court program statewide; state administrative staff expressed strongly the sentiment that certification was designed to build local capacity rather than to punish programs for noncompliance. The certification process generated regular contact between the Tennessee OCJP staff and local programs. By providing technical assistance on certification and grant applications, the state office built relationships and guided local courts in developing successful programs, including the capacity of local programs to collect and report data (Tennessee Office of Criminal Justice Programs 2005, 2008). As the certification process moved forward, the Tennessee OCJP planned to develop local capacity by requiring local courts to prepare examples of documentation such as policy manuals, applications, referral procedures, and mentorship practices. Local administrators suggested that information on successful practices would be widely shared among individual courts. This sharing may facilitate greater standardization as local courts copy existing models, and it will also cut the information costs and development costs of local jurisdictions.

State funding to support local drug court programs has expanded in recent years to include grant funding through the Tennessee OCJP. A state grant program totaling $3.5 million was included in the state budget in 2006 as part of the legislative response to a gubernatorial program to combat methamphetamine use. Of this appropriation, $2 million was earmarked to be divided evenly among four major metropolitan centers— Memphis, Chattanooga, Nashville, and Knoxville—and the remaining $1.5 million was to be available for grants to local drug courts throughout the state. Most drug courts were recipients of state grants through this additional state appropriation. The state grant program significantly expanded the scope of drug court operations across the state and significantly expanded the oversight activity of the TOCJP. The number of local drug courts increased from one program in 1998 to forty-five programs in 2008. Since 2006, the availability of state grant funding through the Tennessee OCJP increased the interaction between local programs and the state office (Tennessee Office of Criminal Justice Programs 2007, 2008).

In Tennessee and in other states, the NADCP's guiding principles were not a magic bullet, but they were a vital framework that encouraged a process of synthesis across state court systems, executive criminal justice agencies, and beyond. These illustrations masked some of the complexity of the process, the difficulties in interpretation, and the sheer amount of time and attention required to reach agreement. Statewide collaborations experienced the same sorts of difficulties as local programs in arriving at statewide interpretations of key components of drug court programs that would apply to all local courts. Statewide groups also encountered the same ambiguities in defining and measuring success that local programs had experienced. The collaborative processes used here brought the potential to produce an end product that was a strong reflection of the general political will and that was also a strong reflection of public sentiment represented by stakeholders. Value was added through the deliberation and exchange of information between stakeholders and across levels of government and the strong connection to local resources.

Conclusion

The examples given in this chapter illustrate the impetus of the national information network in generating new sets of relationships based on the idea of a drug court. The policy template that defined the innovation acted as a process whereby diverse stakeholders collaborated in institutionalizing the drug court concept. Local relationships were forged on the basis of the drug court team. A new form of professionalization connected disparate disciplines and jurisdictions through opportunities for training and skills development. Through collaboration based on the policy template, drug court professionals developed interdisciplinary knowledge and skills. These collaborative efforts provided a platform for information exchange in the development of local drug court programs and the growth of state administrative support. New committees, task forces, and working groups emerged as new institutions expanded the information network more deeply into state and local government agencies.

These new institutions provided new forums in which local drug court programs and state offices negotiated policy content among diverse constituencies and across the power centers of the state judicial and executive branches. The policy template fostered a cycle of information synthesis at the local level, at the state level, and between states, local governments, and the national network. Individual drug court teams, state drug court offices, and a host of task forces engaged in collaborative processes to arrive at a consensus that brought meaning to the policy template and gave life to program content. Interaction among organizations in the information network and state administrators was an essential ingredient in moving the innovation from the local courts to the state level. As a whole, these elements exemplify the theme of synergy between government and key nonprofit organizations in this particular information environment. This synergy is grounded in processes that institutionalized relevant information between states and national nonprofits, between local programs and states and national organizations, and at the local level within programs (boxes 5.3 and 5.4).

BOX 5.3

Dolores Groleaux's Dilemma

Dolores Groleaux's dilemma is a common one for the various professions that cross the boundaries of jurisdiction and profession to work together in the drug court team. Drug court judges and the other members of the drug court team learned new roles and routines. These roles were designed and promoted by the champion organization National Association of Drug Court Professionals. These roles were also reinforced by other professional organizations in the national nonprofit information network. The team was knitted together through its joint participation in professional opportunities that were sponsored by champions and supporters. As the professionalization effort expanded, additional supporter and bystander groups came into touch with an increasing number of new drug court professionals and those who worked with them; as the new profession grew, it became widely acknowledged and accepted as one part of judicial administration. New members of the drug court profession were also aligned with the champion organization. Team members learned to talk to each other across the boundaries of their disciplines. This cross-disciplinary professionalization created new knowledge and skills that elevated the capacity of individual team members and the team in general; this new knowledge also fostered further institutionalization of the innovation and provided a platform to spread the collaborative framework to new policy questions.

BOX 5.4

Taking Advantage of
Collaborative Processes

Alex can take advantage of the collaborative processes that have emerged around the drug court policy template and the interdisciplinary collaborations forged by the new drug court profession. With so many local programs now up and running, a wealth of information exists about how this program has been interpreted in various communities. Local teams have gained experience in resolving the ambiguities of the policy template in ways that can be reconciled with their available resources and policy preferences. At the state level, Alex can organize a similar collaborative process around the policy template in which stakeholders can contribute their unique perspectives and will likely also discover a great deal of common ground. From such a statewide collaboration, subgroups can form to explore issues around legislation, standards, certification, and other issues that concern local programs. Across this process, local interests will continue to be shared with state officials and plans can evolve to further institutionalize the program.

Twenty years after the idea was introduced into the public arena, the various information forms and processes from organizations across the national information network have fostered the drug court concept at the state and local level. The collaborative processes that had their genesis in the policy template and professionalization designed by the champion organization National Association of Drug Court Professionals played a large role in the diffusion of the concept. Supporter organizations collaborated with the new profession and the new program concept and helped local and state administrators integrate it into existing administrative processes. New collaborations were established to address new issues such as state standards, funding support, and enabling legislation; these collaborations drew upon the information generated by organizations in the national information network. As the need for information continued, the national information network and its champions and challengers continued to remain highly engaged. Bystanders remained aware and poised to become involved when issues engage with their organizational purposes; supporters continued to align the work of the drug court movement alongside their own organizational missions.

Notes

1. See Radin (2006) for a detailed analysis of the sociology of professionalism through the work of Eliot Friedson (2001) and others.

2. Some examples of state enabling legislation that incorporated the drug court guiding principles developed by the National Association of Drug Court Professionals either directly or by direct reference include Alabama Act 2003–353; Florida Statutes Section 397.334; Georgia Code Title 15, Chapter 1; Indiana Code 12–23–14.5; Missouri Code Section 478.001; and Tennessee Code Title 16, Chapter 22.

3. Performance indicators and data elements were developed for Florida adult drug court programs in 1999; revisions were made in 2001 and 2004, and the concept was expanded to include juvenile and dependency drug court programs in 2004 (Supreme Court Task Force on Treatment-Based Drug Courts 2004a, 2004b, 2004c).

4. The concept of problem-solving courts has been widely used in discussions about drug courts (Berman and Feinblatt 2005).

5. The RSAT programs were created by the Violent Crime Control and Law Enforcement Act of 1994 (Public Law 103–322). Broadly, RSAT programs were intended to provide individual and group treatment activities for offenders that develop cognitive, behavioral, social, vocation, and other skills to resolve substance abuse and related problems; programs last between six and twelve months and are provided in residential treatment facilities set apart from the general correctional population.

6

Information, Synthesis, and Synergy

A NATIONAL NONPROFIT INFORMATION NETWORK

T**he drug court concept** has been sustained and advanced during the past twenty years by deep, lasting information relationships, forms of information, and decision-making processes. These same influences have created new institutions that foster the ability of local courts and state offices to build upon that success. The intersectoral information network nurtured this synthesis of ideas, relationships, and process involved in drug courts in several important ways. First, the organizations in the information network generated a rich variety of information about emerging trends in criminal justice reform, alternatives to incarceration, and judicial approaches to drug use and crime. Competing ideologies and philosophies about reform were embodied in a wide range of professional associations across disciplines, including judges, court administrators, law enforcement, probation and parole, treatment, prosecutors, and defense counsel. National research organizations studied alternatives and evaluated options, and some groups advocated for sweeping reforms.

From this mix of ideas, perspectives, and values, an array of information positions emerged about drug court policy. Local court and state administrators found policy ideas that they could use, along with information relationships and strategic forms of information that made it easier to implement policy change. The champion organization, the National Association of Drug Court Professionals (NADCP), formed and fostered the growth of drug courts as a policy innovation by creating a cross-professional, interdisciplinary policy group known as a "drug court team" and a new drug court profession along with it. As a champion organization, the NADCP promoted the drug court concept through an array of new institutions that fostered professional ties across local programs, including national training programs and annual conferences that showcased local programs. State professional associations were formed to emulate the national program at the state level. Professional relationships were fostered across the states as well through the Congress of Drug Court Professionals. State and local administrators and elected officials became members of the governing board of the champion organization and of key supporter groups.

These institutional arrangements provided stability for the drug court policy as it grew and spread across the states. The champion organization was supported by the efforts of other national nonprofit organizations and was challenged by others. Across the information network, members of professional groups of judges, lawyers, law enforcement, treatment providers, and criminal justice groups interacted with one another and with the champion group. They shared ideas and learned from one another in multiple venues.

From the information mix surrounding the drug court program, state and local administrators found strategic forms of information that they could use. This information synthesized the experiences of programs across jurisdictions. A policy template developed by the champion organization expressed a set of core values that guided the new policy as it was implemented. These "guiding principles" became examples of best practices in judicial reform and provided administrators with an organizing framework that could be adapted to any drug court setting. The drug court team became a vehicle for generating collaboration and agreement across professions based on a set of core values expressed in the NADCP's guiding principles. The policy template provided general parameters for drug court design and implementation; local drug court teams and state groups collaborated to determine exactly how the design and implementation would proceed. To bring the NADCP's policy template to life, local drug court teams collaborated to determine their own interpretations of the template's various elements. Individual teams and communities had to arrive at a consensus on the meaning that they would give to terms such as "frequent drug testing," "nonviolent" drug offenses, "early" identification, and "prompt" placement. These interdisciplinary and cross-jurisdictional relationships further expanded the information network and fostered new organizations at the state level. State judiciaries and, in some cases, executive branch offices formed task forces and working groups based on the idea of drug courts and worked through the same sorts of definitional issues that had faced local programs.

Drug court teams actually experienced the drug court concept through firsthand observations of model programs. As the program spread across local courts, the policy template served a broader purpose in fostering collaboration among local programs and between local programs and state offices. States passed legislation that incorporated the policy template as a set of core principles and used the template as the basis for developing program performance standards and, in some cases, certification programs. The professionalization of the drug court concept provided new points of connection between the champion organization and supporting organizations in the information network.

The policy template of the NADCP's guiding principles had an undeniable influence on the spread of the program across local courts and on facilitating agreement about program elements at the state and local levels. The influence of the template, however, was broader than the NADCP itself. A fundamental aspect of the influence of this information network was the cumulative interaction of the influence of other nonprofit organizations in the network as implementation was diffused. Figure 6.1 presents a broad illustration of the four primary information positions in the information network and their intersection in relation to the strategic information relationships, strategic forms of information, and strategic processes that were instrumental to drug court diffusion and implementation. Supporters helped institutionalize the drug court concept; challengers' comparisons with other reforms fostered additional research to hone and reinforce the promise of the drug court concept. The champion organization was integrally involved in generating various forms of strategic information and collaborative processes; supporters and challengers contributed to the information mix but were not engaged in every form of information or process identified in this study.

The Continuing Information Cycle: New Challenges in Implementation

The information network illustrated in this book was not static but was part of an evolving cycle of change. This continuous process of change extended the influence of the information relationships, tools, and processes that were developed in the network to new populations and new challenges. These extensions of the network leveraged existing relationships with established public programs, applied the network concepts to new challenges, and established new programs that extended the drug court concept in new directions.

Figure 6.1   Strategic Information, Strategic Processes, and Information Positions across the Network

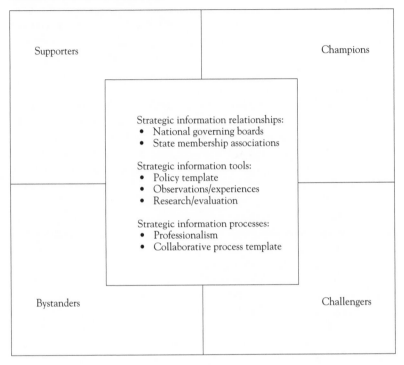

In this process of evolution, administrators—and particularly those at the state level—drew upon the resources and expertise of programs and relationships already in place. Some drug court relationships reported in this study had connections to state or local programs that were developed long before the drug court concept arrived on the scene. At the state level in particular, staff drew upon administrative relationships and resources from existing programs concerned with driving under the influence of alcohol and with court referrals in promoting substance abuse education and treatment to build state institutional support. States also leveraged relationships between the judicial and executive branches in developing state oversight programs. In Tennessee, for example, the information relationships that developed based on federal grants between the executive branch and other criminal justice programs became the model for the relationship between the Tennessee state executive office and local court programs, and the basis for the executive office state certification program. State offices adapted information tools that had been developed to suit earlier initiatives to fit the drug court concept. In Indiana, for example, the state drug court certification program evolved from a certification program for alcohol and drug treatment programs that existed decades before the drug court concept emerged on the scene.

This evolution fostered new relationships, whereby the information network expanded to new areas of influence. The information tools and processes of the drug court model expanded to other programs and populations. New actors became involved in the information network. State and local administrators continued to apply the principles gleaned from the information network to address the emerging implementation issues associated with data and evaluation in state and local programs.

As a part of the natural progression of the drug court program, the information network extended more deeply into the area of performance measurement. State offices and local programs used the tools and collaborative strategies fostered by the information network to navigate the process of identifying performance measures. As with the other aspects of the drug court program, the process was a continuous cycle of definition, measurement, redefinition, and further measurement. States navigated the process of measurement and decisions about how and what to measure through the various collaborative institutions and processes that had been formed to begin local drug court programs, to propose legislation, or to begin state associations.

Across programs and state offices, administrators commented that their pressing challenge was to understand how to identify and define concepts in order to measure some form of impact as well as outputs. Administrators were also working to identify effects that were important to measure and that could be measured in a meaningful way. Through the collaborative processes that were established based on the policy template of guiding principles, and with information from the organizations in the information network, state and local programs identified relevant measures. States worked extensively with the National Center for State Courts (NCSC) to develop state-specific benchmarks and data elements that were central to their statewide programs. Through technical assistance facilitated by the NCSC, states customized their standards using the basic dimensions of the policy template. The NCSC facilitated collaborative decision making about performance measures in a host of various task forces and working groups. More broadly, the NCSC provided assistance in developing state-wide plans for court systems and released a tool kit for problem-solving courts that was made available online.

Administrators realized the importance of developing standards based on data that local jurisdictions were able to collect. One group of administrators described the standards process as a choice between "the perfect and the good." If a state office, or even a local program, thought that a measure was important but local courts were not able to capture that data, "then what have we accomplished? In some cases, it may be to our benefit to simply use indicators that are good enough, even though we know that they aren't perfect." As more than one administrator pointed out, measurement is a necessary element of program success, but measurement alone is never enough; programs succeed because they are based on good ideas that come of age at the right time, they are nurtured in a supportive environment, and they are well executed.

State efforts to measure performance and to conduct evaluations were critically linked to the capacity for data collection and analysis; however, administrators also observed that the overall effort was only as strong as the weakest local link. At the local drug court level, tension between the need for state resources and the desire to retain local control was brought into sharp focus by state budget pressures. Administrators were particularly concerned with their abilities to collect data about their programs. These challenges were at least as severe in local programs as in state offices. Historically, local programs lacked both the financial resources and the technological infrastructure to develop their own data collection systems for court operations in general or for drug court operations in particular. State and local administrators alike expressed concern that local programs might lose funds if they were unable to generate and manage data according to statewide protocols that linked local funding to various standards and reporting requirements. Rural programs appeared to face the greatest pressure in this regard. Administrators noted that state funding for data collection and reporting systems would help alleviate the pressure on local programs in this area. Yet local administrators noted the loss of control that accompanied a central data collection effort at the state level. Some local administrators were wary of ceding authority to a state office concerned with program operating decisions in exchange for state funding support that might not be permanent.

States moved toward data collection in a variety of ways. In some states, drug court management information systems were linked into statewide court data collection or case management systems. Some states added staff to develop management information systems for drug courts and other programs; some state programs added staff to monitor the development of these systems by outside vendors. For example, in Indiana, the state judiciary made available grants to local drug courts for the development of technological infrastructure. Missouri operated a Web-based data collection system as a condition of state funding for local courts. Although the concept of using management information systems to collect and share data in networked environments seemed rather obvious, state and local governments appeared to lack specific technological skill and broad-based expertise in data collection and analysis. The lack of capacity for data collection and analysis hampered local efforts to monitor program activities and also inhibited local program evaluation efforts. In discussions of this issue, administrators reported that data collection had been a slow process and that resources were quite limited. Efforts to standardize or centralize state efforts based on data will be challenged by the uneven data collection capacity of local programs. Some local jurisdictions have developed their own systems but are reluctant (and financially unable) to further invest in a different, statewide approach.

Capacity was also limited by the investment in state staff. In most states, the state-level drug court effort was not a full-time job; administrative responsibilities for drug court programs were frequently blended with responsibilities for other criminal justice initiatives. Approximately half the state-level drug court programs were administered by staff members who had other program responsibilities that consumed more than half their workload. Only about a third of the state programs had at least one staff member whose primary responsibility (more than half time) was the state drug court program. There was no unified course of study or standardized body of drug court education that synthesized its hallmark blend of treatment and law enforcement perspectives.[1] Several state administrators expressed the need for consistent and/or minimum education standards for state and local drug court coordinators. Some state administrators suggested that additional training is needed to support drug court coordinators because of turnover.

Across the country, drug court administrators also recognized that state drug court programs faced potential political challenges despite the popularity and longevity of many local programs. In some states, political momentum gathered to expand local programs and, in tandem, state oversight efforts. In some states, changes in the state's judicial leadership prompted growth in local programs and increased the profile of state efforts to institutionalize and support drug court programs. For example, the election of Sue Bell Cobb in 2006 as the chief justice of the Alabama Supreme Court brought new attention to local court programs. Cobb promised to establish a drug court in every one of Alabama's sixty-seven counties. In Tennessee, the state drug court initiative expanded in the mid-2000s with an influx of state appropriations to local programs to address drug dependency. More than one administrator expressed concern that drug courts would not be a top priority for the next chief justice or governor of their particular state. Across the states, administrators commented that the success of a state office depended upon an embrace of the concept by a critical mass of local trial court judges. Administrators consistently noted that performance measurement and reporting were important dimensions of the political calculus behind judicial support. Public support for drug court programs would not be sustained if local programs were not able to demonstrate accountability and value—however those dimensions of the program might be defined.

The Continuing Information Cycle: Extending Information to New Venues

The content and the processes associated with the drug court model served as a template for other types of courts directed specifically at solving problems for particular groups. Mental health courts and domestic violence courts, for example, became increasingly common across local courts, and their genesis was tied to the drug court movement (Berman and Feinblatt 2005). Some states began to address drug courts in the broader context of what became known as problem-solving courts. The umbrella of problem-solving courts was an attractive method of building capacity across programs by using a similar administrative process for a series of different populations. The problem-solving court approach cut the information costs of developing new programs at the local level and conserved resources in program administration across state and local governments.

Problem-solving courts were also attractive for conceptual reasons. For some, the approach reflected a collection of principles of accountability, informed decision making, and collaboration that were applicable to other types of judicial operations such as small claims and community courts. Some states embraced the problem-solving court concept as an avenue for extrapolating the NADCP's guiding principles to other populations with the expectation of similar positive results in behavioral change. State programs in Alabama and Georgia, for example, adopted the term "accountability courts" as the comprehensive terminology for drug courts, specialty courts, or other problem-solving courts. Administrators in those states remarked that elected officials and the general public were more receptive to the image of accountability than an image of leniency; the concept of accountability was seen as more appropriate for programs seeking state funding.

The champion organization, the NADCP, also extended the drug court model into new populations. In late 2009 the NADCP launched a new treatment initiative, Veterans' Treatment Courts, which combined features of drug courts and the mental health equivalent (mental health courts) to reach veterans with an addiction and/or mental illness. The collaboration included the veterans' health care network along with the now-traditional drug court team and its mental health court counterparts. As this policy initiative moves forward, the universe of organizations in the information network surrounding veterans' treatment courts will most likely also shift to include new groups that focus on veterans' issues. New collaborations will extend the information network in new directions. Other champions, supporters, and challengers will emerge. Some bystanders in the drug court information network may be mobilized to take a more active role either for or against this area of veterans' policy.

The NADCP expanded its efforts to establish new drug court programs in other countries as well. Although this study has focused on the national aspects of the information network and the relationships within the American intergovernmental system, it is worth noting that the drug court concept has been internationally operational since 1998, when the International Association of Drug Treatment Courts was established as a professional membership organization for drug courts outside America. At the time of this study, more than twenty-five drug treatment courts were operational in eleven countries, including Canada, the United Kingdom, Scandinavia, and Atlantic Ocean island nations; and eleven pilot projects were under way in Brazil and Chile. In late 2009, during a visit from the new U.S. drug czar, Gil Kerlikowske, Mexico announced an interest in testing drug courts in its judicial system. In the new environment of another country, information tools and processes from the information network can be expected to provide a basis for moving forward. New information relationships can be expected to evolve as a result of the diffusion of drug courts to other countries, particularly in countries that border American states.

The Continuing Cycle of Information:
New Ideas and New Actors

Some evidence of a shift has occurred in state and federal policy surrounding sentencing practices for drug crimes. Substantial portions of the onerous New York Rockefeller drug laws were repealed in 2008 and 2009; these laws were a blueprint for many states policies that addressed the use and sale of crack cocaine. Interestingly, in conjunction with this repeal, the New York legislature was slated to expand the use of drug courts in the state (Peters 2009). Alongside reform in New York, federal judicial and administrative decisions retreated from previous inflexible interpretations of mandatory federal sentencing guidelines and federal sentence requirements for some crack cocaine offenses (U.S. Sentencing Commission 2007, 2008a, 2008b).

Challenger organizations have continued to present new alternatives for policy change. During the 2008 election cycle, several challenger organizations in the national information network mobilized in spirited debate with the NADCP about the role of drug courts and the need for fidelity to the NADCP's conceptualization of the drug court program. In November 2008 the Drug Policy Alliance and other groups sponsored Proposition 5 on the California ballot as a reform that would expand access to drug treatment across the state's criminal justice system. Proposition 5, also known as the Nonviolent Offender Rehabilitation Act (NORA), proposed mandating treatment instead of prison for most drug offenders, reducing marijuana possession from a misdemeanor to an infraction, and opening treatment to property crime offenders whose crimes are related to drug use. NORA also proposed changing parole and probation requirements for most drug offenses. Last, NORA proposed establishing a new system of oversight boards for the departments of corrections, probation, and parole; the courts; and public treatment programs; staffing requirements for these new oversight boards would include greater citizen participation.[2] NORA was developed in response to steep declines in state funding for drug treatment programs, which had expanded after the success of Proposition 36 in 2000.

NORA was sponsored by the Drug Policy Alliance Network and the Campaign for New Drug Policies. The Drug Policy Alliance (DPA) has continued to advocate for measures such as NORA that broadly decriminalize drug use and tend to treat drug use as a public health issue that reflects a need for greater access to drug treatment both within and outside the criminal justice system. Challenger organizations such as the Sentencing Project and the Open Society Institute were aligned with the DPA's position on NORA.[3] These organizations have continued to press for broader systemic reforms regarding drug use; their positions on NORA reflect the fundamental differences about reform that have percolated through the national information network for the past several decades. Detailed descriptions of the positions of the DPA and the NADCP were widely available on the internet. Both organizations distributed their respective positions and exchanged detailed rebuttals with one another (NADCP 2008; NORA Campaign 2008). These positions reflected fundamental philosophical differences that were apparent when the DPA successfully sponsored California Proposition 36 in 2000 and advocated similar ballot initiatives in other states.

Proposition 5 was defeated by California voters on November 4, 2008, with 60 percent of voters rejecting the initiative (California Secretary of State 2008a); however, the normative debate has continued. Central elements in the controversy remained unresolved, including the role of coercion in treatment generally and the role of a judge in the coercive process more specifically, along with the level of abstinence required to demonstrate success during treatment and subsequent recovery. The fundamental identity of the drug court concept was embedded in the controversy. Was "drug court" a generic label that could be applied to a range of alternatives to incarceration that include some sort of treatment for drug use or abuse and that include all types of offenders and offenses? Or was a "drug court" bounded by the guiding principles of the innovators who conceived the idea and promoted the concept through the NADCP and its guiding principles?

These debates continued to illustrate the shifting nature of an intersectoral information network. New challengers emerged to press against the drug court concept and against the information generated by champions in particular. In the process, new challenger organizations have appeared. In October 2009 the National Association of Criminal Defense Lawyers (NACDL) published a report critical of problem-solving courts and drug courts in particular (NACDL 2009). The NACDL was not identified by public administrators as a source of information about drug courts—in either support or opposition—through the surveys and interviews conducted for this project. Yet, as the drug court program has gained firmer root in many communities, this professional membership organization mobilized to generate information about the drug court program through research and commentary about its findings.

The NACDL's research and report were funded by the Foundation for Criminal Justice and included specific support from the Open Society

Institute, which has assumed a significant challenger posture in the information network.[4] The Open Society Institute has advocated for various forms of drug legalization in its promotion of ballot initiatives in California and other states. One major philosophical premise of the NACDL study was that drug addiction is a public health problem; another was that the appropriate policy solutions include decriminalization and universal free clinics for addiction treatment. The report also raised a number of concerns about the current drug court model that has been advanced by the champion NADCP and supported by so many other organizations in the network. Some of these concerns, such as the nontraditional roles of legal counsel and the drug court judge, were the subject of previous debate within the information network. The study raised the concept of potential ethical questions for members of the defense counsel staff regarding their ability to participate in a team setting, the extensive interaction between program clients and the drug court judge in the absence of legal representation, and various practices in individual drug courts that may foreclose the use of traditional elements of due process and criminal procedure. Overall, the NACDL's report argued that the views of the criminal defense bar have been underrepresented on the drug court team as a whole (NACDL 2009).

In response, information about drug courts emerged from the NADCP in response to the challengers. The NADCP communicated with many members of the information network to clarify its position and "set the record straight." It is premature to examine whether or how the views of these challenger organizations might influence drug court operations or, more broadly, views about the efficacy of drug courts as a policy solution. Given the long-standing information position of the challengers in favor of legalization as a policy, the NACDL's report appeared to signal the extended involvement of the challenger groups in questioning specific aspects of drug court operations. Administrators interviewed during the research for this book observed that it was particularly challenging for drug court teams to gain consistent, active participation by defense attorneys, but they only speculated about why that was the case.

The information generated by these national organizations in this debate will help states and local programs respond to critiques, whether they are raised by the NACDL or come from other sources. This new information may also prompt new relationships or collaborations. For example, one concern raised in the report is that defense lawyers were not sufficiently trained to understand and execute critical aspects of how to represent clients in drug courts, and that drug court defendants should be represented by "senior and highly skilled lawyers" (NACDL 2009, 55). This presented an opportunity for the NACDL to generate training for its members, either alone or in consultation with the NADCP. It also presented an opportunity for members of state and local defense bar associations to form working groups and task forces to address drug court issues in their state. The NACDL report itself suggested a template of best practices for members of the defense counsel to use in drug court representation; if the past application of the NADCP model is prologue, defense bar associations will consider the NACDL's recommendations in a similar way.

The point of these illustrations is not to identify or discuss each concern raised by the challenger organizations or to respond to a particular report or discuss specific program standards but rather to demonstrate that new opportunities for collaboration across professions and jurisdictions have continued to arise that further extend the reach of the information network. These opportunities came about through the efforts of administrators to refine the implementation and operation of the existing drug court initiative and through the development of new programs. The challengers continued to push the champions to produce new information that was more specific than existing information about the drug court program; this information generated pressure for organizations to evaluate, and perhaps shift, their information positions. Throughout, the information network remained influential in providing tools and processes for meeting new challenges.

Considerations for Application to Other Policy Areas

This book has focused on the national information network of nonprofit organizations concerned with a criminal justice policy issue. The influence of the information network derived from multiple dimensions of information connection that are generalizable to other policy areas. The impetus for the drug court movement can also be generalized to other policy questions. The drug court idea grew and spread because the environment was ripe for change across many dimensions of the debate about drugs and crime. Frustration from judges, from treatment professionals, and others involved in the revolving door of drugs and crime combined to focus on a complex and relatively intractable problem. A headwind had built behind the will for change in more than one discipline; this contributed to the overall willingness of participants to take a chance on a new idea.

Like other policy innovations, the drug court example illustrates the influence of a focus concerned with a complex problem—a rich environment of ideas and values that challenge one another, enduring information relationships, information tools, and collaborative processes. Each of these concepts can be broadly applied across policy domains. A few aspects of the drug court example should be considered when comparing this study with others that may follow. These aspects of this example may limit comparison with the policy arenas; these aspects may also suggest important differences between different intergovernmental institutional relationships that support particular policy initiatives.

An initial consideration is the highly localized nature of criminal justice administration. Criminal justice systems are considerably invested in local delivery systems rather than relying on state agencies or offices. Law enforcement, probation, prosecution, and defense are each strongly established functions of local government; treatment services are typically localized to serve specific populations. The courts are creatures of state government, to be sure, but the action here takes place within local criminal trial courts. Some state court systems are more unified in relation to central precepts than others, but the administration of justice occurs at the local level. The grassroots nature of the spread of drug courts has been compatible with this localized delivery system. The idea germinated locally and spread throughout local courts well in advance of state interest. Other policy areas may have greater institutional involvement from states at the outset. Other policy ideas may begin within state government or within national government; the relationships, tools, and collaborative processes may vary from those illustrated through the diffusion and institutionalization of drug courts.

Criminal justice is also an area of public administration that is already highly articulated for a wide range of professions and disciplines. A ready-made framework of local and state public administrators had already been established, along with a multitude of professional membership organizations. These organizations provided ready-made venues for information transmission and exchange and thus also provided an essential mechanism on which to build information relationships; in essence, these organizations provided a foil against which the new professional organization, the National Association of Drug Court Professionals, could position its ideas and values. These organizations also provided a toehold for the new profession to begin building new relationships and methods for diffusing its ideas. Further, collaboration across disciplines—the heart of the drug court policy machine—was possible in part because the administration of justice was already a professionally fragmented enterprise. Specialization has occurred in relation to the administration of law enforcement, probation, and court operations as well as through the treatment, legal, and judicial professions. The concept of an advanced generalist in public service comes from the cross-fertilization of extant professional realms; it may be more difficult (or it may be easier) to achieve collaboration within a broad discipline, without rough edges between different professions, ideas, and values.

Within criminal justice administration, the strong central role of the drug court judge may not translate into a similar authority position in other policy areas. The drug court judge had the authority to begin and conduct a drug court program with limited interference from other actors; in some states, drug courts began under existing state laws. The drug court judge was also first among equals on the drug court team and was ultimately responsible for the program's implementation and success. This strong central actor may not be present—or may not be so obvious—in other interdisciplinary policy arenas, or in other policy initiatives that seek to bridge disciplines, jurisdictions, or professions. Drug court judges were also held politically accountable for their choices in a manner that is relatively direct and transparent in comparison with other administrative realms. This may have influenced the information connections between judges and the national information network in a manner that is different from that which may be observed in other interdisciplinary arenas or with other new policy ideas. In states where citizens elect some or all of their judges, the drug court judge is ultimately held accountable by voters. In states that use judicial appointment, the accountability of a drug court judge was oriented to the appointing authorities, who were often also elected public officials.

Taken together, these characteristics represent a policy environment that had a strong local and autonomous flavor. It may be the case that strong local autonomy is a dimension of successful policy design, or a condition precedent to successful replication. Even if future studies suggest that either is the case, strong local autonomy is not always a feature of public policy. This policy environment also included a national nonprofit information network comprising several organizations that were strongly supported by grants from the federal government. The National Association of Drug Court Professionals is among those. The sustained presence of the NADCP was crucial to the drug court movement across time; the financial support of the federal government was an important aspect of that sustained presence.

Many of these characteristics may exist in the information arrangements that pertain to other policy questions and the diffusion of other policy solutions. One of the goals of this study has been to more carefully specify one type of network—an intersectoral information network—and to analyze its influence on policy diffusion across state and local governments. The state of network research today suggests that multiple types of networks with different characteristics may contribute to their success or failure. In examining this information network and its various information connections with public administrators, one objective has been to specify the characteristics of these connections. As research has moved beyond the consideration of the network as a black box, we have begun to learn more about the individualized characteristics of information exchanges among actors in networked arrangements. One goal is to conceptualize distinctive features of this information network as compared with others that may be studied in the future, and to identify potential distinctions that may make a difference in some aspect of solving public problems. The distinctions about the information network that pertains to drug courts are grounded to some degree in characteristics of the criminal justice policy system, to some degree in the organizations that make up the information network, and to some degree in the characteristics of the individual actors engaged in information exchanges. Potential points of distinction are specified here to provide an additional context for the information relationships between public administrators and the national nonprofit organizations in the information network, to provide a degree of clarification about the conditions that fostered the diffusion of drug court innovation across state and local governments, and to provide researchers with a basis for comparison in future studies. These distinctions also give us further insight into the information network itself.

Notes

1. Several administrators mentioned that a series of academic courses or a degree for drug court professionals had been discussed in general terms, but specifics had not been determined.

2. The voter information about NORA stated that the initiative would require (1) increased funding and oversight for individualized treatment and rehabilitation programs for nonviolent drug offenders and parolees; (2) multiple-tiered probation with treatment; (3) case dismissal and/or sealing of records after probation; (4) limitations on court authority to incarcerate offenders who violated probation or parole; (5) shortened parole for most drug offenses, including sales and for nonviolent property crimes; (6) new administrative infrastructure and reporting requirements regarding drug treatment and rehabilitation; and (7) charging certain

marijuana misdemeanors as infractions rather than misdemeanors (California Secretary of State 2008b).

3. Many organizations have indicated support for NORA. The Sentencing Project is one of the national nonprofit organizations in the national information network that is the subject of this study. The Open Society is also an organization in the national nonprofit information network; NORA materials identify George Soros as a major funder of the NORA Campaign. Other organizations engaged in the NORA campaign in favor of Proposition 5 also have ties to the national information network; e.g., the California Association of Alcoholism and Drug Abuse Counselors is the state association affiliated with the National Association of Alcoholism and Drug Abuse Counselors, one of the organizations interviewed in the exploratory phase of this study.

4. The study was also funded by the Ford Foundation, which was not identified as part of the national nonprofit information network and was not identified with any particular information position related to this research.

7

Bringing Value to Public Decisions

INFORMATION RELATIONSHIPS, TOOLS, AND PROCESSES

The overarching objective of this book has been to illustrate how information matters in the interdependent and complex environment of public administration and to identify potential productive connections between the work of the nonprofit sector and the work of government. As the preceding chapters illustrate, the information relationships, tools, and processes that developed between national nonprofit organizations and public administrators were instrumental in the design, diffusion, and implementation of policy change. These information relationships, tools, and processes developed within and through an intersectoral information network that combined the efforts of national nonprofit organizations with those of public administrators. Across state and local governments, administrators synthesized ideas through a web of relationships and collaborative processes that built government capacity to deliver public policy solutions. This volume has focused on one area of criminal justice reform, but the lessons here apply beyond a single policy realm. The relationships, tools, and processes of this information network and its interaction with administrators have illustrated successful practices and lessons that can be applied to other policy questions and in other policy arenas. Further, the information linkages between the nonprofit sector and government offices have also expanded the way we understand networked arrangements and sources of information related to policy change.

The Typology of Information Positions
as a Resource for Policy Change

Considerable research has established the importance of information in spreading innovative policy ideas and bringing about policy change within government (Agranoff 2007; Rogers 1995; Walker 1969). A major premise of this book has been that nonprofit organizations are uniquely suited to producing information that speaks to multiple constituencies. This information typically synthesizes the experiences of multiple participants and illustrates the comparative advantage and value of a particular initiative or policy direction. Synthesized information provides a form of information shorthand that is a particularly important resource for administrators in designing and implementing new public programs (Mossberger and Hale 2002). Nonprofits are a key source for synthesized information, which includes research studies and examples of success through best practices and model initiatives. Of course, the nonprofit sector is itself a highly diverse collection of organizations formed on the basis of missions that reflect unique points of view about policy and the need for policy change. The typology of information positions explored in this study provides new insight into the information that nonprofit organizations produce and how this information influences state and local policy decisions.

The typology considers an information network of nonprofit organizations and the information disseminated to public administrators in terms of an organization's engagement with an innovative idea and their support or opposition to it. This typology is one way of considering the motivations that organizations may have in generating information about a policy idea. Motivation is an important consideration, because information itself is not a neutral concept; information is developed for various purposes and by people within organizations with differing ideologies and goals (Radin 2006). As is illustrated by the four organizational archetypes—champions, supporters, challengers, and bystanders—organizational motivations will vary across a typical national information network. These motivations may have implications for the work of administrators engaged with the information generated by these types of organizations.

Champion organizations are highly engaged in the policy debate concerned with a particular policy question and also strongly in favor of a particular innovation as the solution to the dilemma at hand. Champions can be expected to generate information that demonstrates the need for policy change. Champions can be expected to be heavily involved in the design of an innovative policy solution and in providing assistance for implementation. Policy templates of best practices, model programs, and policy experiences are examples of the forms of information that emerge from champion groups. Champions may also be involved in generating information that demonstrates the relative worth of a particular solution in comparison with other ideas. Champions may generate or sponsor research or evaluative data that demonstrate the performance of a new idea relative to other options.

Supporter organizations find ways to advance their missions by linking some of their work to the policy innovation, although the innovation itself is not a specific goal of these groups. Organizations that conduct training and education programs may find a need to develop materials and sessions on the new idea. Organizations that provide general technical or administrative support to government offices may find a niche in resolving technical or administrative issues that arise during the implementation of a new policy approach. Organizations that conduct policy research may become involved in studies that evaluate the design, implementation, and/or performance of a new idea.

Challengers generate information that pushes back on champions' arguments in favor of a particular solution. Challengers may argue in favor of a different solution or may define the problem in entirely different terms. Challengers' information may suggest different methods of design or implementation. Challengers may also evaluate the innovation. Challengers may be opposed to an entire approach or to key aspects of a policy solution; their work is characterized by ideological differences about problem definition. Challengers may be champions of other policy innovations that are based on very different ideas from the rest of the network.

Bystanders remain on the sidelines of a policy issue. Bystander organizations are highly informed about issues and about the positions of other organizations. However, bystanders are not engaged either in support or opposition to a particular innovation. This lack of engagement is related to mission and organizational focus rather than a lack of general interest. Bystander organizations can choose to engage in the information debate at any point.

Because each type of organization generates information that reflects its views and mission, the potential exists that the information will reflect some degree of organizational bias or self-interest. Champions and challengers produce information that encourages or discourages a potential solution. Supporters generate information that will link their current work to a new idea. Bystanders observe and decide whether a current situation implicates their core mission. However, the juxtaposition of these different orientations within the information network helps mediate concerns about the accuracy and legitimacy of the information that is disseminated and whether it is aligned with the agenda of any particular organization. The typology of information positions reflects an environment of complementary and competing ideas in which nonprofit organizations strive for currency with and acceptance by public administrators as well as with their other stakeholder constituencies. Because administrators have access to multiple sources of expertise, each organization is motivated to be considered an accurate, responsive, and trustworthy information source.

Moreover, the information that flows through the information network from any one organization does not exist in isolation; the information is iterative, cumulative, and interactive between organizations. Organizations in the information network operate in a web of communication with public administrators and with one another. Champions respond to challengers' claims in order to reinforce the merits of the innovation; challengers continue to push champions to refine their messages and demonstrate success in specific terms. The information claims of one group do not stand alone but instead are engaged in an evolving information environment. This interaction helps maintain the integrity of the information for public administrators.

A generic hypothetical example illustrates this point. To begin the example, assume that a champion organization has advanced a policy solution and a prototype has been initiated by administrators in one jurisdiction. The idea is novel and provokes reactions from both detractors and attractors. Administrators are interested in whether the new idea "works" and conduct an evaluation of the prototype. A champion organization or a supporter group seeks an evaluation study as well; the results will assist administrators in learning about whether and how the idea can work. The idea is a success according to these few initial studies. However, even if these studies are conducted at arms' length from champions, the findings could be linked to champions or supporters, and so administrators may have reservations about the results. Supporters, challengers, and even bystanders may conduct additional evaluations.

Ultimately, a body of information is available to administrators, and the collective results differ in key respects. Champions and some supporters examine the issues identified in the various competing studies and implement solutions. More jurisdictions become involved; administrators begin to contribute to the development of specific practices that they believe will be appropriate for their localities. Supporters incorporate the new idea into work that they are doing in other jurisdictions to test the idea with other administrators. Champions fine-tune their best practices information to develop solutions to some of the findings of the studies conducted by other groups and incorporate these solutions into their work. Supporters offer additional insight into connections between the new idea and existing practices. New practices emerge to reflect the synthesis of the information as it accumulates. Bystanders watch with interest and may observe the new idea in practice. Bystanders often find a point of commonality between the new idea and their own missions. Bystanders generate information to illustrate the ways in which this new idea supports or opposes the work of their groups—becoming supporters, challengers, or even champions through this process.

The body of information available to administrators continues to evolve against the point/counterpoint of the different information positions in the information network. The organizations continue to maintain work that is consistent with their missions and remain tied to their various stakeholders and constituencies that support their work as nonprofits. Administrators that access information from many and diverse positions in the information network thus gain access to a rich and evolving field of competing ideas that is broadly supported by many stakeholder communities with different points of view. As time passes, administrators may also gain more experience as information consumers and may become more sophisticated in their ability to interpret information. This experience itself builds capacity within the ranks of public administrators. Ultimately, of course, administrators choose whether to act on the information they obtain; however, the rich competition of ideas, multiple perspectives, and sources of information suggests that the motivations of any one organization are tempered by the information network as a whole.

The interplay between administrators and organizations that are variously engaged in a reform initiative, as either proponents or opponents, may be a condition precedent or a necessary catalyst for the spread of an innovation. An information network that includes a collection of professional membership organizations comprising various groups of public administrators may provide an important means of communicating about new ideas. The professional membership component of the information network may also be an important element of bringing to scale new policy ideas that involve the work of those constituencies.

The typology of competing and complementary information positions also suggests that administrators receive a relatively comprehensive view about political support for and opposition to an idea. Competing ideologies, support for the status quo, and perhaps even partisan alliances will be apparent in the various stances taken by organizations in the information network. Gauging the political will behind an idea is important for administrators; they conduct their work in political environments, and ideas that lack any political support are unlikely to gain significant traction.

The data, illustrations, and vignettes presented in this volume also underscore several themes about how the information generated by national nonprofit organizations matters in bringing about policy change and about information relationships, tools, and processes that can be applied to other policy areas. These themes include the value of synergies across governments and disciplines, tools for embracing ambiguity, and sustained energy to bring about policy change. These themes also include a strong relationship between central organizing tools, reinforcement, and synthesis. And finally, these themes transcend the particular policy questions facing state and local administrators that concern drug use and crime and can be applied to other policy areas.

Synergies across Governments and Disciplines

A national nonprofit information network can be more than just a vehicle for information exchange, although that certainly will occur. The information network explored in this volume integrated policy information with the professional associations of public administrators and public officials. The tools that public administrators used to bring about this integration provided a structure for interaction and collaboration across local government and between local governments and state offices. This structure led to the institutionalization of a new idea that provided stability for the innovation over time. These tools also fostered new institutional relationships that served as a platform for new ideas beyond the current policy innovation. These tools were particularly important because they arose within an information network of loosely linked organizations. And these tools may be especially useful in helping public administrators navigate other similar collections of organizations that are that are not bound by formal ties—in other words, some of the networked arrangements that are common in public administration today.

The information relationships, tools, and processes that emerged from this information network also transcended disciplines. The diversity of interdisciplinary initiatives appeared to foster a competition of information perspectives that contributed to collaboration and synthesis. The interdisciplinary focus of innovation reinforced the need for multiple points of view and the involvement of multiple organizations. Some innovations may move forward and grow precisely because of their interdisciplinary nature; the need for multiple perspectives may mobilize a broader constituency that becomes invested in the innovation whether to support it, oppose it, or align with it. The efforts of champions of innovation became stronger when supporter organizations became involved. The collective efforts of champions and supporters became more finely tuned when challenged by other groups. The interdisciplinary perspective contributed to a diverse collection of information; from this diversity, various organizations found some aspect of an innovative idea that aligned with their mission and took action to move it forward.

Within this informal collection of organizations, the information relationships, tools, and processes merged in a self-reinforcing fashion to institutionalize certain concepts such as an interdisciplinary policy team and interdisciplinary professional identity and a policy template for design and operation. These concepts served as a common language, on the basis of which decisions were made. These concepts—which are by nature collaborative—fostered further collaboration to institutionalize the innovation within the work practices of public administrators. From the information network, a language of collaboration evolved that was used to address other issues. Similarly, new collaborative arrangements continued to emerge to address emerging issues within the innovation itself. In turn, these collaborative arrangements were a tool for establishing a strategy for future collaboration and information exchange that further promoted the model.

The interdisciplinary approach appears to align closely with the focus of the nonprofit sector. One of the inherent values of the nonprofit sector is its grounding in community and in collaboration across diverse constituencies. The work of public administrators in complex, interdependent environments can be enhanced by embracing the information relationships, tools, and processes that evolve from information connections with national nonprofit organizations. The relatively intractable nature of public problems suggests that future efforts at solutions will attempt to bring together more rather than fewer perspectives. There will always be a degree of uncertainty in the collaborative process of bringing multiple stakeholders together to reach a consensus. Interdisciplinary initiatives will continue to present the obstacle of communicating across disciplines and professional orientations. It will continue to be difficult and expensive—and sometimes, impossible—to define and measure some concepts.

Further, measurement alone is not sufficient to establish that particular results (good or bad) can be attributed to a public program. Effectiveness will tend to mean whatever significant stakeholders and constituencies think it should mean. It will become more complicated to analyze results when stakeholder groups represent different professional perspectives. And yet, as diverse groups learn how to talk with one another, they learn new languages and new capacity is generated. The nonprofit orientation of serving diverse constituencies seems to add continuing value to government efforts to become more capable within complex, interdependent collaborative processes. The power of interdisciplinary and cross-jurisdictional collaboration between a national information network and public administrators suggests that we should define problems in more expansive terms and bring more ideas and interests to the table.

Synthesis, Reinforcement, and Centrality

Synthesized information and collaborative decision-making processes are important organizing resources for policy change in complex, interdependent environments. Provan and Milward (1995, 2001) demonstrated the importance of certain centralizing forces in successful network performance in their studies of certain intergovernmental social service networks. In particular, they found that a centralized funding source was important, not only for financial support but also for the ancillary support that this central source could provide in coordinating reporting and other information. The information network studied in this volume exemplifies a form of this centralization that occurs through a process of reinforcement and synthesis at two different levels. At the network level, the efforts of champions and supporters reinforced one another as each pursued their respective missions. Complementary ideas and strategies were transferred across organizations and into state and local offices. At the program level, the policy template and policy experience had a strong centralizing effect on policy content and literally brought people together in the same physical space; moreover, these tools reinforced one another. The tenets of the policy template served as an organizing tool for developing and arranging policy content. The policy experience reinforced the policy template. Together, these tools promoted local policy implementation and new platforms for collaborative decision making. Local networks evolved based on the information tools promoted by the national nonprofit information network, and multiple state networks evolved based on the same information.

The centralizing and reinforcing interactions of the information network kept programs moving in the same direction and facilitated replication.

Customization through Ambiguity

The information relationships, tools, and process that were fostered through the information network were relatively ambiguous. New spaces were created for experimentation and further innovation within the concepts of the interdisciplinary team, the interdisciplinary professional identity, and the policy template. A central benefit of this ambiguity was that it fostered local support and control. The power of local decision making was promoted and institutionalized by the synthesized forms of information that flowed through the information network. Best practices, model programs, and locally based program evaluations enhanced a culture of local decisions. The policy template for program design and operation forced a decision-making process that was grounded in local communities. This type of approach encouraged communication across diverse perspectives within local communities in order to determine the actual parameters of program design and operation. The concept of observation encouraged interested administrators and community members to see innovation in action. These observations provided an information base for discussion and further collaboration about how innovation could take shape in local communities and become customized to suit local preferences. Through customization, ideas can be supported by local political conditions, ideologies, values, and customs. Local communities can assume both the ownership of innovation and control its growth and application within local political constraints, resource limitations, and citizen pressures for change.

Local support and local control can foster accountability in an otherwise diffuse intergovernmental environment. Localized involvement keeps information and decisions close to the communities in which programs are carried out. Local collaborations should tend to produce program operations that are aligned with local resources. Local collaborations should also tend to generate measures of program success that have broad public support. Strong public support for local programs should alleviate some measure of concern about accountability for results, particularly in cases where performance standards are established at the local level or with substantial local input. Resolving ambiguity also generates new local capacity. This is important because growth in local capacity appears to prime the pump up the line; investment in local capacity can also lead to the development of additional capacity in state offices.

Sustained Voluntary Commitment

The nonprofit organizations in the information network detailed in this volume enthusiastically pursued their missions with respect to the drug court concept and, more broadly, with respect to other policy ideas at the intersection of drug use and crime. This voluntary commitment to an organizational mission is unique to the nonprofit sector. It is also distinct from the political environment that defines the public sector. The work of the public sector is defined and shaped by a political environment and political commitments to particular initiatives. However, the nature of the public sector is that political oversight changes on a regular and relatively frequent schedule. The work of a public office shifts with changes in political leadership. Program support shifts as political leadership shifts. The national nonprofit information network and its information tools and processes provided a source of sustained commitment to mission that is not inherent in the public-sector environment.

The independence of the nonprofit mission is also an important consideration. Because nonprofit organizations are essentially self-defining organizations, the work they choose to do is up to them. Their interests, missions, and activities are chosen voluntarily. These organizations pursue missions and interests that do not necessarily align with the views of the political majority at any particular point in time. To the extent that these organizations are inclined to pursue policy reform, they may have a greater ability to take risks in pursuing policy solutions. Risk taking can show up in novel institutional arrangements, processes, and approaches to problems. Nonprofit organizations can pursue innovation relatively free from political restriction or the will of the majority.

Advancing the Study of Networks, Public Administration, and Policy

This volume extends our understanding of networked arrangements in the context of public administration in two ways. It illuminates the intersectoral information network as an arrangement that is both similar to and different from other network arrangements that have been observed. The national nonprofit information network illustrated some characteristics of other types of networks that have been the subject of recent exploration. The information exchanges between the national nonprofit organizations and public administrators were clearly oriented toward public policy. Yet the national nonprofit information network was not a policy network in the nature of the policy networks that are the basis of much of the academic analysis of the public policy process (e.g., Kickert, Klijn, and Koppenjan 1999). The national nonprofit information network was not a policy-making network, although organizations in the network held distinct policy positions. The national nonprofit information network also illustrated each of the different orientations that public management networks possess (Agranoff 2007). In the intersectoral arrangement, however, these functions were far more blended than distinct. Organizations in the information network were involved simultaneously with seeking or providing information, development, action, and outreach. At any particular time, many of the organizations in the national nonprofit information network were working with public administrators to establish local programs, to establish state institutional supports, and to evaluate their efforts.

The national nonprofit information network also had no authority or responsibility for governance or administration. Many of the network organizations, however, were deeply involved with public administrators in structuring policy design and implementation, and in the work of administering an innovative idea. The relationships between public administrators and the information resources that they used to implement new programs illustrate a strong connection between the practice of public administration and the practice of policy implementation. The tools of the information network reinforced the connections between administrators and the overall network and promoted new and continuing relationships. This integration between the network and public administrators extends deeply into the traditional understanding of the public policy process; it implicates the network in many stages of the public policy process, from problem definition to solution, through design, implementation, and evaluation. The synthesis that occurred between administrators and these national organizations blurred the differences between the functions of policymaking, implementation, and administration. The synthesis of these functions generated significant and positive policy change on a national scale.

A related observation about networked arrangements and public administrators concerns the issue of the potential loss of government sovereignty in networked arrangements. The concept of an intersectoral information network suggests that the national nonprofit information network studied in this volume is integrated with the work of government but is also somehow apart from government proper. A concern might be that the information from the network would preempt the public will and somehow replace people's public policy preferences with ideas that do not have popular support. The national nonprofit information network illuminates a new dimension in the relationship between the sectors. The nonprofit organizations were formed individually based on unique missions that touch upon areas of public concern, but these organizations find their central purpose outside government. And yet a substantial number of organizations in the information network were professional membership organizations whose members were public administrators. These administrators remained accountable within their own offices, either through election or by appointment. Rather than removing authority from government, this information arrangement infused government administrators with the critical information relationships, tools, and processes necessary for navigating networked arrangements. The information network itself seemed to serve as a check against the loss of governing power. The actions taken by administrators were more informed by the national information network, and they were made possible in large part by the tools that flowed from the network. But the actions of public administrators remained the actions of government—with all the authority and legitimacy that government action implies.

Future Challenges

This book began with a series of questions about the nature and influence of information relationships between a national network of nonprofit organizations and the spread of a policy innovation. The answers to these questions produced an information network and demonstrated the value of this network for policy implementation and outcomes. The process of describing and identifying nonprofit organizations as a national nonprofit information network revealed an information resource and much more. The national nonprofit information network made a difference in the way that public administrators made decisions. Specific forms of synthesized information were especially useful and also fostered collaboration. The interaction of these synthesized forms of information with interdisciplinary concepts such as drug court professionalization also promoted collaborations and synergy. High-information states—those that were more engaged in the information relationships, tools, and processes that derived from the information network—were more likely to be more extensive implementers and have better outcomes. The collaborative nature of the drug court concept was strongly evident throughout local programs and state offices.

As a whole, the answers to these questions suggest a sort of information literacy in which administrators have an awareness of a healthy competition of ideas and organizational resources that can be applied to both policy questions and solutions. The national nonprofit information network created a framework for translating raw information into knowledge, and for translating knowledge into action. By drawing upon the information network, public-sector organizations generated formal and informal relationships that built capacity for implementation and for future policy action. The information network built a knowledge infrastructure that can be applied to other questions. This infrastructure is important in the current information environment, where information is more voluminous and readily accessible than ever before.

Understanding more about specific ways in which intersectoral information relationships translate into policy success is particularly important in the twenty-first-century information environment. Wide-scale electronic methods of information exchange have produced an environment in which most all organizations are able to access virtually unlimited information about a particular policy idea. In this environment, the information that matters will be information that solves problems and produces results. The nonprofit sector holds a wealth of information resources—relationships, tools, and processes that can be tapped to enhance the capacity of public-sector organizations.

In studying information in the context of intersectoral networks, we learn more about how theory is articulated through practice. We also hope to gain insight about tools and relationships that are used in practice and that improve the possibilities for responsive and successful policy change. The national nonprofit information network examined here illustrates several qualities of the intersectoral information relationship that contribute to the capacity of public agencies for current and future policy initiatives. The information relationships, tools, and processes that make up this information network have been critical to the diffusion of one policy innovation. They have been instrumental in providing stability in demonstrating the merits of an idea, in taking the steps to implement it, and in taking the steps for administrative institutionalization. More broadly, the information network has been essential in integrating innovative policy ideas with overarching criminal justice system goals and establishing platforms for further policy development.

The relationship between the information network and government has been studied here as an intersectoral one. Within this description, there is perhaps an underlying tendency to consider government as an equal actor in comparison with the nonprofit sector, and to consider state or local programs on par with organizations outside the state. However, the sovereign authority and responsibility to govern remain with government. Government offices are inherently unequal and weightier players in networked arrangements, with responsibilities to remain accountable for their actions in accordance with the principles of an elected government in a representative republic. By looking at the information relationships and collaborative tools that promote synergy and further collaboration within government programs, this research takes one step toward identifying the internal aspects of one kind of network arrangement that can make a difference in how government operates. By understanding how this information network has contributed to intergovernmental capacity, we learn more about productive relationships between the public and nonprofit sectors. The tools used in this information network can be replicated in other policy arenas. In further studies that go "inside" network relationships and examine tools for success, the tools and processes examined here may emerge as a form of best practices for decision making and policy implementation.

There remains much to learn about information and networks and about the intersectoral relationship. This study has been limited to a single policy innovation and a single conceptualization of an information network based on that idea. However, the relationships, tools, and processes that were embraced by public administrators clearly contributed to the diffusion and implementation of a successful program across state and local government. Information clearly mattered in the case of this information network and this policy innovation.

Appendix: Methodology

The questions used to guide the semistructured interviews with key informants in national nonprofit organizations are reported in figure A.1. Key informants were asked to provide a general identification and description of the national nonprofit organizations that exchanged information about alternatives to incarceration, drug court policy, and criminal justice reform initiatives, and to discuss their organizational involvement within the broader collection of organizations. Key informants were asked to describe the extent to which these organizations constituted a national information network, and the extent to which the network, if present, was concerned with alternatives to incarceration, community corrections, drug courts, or other recent reforms. They were also asked to discuss the types of information they developed to disseminate to state administrators and policymakers, and how they shared this information with them.

Comments on Data Collection

Descriptive data on the organizations in the national information network were widely available on organizational websites and through information filed with the Internal Revenue Service. Information returns (i.e., Internal Revenue Service Form 990 and Form 990, Schedule A) are filed by nonprofit organizations that operate as public charities under Section 501(c)(3) of the Internal Revenue Code and that have gross annual revenues in excess of $25,000 (i.e., one of the various types of Internal Revenue Service Form 990). The data used in this research are available to the public without charge. All organizations had websites; the information returns were available for 90 percent of the organizations. The response to requests for telephone interviews was also high; these interviews were conducted with staff members from 80 percent of the organizations.

Figure A.1. Interview Questions for Key Informants of National Nonprofit Organizations

1. Who and/or what are the main nonprofit organizations or groups involved in the area of alternative sentencing policy and similar criminal justice reforms?

2. How would you describe the groups working in this area? Would you describe this as an alternative sentencing network, a community corrections network, a criminal justice network, or people working on their own?

3. If you describe these groups as a network, does this network include discussion and information about drug courts? How would you describe that?

4. If you describe these groups as a network, does this network include discussion and information about re-entry issues?

5. If you describe these groups as a network, how is your organization involved in this network?

6. How would you describe your organization's involvement in alternative sentencing policies or similar criminal justice reforms? Do you have dedicated staff or policy priorities?

7. What kinds of information does your organization disseminate?

8. Can you comment on the methods that your organization uses to communicate with state policymakers or administrators? Does your organization communicate with state policymakers or administrators through any of the following methods?

   Examples:
   a. Newsletters, journals
   b. Membership surveys
   c. Committees, subcommittees, working groups
   d. Annual conferences
   e. Seminars
   f. In-service training and staff workshops
   g. Certification standards
   h. Licensing activities
   i. Codification, manuals, handbooks
   j. Joint sponsorship
   k. Formal exchange of personnel
   l. Sharing resources (facilities, mailing lists, support services)
   m. Coordination of professional activities
   n. Participation of nonmembers
   o. Advisory boards

9. Can you comment on the types of information that state policymakers or administrators could receive from your organization? Does your organization communicate with state policymakers or administrators about any of the following topics?

Examples:
a. Best practices
b. Capacity building
c. Funding alternatives
d. Member services
e. Program evaluation
f. Research
g. Training and other types of professional development
h. Public education (fact sheets, prepared statements, briefing papers)

The survey of state administrators was purposively administered in a Web-based format to fifty respondents identified by the National Association of Drug Court Professionals (NADCP) as the key drug court contacts for each state (Huddleston, Freeman-Wilson, and Boone 2004). The initial contact list published by the NADCP was updated by the author via e-mail and telephone to obtain current contact information for all fifty states. These current contacts were asked to complete the survey or to forward it to the individual in their state who was most responsible for state-level activities pertaining to drug courts. Administrators from each of the fifty states identified national nonprofit organizations that were sources of information about drug courts, the types of information that they sought from these organizations, the types of information that they found most useful, and the frequency with which they sought information. The survey also collected data about the activities that states have taken to support drug court operations, including establishing various types of legislation, state conferences, advisory councils, standards, and other measures.

Responses were collected through a web link to the survey from July 24, 2004, through November 5, 2004. The survey was distributed initially via e-mail messages that contained a hyperlink to an online response form. The web-based survey service was made available through Flashlight Online, a web-based system for creating surveys, gathering responses, and gathering data. Flashlight Online is a product of the Center for Teaching and Learning at Washington State University and was available through a subscription to the service by Kent State University. Follow-up was conducted by e-mail and telephone. Respondents completed the survey primarily through response to the web-based survey format. Responses to follow up requests for participation were also provided primarily through the web-based format; some states provided responses by fax, and some states provided responses by completing the survey over the telephone. With a response rate of 100 percent ($N = 50$), the data suggest a valid and reliable illustration of state-level involvement in drug court administration. All respondents reported active engagement in drug court operations at the state level and reported significant responsibility for state-level implementation efforts, including policy leadership and administrative support. Most state administrators (76 percent) reported personal involvement in drug court grant applications.

The total number of organizations identified by state administrators from any source ranged from zero to nineteen. The mean number of nonprofit organization contacts was 7.4. One-quarter of the states reported contact with twelve or more nonprofit organizations regarding drug court programs. Only one state reported no contact with any nonprofit organizations in the national nonprofit information network. The survey questions are presented in figure A.2.

Additional data were collected about the diffusion of drug courts in six states (Alabama, Florida, Georgia, Indiana, Missouri, and Tennessee). These states were selected for additional study based on responses to the national survey. These states were selected to provide variation on factors of interest that may explain approaches to the statewide governance and management of drug court initiatives. These states were chosen to illustrate a range of different approaches to the use of information from the information network. The states were also chosen to illustrate governing and management responsibilities in the executive branch and the incorporation of nonprofit organizations into the process. Finally, the states were selected to illustrate potential differences between earlier and later adopters of state support.

These six states do not illustrate every approach to the use of information in institutionalizing drug court programs; the quantitative and qualitative data from multiple sources that are analyzed here suggest that these states are representative of the approaches taken in other states. Data were also drawn from public documents and semistructured interviews conducted with state officials responsible for drug court administration at the state level. Written documents provided a check on the validity of personal recall in the state-specific interviews (Stake 1995; Yin 2002). Documents included legislation, testimony, meeting minutes, analyses, news accounts, press releases, grant applications, and agency summaries of drug court programs at the state and local levels. Figure A.3 presents the list of primary administrative contacts for each of these states and the semistructured interview questions.

Figure A.2. Survey of State Drug Court Administrators

1. Identify your state either by full name or abbreviation (there is no drop-down list of states with this survey).
2. Please list your department or agency, and your title.
3. Identify the role that your agency plays in drug court operations in your state. Check all that apply.
   a. Lead administrative agency
   b. Key source/pass through for funding
   c. Policy leadership and direction
   d. Supporting agency with program/activities that support drug court operations
   e. Aware of drug courts by agency programs/activities are not related
4. Were you as an individual involved in any of the drug court grant applications or other ways of seeking drug court funding for your state?
5. Did your agency contact any other state to learn more about drug courts?
6. Please list all states that your agency contacted regarding their drug court operations.
7. Check all ways in which your state has obtained information about drug courts from professional associations, membership groups, nonprofit or other nongovernmental organizations. Do not include information from government agencies.
   a. National conferences
   b. Regional conferences
   c. Professional meetings
   d. Websites
   e. Newsletters
   f. Listservs
   g. Research publications
   h. Personal contacts
8. Please identify any other ways in which your agency or department obtained information from nongovernmental organizations that were not listed in your response above.

Figure A.2. Survey of State Drug Court Administrators (Continued)

Please indicate how frequently you sought or obtained information from professional associations, membership groups, nonprofit organizations, or other nongovernmental sources:

	Check only one response for each item:			
	>6 times per year	3–6 times per year	1–2 times per year	Not at all
9. Best practices				
10. Model programs				
11. Program evaluation research				
12. Information about what other states are doing				
13. Staff development				
14. State legislative trends				
15. Federal legislative trends				
16. Funding sources				
17. Information systems				

Please indicate the usefulness of any of the following types of information about drug courts that your agency has used from professional associations, membership groups, nonprofit organizations or other nongovernmental sources:

	If you used the information, how useful was it?				
	Very useful	Somewhat useful	Not very useful	Not at all useful	Did not use	No opinion
18. Best practices						
19. Model programs						
20. Program evaluation research						
21. Information about what other states are doing						
22. Staff development						
23. State legislative trends						
24. Federal legislative trends						
25. Funding sources						
26. Information systems						

27. Of all of the types of information, which was most useful? List only one item.
28. Please provide your comments about why the information that you selected was the most useful.
29. Check below all of the court-related professional or membership organizations that provided your agency with information on drug court issues, whether or not that information influenced your state's drug court operations.

a. American Probation and Parole Association
b. National Association of Drug Court Professionals
c. National Association of Probation Executives
d. National Center for State Courts
e. National Council of Juvenile and Family Court Judges
f. National Judicial College
g. National District Attorneys Association
h. National Legal Aid and Defender Association

Figure A.2. Survey of State Drug Court Administrators (Continued)

30. Check below all of the research/policy organizations that provided your agency with information on drug court issues, whether or not that information influenced your state's drug court operations.
   a. Drug Policy Alliance
   b. Justice Policy Institute
   c. National Association of State Sentencing Commissions
   d. National Center for Institutions and Alternatives
   e. Open Society Institute
   f. The Sentencing Project
   g. Urban Institute
   h. Vera Institute of Justice

31. Check below all of the criminal justice or drug treatment organizations that provided your agency with information on drug court issues, whether or not that information influenced your state's drug court operations.
   a. American Correctional Association
   b. International Community Corrections Association
   c. National Association of State Alcohol/Drug Abuse Directors

32. List any other nongovernmental organization that was a source of information used in the design or implementation of your state's drug court program.

33. Name the two nongovernmental organizations that were your most important sources of information about drug court programs.

34. Check below all of the activities that have been implemented in your state to support drug court programs.
   a. State agency-sponsored conference/training about drug courts
   b. State standards for drug courts
   c. New state level department or office for drug courts
   d. Collaborations or working groups of agency experts and/or professionals
   e. Management information systems
   f. Other (list in next question)

35. Please list the other steps that your state has taken to implement, fund, or otherwise support drug court operations.

36. Please estimate the number of staff positions (FTEs) at the state level with job responsibilities that involve drug courts (at least 50% of time on drug courts).
    a. 0
    b. 1–2
    c. 3–5
    d. 6–9
    e. 10–14
    f. 15–19
    g. 20–24
    h. 25 or more

37. Please estimate the number of staff positions (FTEs) at the state level with job responsibilities that involve drug courts and one or more other programs (less than 50% of time on drug courts).
    a. 0
    b. 1–2
    c. 3–5
    d. 6–9
    e. 10–14
    f. 15–19
    g. 20–24
    h. 25 or more

38. Are other specialty courts in operation in your state (e.g., mental health courts, domestic violence courts)?

39. Does your department, agency, or office have any responsibility for other specialty court programs (e.g., mental health courts, domestic violent courts)?

40. Thank you for participating in this research. Please provide any other information about your state's drug court operations that you think would be helpful in this research.

Figure A.3   Interview Questions and Administrative Contacts for Drug Court Programs in Six States

Semistructured Interview Questions

1. What kinds of decisions does your office make about the state drug court program?
2. Who are the regular participants in those decisions? What are their responsibilities? How are they selected?
3. What sources of information do you use to make decisions about state-level activities?
4. What forum and/or process do you use to make decisions about the state drug court program?
5. How does your office interact with local drug court programs in your state? Does your office have formal/informal responsibility for any local program decisions? If so, who is involved in those decisions?
6. Does your office get involved with funding decisions for local drug court programs?
7. How has the state-level decision process evolved over time?
8. Have the state goals and objectives changed since the state office was first established? What factors influenced those changes?
9. What changes, if any, do you plan to make to the decision processes that you are using now?
10. What are the challenges facing the state drug court program? What are the challenges facing local drug court programs?

Primary Administrative Contacts for State Drug Court Operations

Michael Gregory, Drug Court Program Manager
Alabama Administrative Office of Courts

Jane Martin, Associate Director
Division of Children, Families and the Courts
Georgia Administrative Office of the Courts

Jennifer Grandal, Court Operations Consultant
Florida Office of the State Courts Administrator

Mary Kay Hudson, Problem-Solving Court Administrator
Indiana Judicial Center

Ann Wilson, Alcohol and Drug Abuse Coordinator (retired 2008)
Division Court Programs and Research
Missouri Office of State Courts Administrator

Marie Crosson, State Drug Court Coordinator
Office of Criminal Justice Programs
Tennessee Department of Finance and Administration

The Multivariate Analyses

Two forms of multivariate models are used to analyze the influence of information on implementation and policy outcomes. The multivariate analyses employ control variables to minimize the influence of competing explanations for any findings and include demographic and policy-specific conditions that vary across the states. A cross-sectional model is used to analyze the influence of information on implementation at the time of the national survey. Definitions, descriptive statistics, and source information are presented in table A.1 for the cross-sectional model.

A time-series model tests the influence of information over time, covering the period from the inception of local drug courts in 1989 through 2004. Annual data from the fifty states are used in six separate two-stage, pooled, cross-sectional time-series analyses. The two-stage cross-sectional time series models control for endogeneity between information and implementation, and they increase the robustness of the findings in relation to the theoretical framework. A two-stage model is desirable in the cross-sectional regression analysis as well; however, the small n (fifty cases) in such a model is more likely to produce null results than to support findings of statistical significance in the independent variables. Conceptually, the two-stage model generates predicted values of implementation, which are then tested against changes in criminal justice policy outcomes. In the second-stage analysis, additional controls are used to account for factors expected to influence the effect of implementation on these policy outcomes. It is important to note that this study captured only a portion of the universe of information relationships between state and local administrators and the national nonprofit information network. By definition, network relationships are fluid and relatively unbounded, so this limitation is not unusual. In fact, information relationships should be expected to be more extensive between administrators and national organizations than those that were quantified in this study.

Because the dependent variable in the time series models is continuous and measured over time, data are analyzed using a pooled, time-series, cross-sectional model to analyze repeated observations of fixed units over time. Time-series, cross-sectional data are pooled for the observed states and years from 1989 through 2004 in a series of comparative analyses. The generic equation for this time-series cross-section model is expressed as

$$y = x_{i,t}\beta + \epsilon_{i,t;\ i} = 1, \ldots, N;\ t = 1, \ldots, T$$

Table A.1 Data Descriptions and Sources

Variable	Definition	Source
Information network		
Information sources	Number of nonprofit organizations in the national information network reported by state drug court administrators in 2004	Survey of state drug court administrators
NADCP Board	Membership on the National Association of Drug Court Professionals board of directors by state by year 1989–2004 (0 = no board members; 1 = one or more board members)	National Association of Drug Court Professionals, Internal Revenue Service Form 990
NCSC Board	Membership on the National Center for State Courts board of directors by state by year 1989–2004 (0 = no board members; 1 = one or more board members)	National Center for State Courts
State associations	Incorporation of state association of drug court professionals by state by year 1989–2004 (0 = no state association incorporated; 1 = state association incorporated)	Internal Revenue Service Form 990, state corporate registrations
Implementation		
State implementation	Number of state-level acts taken to institutionalize drug courts by 2004, and by state by year 1989–2004	Survey of state drug court administrators; Office of Justice Programs; Huddleston, Freeman-Wilson, and Boone 2004
Local implementation	Annual number of local drug courts in operation by state by year per 100,000 population	Office of Justice Programs
Outcomes		
Property crime	Property crime index offenses per 100,000 population by state by year 1989–2004; adults and juveniles[a]	Uniform Crime Reports, U.S. Department of Justice
Drug abuse arrests	Arrests for drug abuse violations per 100,000 population by state by year 1989–2004; adults and juveniles[b]	Uniform Crime Reports, U.S. Department of Justice

State violent crime rate	Violent crime index offenses per 100,000 population by state by year 1989–2004; adults and juveniles[c]	ICPSR Uniform Crime Reports, U.S. Department of Justice
Controls		
Education	Percent of population with high school diploma or greater level of educational attainment by state by year 1989–2004	U.S. Bureau of the Census
Unemployment	Rate of unemployment by state by year 1989–2004	U.S. Bureau of the Census
Urban population	Percent of population living in urban areas by state by decade 1989–2004	U.S. Bureau of the Census
Age	Percent of population ages 18–24 by state by year 1989–2004	U.S. Bureau of the Census
Racial diversity	Index of racial diversity by state ranging from 0 to 1, measuring the proportion of black, Asian, Latino and white non-Hispanic in the population	Hero and Tolbert 1996; U.S. Bureau of the Census
Institutional ideology	Index of ideology of state officials and political leaders by state by year 1989–2004 (0 = conservative; 100 = liberal)	Berry et al. 1998, 2001
Income	Median household income by state by year 1989–2004	U.S. Bureau of the Census

[a] Index offenses for property crimes reported under the Uniform Crime Reporting system (UCR) include burglary, larceny/theft, and motor vehicle theft. Supplemental data were drawn from state criminal justice reports for Florida, Illinois, and Wisconsin (Florida Statistical Analysis Center of the Florida Department of Law Enforcement, available at www.fdle.state.fl.us; Illinois State Police and Chicago Police Department *Crime in Illinois* reports, available at http://oja.state.il.us; and Office of Justice Assistance of the State of Wisconsin, available at http://oja.state.wi.us).

[b] Drug abuse violations include the sale, manufacture, or possession of narcotics (opium or cocaine and derivatives morphine, heroin, and codeine), marijuana, synthetic narcotics (manufactured narcotics that can cause drug addiction such as Demerol and methadone) and other dangerous nonnarcotic drugs (e.g., barbiturates and Benzedrine); includes adults and juveniles. Supplemental data were drawn from state criminal justice reports for Florida, Illinois, and Wisconsin, as listed in note 1.

[c] Index offenses for violent crimes established under the UCR system (murder and nonnegligent homicide, forcible rape, robbery, and aggravated assault); includes adults and juveniles. Supplemental data were drawn from state criminal justice reports for Florida, Illinois, and Wisconsin, as listed in note 1.

where $x_{i,t}$ is a vector of one or more endogenous variables and observations are indexed both by unit (i) and time (t) (Beck and Katz 1995, 635–36; Stimson 1985). The number of cross sections (N) is equal to the number of states in which observations are made in each time period and ranges from one to fifty. The number of time periods (T) ranges from one to sixteen, equal to the number of observations taken at annual intervals from 1989 through 2004.

The analysis is conducted using ordinary least squares (OLS) regression with panel-corrected standard errors (PCSEs), which correct for temporally and spatially correlated errors and for the heteroskedasticity present in OLS modeling of panel data (Beck and Katz 1995, 634). The use of PCSEs also controls for variation in the conditions that produce the error terms across cross-sectional units. And the use of PCSEs is preferred to random effects models for pooled data when the number of time periods is relatively small in comparison with the number of panels (Beck and Katz 1995). Here, the models have sixteen time periods (T) in comparison with fifty panels (N). Definitions, descriptive statistics, and source information are presented in table A.2 for the cross-sectional model.

Assessments were conducted to determine the expected effects of different levels of the key explanatory variables. Assessments of the level of influence of information on implementation are calculated through a simulation of expected values of the scope of implementation. In the simulation, a baseline model is calculated for each second-stage regression equation by setting the coefficient of each variable at its mean value. The baseline equation yields an expected value for Y. In a series of simulations, the predicated values of state and local implementation are then varied around their means, from very low (2 standard deviations below the mean) to low (1 standard deviation below the mean), mean, high (1 standard deviation above the mean), and very high (2 standard deviations above the mean), while holding all other variables constant at their means. These varied expected values of Y are then compared with the mean value of Y, and the difference is expressed as an effect, which is the effect of the change in implementation on each particular criminal justice policy outcome. This process is repeated to assess the influence of changing levels of state and local implementation on each of the three policy outcomes. Estimations were produced using Clarify Software for Interpreting and Presenting Statistical Results (King, Tomz, and Wittenberg 2000).

Table A.2 Descriptive Statistics

Variable	Mean	Standard Deviation	Minimum	Maximum
Information sources	7.4	5.142	0	19
Frequency of contact	23.52	6.885	10	36
State implementation	.738	1.0	0	5
Local implementation	.174.	336	0	2.993
Education	81.022	5.975	67.1	92.8
Income	35,615.45	7,719.02	18,166	56,407
Unemployment rate	5.262	1.424	2.2	11.3
Racial diversity	.331	.171	.02	.77
Institutional ideology	47.505	25.264	0	97.917
Urban areas	69.196	14.692	32.2	94.4
Age	9.983	.999	7.56	16.75
Property crime rate[a]	4,102.684	1,078.441	2,001.7	7,969.1
Rate of arrests for drug abuse violations[b]	411.676	196.660	3.65	1,076.78
Violent crime rate[c]	484.867	2,347.345	63.2	1,244.3

N = 800 observations

[a] Includes index offenses for property crimes established under the Uniform Crime Reporting system (burglary, larceny/theft, and motor vehicle theft); includes adults and juveniles.

[b] Drug abuse arrest data were taken from county-level files produced and distributed in electronic form by the Inter-university Consortium for Political and Social Research; see Federal Bureau of Investigation 2006. Missing data were supplemented through state criminal justice reports for Florida, Illinois, and Wisconsin. Drug abuse violations include the sale, manufacture, or possession of narcotics (opium or cocaine and derivatives morphine, heroin, and codeine), marijuana, synthetic narcotics (manufactured narcotics that can cause drug addiction such as Demerol and methadone), and other dangerous nonnarcotic drugs (such as barbiturates and Benzedrine); includes adults and juveniles.

[c] Includes index offenses for violent crimes established under the Uniform Crime Reporting system (murder and nonnegligent homicide, forcible rape, robbery, and aggravated assault); includes adults and juveniles.

References

Agranoff, Robert. 2007. *Managing within networks: Adding value to public organizations.* Washington, DC: Georgetown University Press.

Agranoff, Robert, and Michael McGuire. 1998. Multinetwork management: Collaboration and the hollow state in local economic policy. *Journal of Public Administration Research and Theory* 8 (1): 67–92.

———. 2003. *Collaborative public management: New strategies for local governments.* Washington, DC: Georgetown University Press.

Alabama Administrative Office of the Courts. 1998. Alabama drug court association meets. *Alabama Court News* 6 (1): 11.

———. 2008. *Alabama Unified Judicial System FY 2007 annual report and statistics.* Montgomery: Alabama Administrative Office of the Courts.

ASC (Alabama Sentencing Commission). 2002. *Sentencing reform: Initial report to the Alabama Legislature, January 7, 2002.* Montgomery: ASC.

———. 2003 *Recommendations for reform of Alabama's criminal justice system, 2004 report: A rational approach to sentence reform.* Montgomery: ASC.

———. 2004. *Recommendations for reform of Alabama's criminal justice system, 2004 report: A rational approach to sentence reform.* Montgomery: ASC.

———. 2007. *2007 Report, collaborative success: Alabama implements sentencing standards.* Montgomery: ASC.

———. 2008. *2008 report, sentencing standards implementation: Emphasis on data quality, collection and analysis.* Montgomery: ASC.

Anheier, Helmut K., Stefan Toepler, and S. Wojciech Sokolowski. 1997. The implications of government funding for nonprofit organizations: Three propositions. *International Journal of Public Sector Management* 10 (3): 190–213.

Austin, James E. 2000. *The collaboration challenge: How nonprofits and businesses succeed through strategic alliances.* San Francisco: Jossey-Bass.

Balla, Steven J. 2001. Interstate professional associations and the diffusion of policy innovations. *American Politics Research* 29 (3): 221–45.

Bean, Philip. 2002. Drug courts, the judge and the rehabilitative ideal. In *Drug courts in theory and in practice*, edited by James L. Nolan Jr., 235–54. Hawthorne, NY: Aldine de Gruyter.

Beatty, Phillip, Amanda Petteruti, and Jason Ziedenberg. 2007. *The vortex: The concentrated racial impact of drug imprisonment and the characteristics of punitive counties.* Washington, DC: Justice Policy Institute.

Beck, Nathaniel, and Jonathan N. Katz. 1995. What to do (and not to do) with time-series cross-section data. *American Political Science Review* 89 (3): 634–47.

Bedrick, Brooke, and Jerome H. Skolnick. 1999. From "treatment" to "justice" in Oakland, California. In *The early drug courts: Case studies in judicial innovation, Drugs, Health and Social Policy Series, Vol. 1*, edited by W. Clinton Terry III, 43–76. Thousand Oaks, CA: Sage.

Belenko, Steven. 1998. Research on drug courts: A critical review. *National Drug Court Institute Review* 1 (1): 1–42.

———. 1999a. Diverting drug offenders to treatment courts. In *Case studies in judicial innovation, Drugs, Health and Social Policy Series, Vol. 1*, edited by W. Clinton Terry III, 108–38. Thousand Oaks, CA: Sage Publications.

———. 1999b. Research on drug courts: A critical review 1999 update. *National Drug Court Institute Review* 2 (1): 1–58.

Berman, Evan M. 2006. *Performance and productivity in public and nonprofit organizations*, 2nd ed. Armonk, NY: M. E. Sharpe.

Berman, Greg, and John Feinblatt, with Sarah Glazer. 2005. *Good courts: A case for problem-solving justice*. New York: New Press.

Bernard, H. Russell. 2000. *Social research methods*. Thousand Oaks, CA: Sage.

Berry, Frances Stokes, and William D. Berry. 1990. State lottery policy adoptions as policy innovation: An event history analysis of living-will laws. *American Political Science Review*. 84 (2): 395–415.

———. 1999. Innovation and diffusion models in policy research. In *Theories of the policy process*, edited by Paul A. Sabatier, 169–200. Boulder, CO: Westview Press.

Berry, William D., Evan J. Ringquist, Richard C. Fording, and Russell L. Hanson. 1998. Measuring citizen and government ideology in the American states, 1960–1993. *American Journal of Political Science* 41 (4): 327–48.

———. 2001. Measuring citizen and government ideology in the United States. ICPSR study 1208. Available at http://icspr.umich.edu.

Bhati, Avinash Singh, John K. Roman, and Aaron Chalfin. 2008. *To treat or not to treat: Evidence on the prospects of expanding treatment to drug-involved offenders*. Washington, DC: Urban Institute Justice Policy Center.

Boldt, Richard. 1998. Rehabilitative punishment and the drug court treatment movement. *Washington University Law Quarterly* 76 (4): 1205–1306.

Boris, Elizabeth T. 2006. Nonprofit organizations in a democracy: Varied roles and responsibilities. In *Nonprofits and government: Collaboration and conflict*, 2nd ed., edited by Elizabeth T. Boris and C. Eugene Steuerle, 257–76. Washington, DC: Urban Institute Press.

Boyum, David A., and Mark A. R. Kleiman. 2002. Substance abuse policy from a crime-control perspective. In *Crime: Public policies for crime control*, edited by James Q. Wilson and Joan Petersilia, 351–82. Oakland, CA: ICS Press.

Braddock, David L., Richard E. Hemp, and Mary C. Richards. 2008. *The state of the state in developmental disabilities*. Washington, DC: American Association on Intellectual and Developmental Disabilities.

Brooks, Arthur C. 2000. Is there a dark side to government support for nonprofits? *Public Administration Review* 60 (3): 211–18.

———. 2004. Can nonprofit management help answer public management's "big questions"? *Public Administration Review* 62 (3): 259–66.

Bureau of Justice Assistance. 2005. *Drug court discretionary grant program: FY 2005 resource guide for drug court applicants*. Washington, DC: Bureau of Justice Assistance, U.S. Department of Justice.

Burgess, Philip M. 1975. Capacity building and the elements of public management. *Public Administration Review* 35 (6): 705–16.

California Secretary of State. 2008a. *General election; Election night results*. Sacramento: California Secretary of State. Available at http://vote.sos.ca.gov.

———. 2008b. *Prop 5: Nonviolent drug offenses—sentencing, parole and rehabilitation—Initiative statute*. Sacramento: California Secretary of State.

Camp, Robert C. 1995. *Business process benchmarking: Finding and implementing best practices*. Milwaukee: ASQC Quality Press.

Carey, Shannon M., and Michael W. Finigan. 2007. *Indiana drug courts: Vigo County drug court process, outcome and cost evaluation*. Portland: NPC Research.

Carey, Shannon M., Michael W. Finigan, and Kimberly Pukstas. 2008. *Exploring the key components of drug courts: A comparative study of 18 adult drug courts on practices, outcomes, and costs*. Washington, DC: U.S. Department of Justice.

Carman, Joanne G. 2001. Community foundations: A growing resource for community development. *Nonprofit Management and Leadership* 12 (1) (Fall 2001): 7–24.

———. 2007. Evaluation practice among community-based organizations. *American Journal of Evaluation* 28 (1): 60–75.

———. 2009. Nonprofits, funders and evaluation: Accountability in action. *American Review of Public Administration* 39 (4): 374–90.

Casey, Pamela M., and David B. Rottman. 2003. *Problem-solving courts: Models and trends*. Williamsburg, VA: National Center for State Courts.

Casey, Pamela M., David B. Rottman, and Chantal G. Bromage. 2007. *Problem-solving justice toolkit*. Williamsburg, VA: National Center for State Courts.

Cayer, N. Joseph. 2004. *Public personnel administration*, 4th ed. Belmont, CA: Thomson Wadsworth.

Chait, Richard P., Thomas P. Holland, and Barbara E. Taylor. 1996. *Improving the performance of governing boards*. Phoenix: Oryz Press.

Cheesman, Fred L., II, and Dawn Marie Rubio. 2004. *Tennessee technical assistance project: Performance measures for Tennessee drug courts final report*. Williamsburg, VA: National Center for State Courts.

Cigler, Beverly A. 1999. Pre-conditions for the emergence of multi-community collaborative organizations. *Policy Studies Review* 16 (1): 86–102.

Cissner, Amanda B., and Michael Rempel. 2005. *The state of drug court research: Moving beyond "do they work?"* New York: Center for Court Innovation.

Conlan, Timothy. 1998. *From new federalism to devolution: Twenty-five years of intergovernmental reform*. Washington, DC: Brookings Institution Press.

Conroy, Theresa. 2002. Let's hear it for the ex-drug offenders! *Philadelphia Daily News*, January 4.

Cooper, Caroline S. 1997. *Drug courts: 1997 Overview of operational characteristics and implementation issues, Volume one: Preliminary Report*. Washington, DC: American University Office of Justice Programs.

Derthick, Martha. 1970. *The influence of federal grants: Public assistance in Massachusetts*. Cambridge, MA: Harvard University Press.

Deschenes, Elizabeth Piper, with Robert Mimura, Ralph Rogers, Beverly Marksbury, Mack Jenkins, and Rochelle Newble. 2000. Countywide approaches to drug court program implementation: A comparison of Los Angeles and Orange counties, California. *National Drug Court Institute Review* 3: 57–99.

Deschenes, Elizabeth Piper, and Rebecca D. Peterson. 1999. Experimenting with the drug court model: Implementation and change. In *The early drug courts: Case studies in judicial innovation, Drugs, Health and Social Policy Series, Vol. 1*, edited by W. Clinton Terry III, 139–65. Thousand Oaks, CA: Sage.

de Tocqueville, Alexis. 1835/1945. *Democracy in America*, the Henry Reeve text as revised by Francis Bowen. 2 vols. New York: Alfred A. Knopf. Orig. pub. 1835.

DeVita, Carol J. 1999. Nonprofits and devolution: What do we know? In *Nonprofits and government: Collaboration and conflict*, edited by Elizabeth T. Boris and C. Eugene Steuerle, 213–33. Washington, DC: Urban Institute Press.

DeVita, Carol J., and Eric C. Twombly. 2006. Nonprofits and federalism. In *Nonprofits and government: Collaboration and conflict*, 2nd ed., edited by Elizabeth T. Boris and C. Eugene Steuerle, 257–76. Washington, DC: Urban Institute Press.

DiMascio, William M., with Marc Mauer, Kathleen DiJulia, and Karen Davidson. 1997. *Seeking justice: Crime and punishment in America*. New York: Edna McConnell Clark Foundation.

Dowie, Mark. 2001. *American foundations: An investigative history*. Cambridge, MA: MIT Press.

Downs, George W., Jr. 1976. *Bureaucracy, innovation and public policy*. Lexington, MA: Lexington Books.

Downs, George W., Jr., and Lawrence B. Mohr. 1976. Conceptual issues in the study of innovation. *Administrative Science Quarterly* 21 (4): 700–714.

Edwards, Erika. 2004. *Drug court prevents overdoses in South Boston*. Boston: Join Together Project, School of Public Health, Boston University.

Edwards, Leonard P. 2004. Remarks of Judge Leonard P. Edwards at the presentation of the William H. Rehnquist Award for Excellence. *Journal of the Center for Families, Children and the Courts* 5: 169–80.

Eyestone, Robert. 1977. Confusion, diffusion and innovation. *American Political Science Review* 71 (2): 441–47.

Federal Bureau of Investigation, U.S. Department of Justice. 2006. *Uniform Crime Reporting Program Data [United States]: County-Level Detailed Arrest and Offense Data*, computer file, 2nd ICPSR ed. Ann Arbor: Inter-University Consortium for Political and Social Research.

First Judicial District of Pennsylvania. 2001. Drug treatment court recognized by Justice Dept. *The Courterly* 3 (2): 6.

Flango, Victor E., and David B. Rottman. 1992. Measuring trial court consolidation. *Justice System Journal* 16 (4): 65–74.

Fluellen, Reginald, and Jennifer Trone. 2000. *Issue brief: Do drug courts save jail and prison beds?* New York: Vera Institute of Justice.

Fox, Aubrey, and Robert V. Wolf. 2004. *The future of drug courts: How states are mainstreaming the drug court model.* New York: Center for Court Innovation.

Frederickson, David G., and H. George Frederickson 2006. *Measuring the performance of the hollow state.* Washington, DC: Georgetown University Press.

Friedson, Eliot. 2001.*Professionalism, the third logic: On the practice of knowledge.* Chicago: University of Chicago Press.

Gargan, John J. 1981. Consideration of local government capacity. *Public Administration Review* 41 (6): 649–58.

Gebelein, Richard S. 2000. *The rebirth of rehabilitation: Problems and perils of drug courts.* Washington, DC: National Institute of Justice.

Glaeser, Edward L., and Bruce Sacerdote. 1999. Why is there more crime in cities? *Journal of Political Economy* 107 (6, part 2): S225–S258.

Glick, Henry R. 1981. Innovation in state judicial administration: Effects on court management and organization. *American Politics Quarterly* 9 (1): 49–69.

Goldkamp, John S. 1999. The origin of the drug treatment court in Miami. In *The early drug courts: Case studies in judicial innovation, Drugs, Health and Social Policy Series, Vol. 1,* edited by W. Clinton Terry III, 19–42. Thousand Oaks, CA: Sage.

———. 2003. The impact of drug courts. *Criminology and Public Policy* 2 (2): 197–206.

Goldsmith, Stephen, and William D. Eggers. 2004. *Governing by network: The new shape of the public sector.* Washington, DC: Brookings Institution Press.

Gore, Al. 1993. *National performance review.* Washington, DC: U.S. Government Printing Office.

Gray, Virginia. 1973. Innovation in the states: A diffusion study. *American Political Science Review* 67 (4): 1174–85.

Green, Judith, and Kevin Pranis. 2005. *Alabama prison crisis: A Justice Strategies policy report commissioned by the Drug Policy Alliance.* Washington, DC: Justice Strategies.

Guydish, Joseph, Ellen Wolfe, Barbara Tiajim, and William J. Woods. 2001. Drug court effectiveness: A review of California evaluation reports, 1995–1999. *Journal of Psychoactive Drugs* 33 (4): 369–78.

Hall, Peter Dobkin. 1992. *Inventing the nonprofit sector and other essays on philanthropy, voluntarism and nonprofit organizations.* Baltimore: Johns Hopkins University Press.

Hammack, David C. 1998. *Making the nonprofit sector in the United States: A reader.* Bloomington: Indiana University Press.

Harmon, Michael M., and Richard T. Mayer. 1986. *Organization theory for public administration.* Glenview, IL: Scott-Foresman.

Harrell, Adele, John Roman, and Emily Sack. 2001. Drug court services for female offenders, 1996–1999: *Evaluation of the Brooklyn treatment court*. Washington, DC: Urban Institute Press.

Hart, Peter, and Associates. 2002. *Changing public attitudes toward the criminal justice system, February 2002*. New York: Open Society Institute.

Hartney, Christopher, and Susan Marchionna. 2009. *Attitudes of U.S. voters toward nonserious offenders and alternatives to incarceration*. Oakland: National Council on Crime and Delinquency.

Hatry, Harry P., Jake Cowan, and Michael Hendricks. 2004. *Analyzing outcome information: Getting the most from data*. Washington, DC: Urban Institute Press.

Heck, Cary, and Aaron Roussell. 2007. State administration of drug courts: Exploring issues of authority, funding and legitimacy. *Criminal Justice Policy Review* 18 (4): 418–33.

Hennessey, James J. 2001. Drug courts in operation. *Journal of Offender Rehabilitation* 33 (4): 1–10.

Hero, Rodney E., and Caroline J. Tolbert. 1996. A racial/ethnic diversity interpretation of politics and policy in the states of the U.S. *American Journal of Political Science* 40 (3): 851–71.

———. 2003. Racial ethnic diversity and states' public policies: Social policies as context for welfare policies. In *Race and the politics of welfare reform*, edited by Sanford Schram, Joe Soss, and Richard Fording, 298–319. Ann Arbor: University of Michigan Press.

Hodgkinson, Virginia A., and Murray S. Weitzman. 1996. *Nonprofit almanac 1996/1997*. Washington, DC: Independent Sector.

Hoefer, Richard. 2000. Accountability in action? Program evaluation in nonprofit human service agencies. *Nonprofit Management and Leadership* 11(2): 167–77.

Hoffman, Morris B. 2000. The drug court scandal. *North Carolina Law Review* 78: 1437–1527.

———. 2002. The Denver drug court and its unintended consequences. In *Drug courts in theory and in practice*, edited by James L. Nolan Jr., 67–87. New York: Walter de Gruyter.

Honadle, Beth Walter. 1981. A capacity-building framework: A search for concept and purpose. *Public Administration Review* 41 (5): 575–80.

Hora, Peggy F., William G. Schma, and Jonathan Terrence A. Rosenthal. 1999. Therapeutic jurisprudence and the drug treatment court movement: Revolutionizing the criminal justice system's response to drug abuse and crime in America. *Notre Dame Law Review* 74 (2): 439–537.

Huddleston, C. West, III, Karen Freeman-Wilson, and Donna L. Boone. 2004. *Painting the current picture: A national report card on drug courts and other problem solving courts*. Alexandria, VA: National Drug Court Institute.

Huddleston, C. West, III, Douglas B. Marlowe, and Rachel Casebolt. 2008. *Painting the current picture: A national report card on drug courts and other problem-solving court programs in the United States*. Alexandria, VA: National Drug Court Institute.

Hula, Richard, Cynthia Jackson-Elmore, and Laura Reese. 2007. Mixing God's work and the public business: A framework for the analysis of faith-based service delivery. *Review of Policy Research* 24 (1): 67–89.

IJC (Indiana Judicial Center). 2007a. *Drug court certification checklist.* Indianapolis: Indiana Judicial Center.

———. 2007b. *Indiana Drug Courts: A summary of evaluation findings in five adult programs.* Indianapolis: Indiana Judicial Center.

———. 2008. *Application for initial certification as a drug court.* Indianapolis: Indiana Judicial Center.

Judicial Conference of Indiana. 2008. Drug court rules. Indianapolis: Indiana Judicial Center.

Judicial Council of Georgia Standing Committee on Drug Courts. 2008a. *FY2009 grant application and budget for start-up and operational programs.* Atlanta: Judicial Council of Georgia Standing Committee on Drug Courts. Provided July 10, 2008, by e-mail to the author by Jane Martin, associate director, Division of Children, Families, and the Courts, Administrative Office of the Courts, Judicial Council of Georgia.

———. 2008b. *Judicial Council of Georgia Standing Committee on Drug Courts Treatment Standards.* Atlanta: Administrative Office of the Courts, Judicial Council of Georgia.

Karberg, Jennifer C., and Doris J. James. 2005. *Substance dependence, abuse and treatment of jail inmates, 2002.* Washington, DC: Office of Justice Programs, Bureau of Justice Statistics, U.S. Department of Justice.

Kettl, Donald F. 1995. Building lasting reform: Enduring questions, missing answers. In *Inside the reinvention machine: Appraising governmental reform,* edited by Donald F. Kettl and John J. DiIulio, 8–83. Washington, DC: Brookings Institution Press.

———. 2002. *The transformation of governance: Public administration for the twenty-first century.* Baltimore: Johns Hopkins University Press.

———. 2005. *The worst is yet to come: Lessons from September 11 and Hurricane Katrina.* Fels Government Research Service Report 05–01. Philadelphia: Fels Institute of Government, University of Pennsylvania.

Kickert, Walter J. M., Eric-Hans Klijn, and Joop F. M. Koppenjan. 1999. Introduction: A management perspective on policy networks. In *Managing complex networks: Strategies for the public sector,* 2nd ed., edited by Walter J. M. Kickert, Erik-Hans Klijn, and Joop F. M. Koppenjan, 1–13. Thousand Oaks, CA: Sage.

King, Gary, Michael Tomz, and Jason Wittenberg. 2000. Making the most of statistical analysis: Improving interpretation and presentation. *American Journal of Political Science* 44 (2): 347–61.

King, Ryan S., and Marc Mauer. 2002. *Distorted priorities: Drug offenders in state prisons.* Washington, DC: Sentencing Project.

King, Ryan S., and Jill Pasquarella. 2009. *Drug courts: A review of the evidence.* Washington, DC: Sentencing Project.

Klinger, Donald E., and John Nalbandian. 2003. *Public personnel management: Contexts and strategies*, 5th ed. Upper Saddle River, NJ: Prentice Hall.

Krisberg, Barry, and Susan Marchionna. 2006. *Attitudes of U.S. voters toward prisoner rehabilitation and reentry policies*. Oakland: National Council on Crime and Delinquency.

Latimer, Jeff, Kelly Morton-Bourgon, and Jo-Anne Chrétien. 2006. *A meta-analytic examination of drug treatment courts: Do they reduce recidivism?* Ottawa: Department of Justice Canada, Government of Canada.

Leone, Matthew, Belinda Rodgers McCarthy, and Bernard McCarthy. 2007. *Community-Based Corrections*. Belmont, CA: Wadsworth.

Lester, James P., James L. Franke, Ann O'M. Bowman, and Kenneth Kramer. 1983. Hazardous wastes, politics and public policy: A comparative state analysis. *Western Political Quarterly* 36 (2): 257–85.

Letts, Christine, William P. Ryan, and Allen Grossman. 1999. *High performance nonprofit organizations: Managing upstream for greater impact*. New York: John Wiley & Sons.

Light, Paul C. 1998. *Sustaining innovation: Creating nonprofit and government organizations that innovate naturally*. San Francisco: Jossey-Bass.

———. 2000. *Making nonprofits work: A report on the tides of nonprofit management reform*. Washington, DC: Brookings Institution Press.

———. 2004. *Sustaining nonprofit performance: The case for capacity building and the evidence to support it*. Washington, DC: Brookings Institution Press.

Mandell, Myrna. 1994. Managing interdependencies through program structures: A revised paradigm. *American Journal of Public Administration* 24 (1): 99–121.

———. 1999. Community collaborations: Working through network structures. *Policy Studies Review* 16 (1): 42–64.

Marion, Nancy. 2002. *Community corrections in Ohio: Cost savings and program effectiveness*. Washington, DC: Justice Policy Institute.

Marlowe, Douglas B., David S. DeMatteo, and David S. Festinger. 2003. A sober assessment of drug courts. *Federal Sentencing Reporter* 16 (1): 113–28.

Marlowe, Douglas B., David S. Festinger, Patricia A. Lee, Karen L. Dugosh, and Kathleen M. Benasutti. 2006. Matching judicial supervision to clients' risk status in drug court. *Crime & Delinquency* 52 (1): 52–76.

Marlowe, Douglas B., Cary Heck, C. West Huddleston, III, and Rachel Casebolt. 2006. A national research agenda for drug courts: Plotting the course for second-generation scientific inquiry. *Drug Court Review* 5 (2) (Special Research Edition): 1–32.

Mauer, Mark. 1999. *The race to incarcerate*. New York: New Press and Sentencing Project.

McGuire, Michael. 2002. Managing networks: Propositions on what managers do and why they do it. *Public Administration Review* 62 (5): 599–609.

Meier, Kenneth J. 1994. *The politics of sin: Drugs, alcohol and public policy*. Armonk, NY: M. E. Sharpe.

Milward, H. Brinton, and Keith Provan. 1998a. Measuring network structure. *Public Administration Review* 76 (2): 387–407.

———. 1998b. Principles for controlling agents: The political economy of network structures. *Journal of Public Administration Research and Theory* 8 (2): 203–21.

Mintrom, Michael. 2000. *Policy entrepreneurs and school choice.* Washington, DC: Georgetown University Press.

Mintrom, Michael, and Sandra Vergari. 1998. Policy networks and innovation diffusion: The case of state education reform. *Journal of Politics* 60 (1): 126–48.

Missouri Association of Drug Court Professionals. 2008. *MADCP board members.* Jefferson City: Missouri Association of Drug Court Professionals.

Missouri Drug Courts Coordinating Commission. 2008. *Drug court facts.* Jefferson City: Drug Courts Coordinating Commission, Supreme Court of Missouri.

Missouri Office of the State Courts Administrator. 1998. *Missouri resource manual for the development and implementation of drug courts.* Jefferson City: Division of Court Programs and Research, Office of State Courts Administrator.

———. 2008. *Summary of drug court site visit.* Jefferson City: Division of Court Programs and Research, Office of State Courts Administrator.

Mooney, Christopher Z. 2001. Modeling regional effects on state policy diffusion. *Political Research Quarterly* 54 (1):103–24.

Mooney, Christopher Z., and Mei–Hsien Lee. 1995. Legislating morality in the American states: The case of pre-Roe abortion regulation reform. *American Journal of Political Science* 39 (3): 599–627.

Mossberger, Karen. 2000. *The politics of ideas and the spread of the enterprise zones.* Washington, DC: Georgetown University Press.

Mossberger, Karen, and Kathleen Hale. 2002. Polydiffusion in intergovernmental programs: Information diffusion in school-to-work programs. *American Review of Public Administration* 32 (4): 398–422.

Mumola, Christopher J., and Jennifer C. Karberg. 2006. *Drug use and dependence: State and federal prisoners, 2004.* Washington, DC: Office of Justice Programs, Bureau of Justice Statistics, U.S. Department of Justice.

NACDL (National Association of Criminal Defense Lawyers). 2009. *America's problem-solving courts: The criminal costs of treatment and the case for reform.* Washington, DC: NACDL.

NADCP (National Association of Drug Court Professionals). 1997. *Defining drug courts: The key components.* Alexandria, VA: National Association of Drug Court Professionals.

———. 2004. *Defining drug courts: The key components.* Published under Grant 96-DC-MX–K001, Drug Courts Program Office, Office of Justice Programs. Alexandria, VA: NADCP.

———. 2008. *Position statement on the Nonviolent Offender Rehabilitation Act (NORA).* Alexandria, VA: NADCP.

———. Various years. *NADCP News.* Alexandria, VA: NADCP.

National Center for State Courts. Various years. *Annual report (1988–2005)*. Williamsburg, VA: National Center for State Courts.

National Council of Juvenile and Family Court Judges. 2009. *The model court effect: Proven strategies in systems' change*. Reno: National Council of Juvenile and Family Court Judges.

National District Attorneys Association. 2005. *Drug prosecution and prevention programs: A descriptive overview*. Alexandria, VA: National District Attorneys Association.

Noble, Mary C., and Connie Reed. 1999. Kentucky drug courts: Court supervision of a drug treatment program. *The Advocate* 21 (2): 6.

Nolan, James L., Jr. 2001. *Reinventing justice: The American drug court movement*. Princeton, NJ: Princeton University Press.

———. 2002. *Drug courts in theory and in practice*. New York: Walter de Gruyter.

NORA Campaign. 2008. *Response to the NADCP position paper on NORA (Prop. 5)*. Los Angeles and Sacramento: Campaign for New Drug Policies and Drug Policy Alliance Network.

Office of Justice Programs. 2000. *Summary of drug court activity by state and county*. Washington, DC: Drug Court Clearinghouse and Technical Assistance Project at American University, Bureau of Justice Assistance, U.S. Department of Justice.

———. 2001a. *Background information on state court administrative office activities in support of local drug court programs, May 2001*. Washington, DC: Drug Court Clearinghouse and Technical Assistance Project at American University, Bureau of Justice Assistance, U.S. Department of Justice.

———. 2001b. *Court rules enacted for state and local courts relating to drug courts, May 2001*. Washington, DC: Drug Court Clearinghouse and Technical Assistance Project at American University, Bureau of Justice Assistance, U.S. Department of Justice.

———. 2003. *State level activity relating to drug court programs as of December 15, 2003*. Washington, DC: Drug Court Clearinghouse and Technical Assistance Project at American University, Bureau of Justice Assistance, U.S. Department of Justice.

———. 2004a. *Statutes enacted in state legislatures and tribal councils relating to drug courts as of May 1, 2004*. Washington, DC: Drug Court Clearinghouse and Technical Assistance Project at American University, Bureau of Justice Assistance, U.S. Department of Justice.

———. 2004b. *Summary of drug court activity by state and county*. Washington, DC: Drug Court Clearinghouse and Technical Assistance Project at American University, Bureau of Justice Assistance, U.S. Department of Justice.

———. 2004c. Summary of drug court activity by state and county. Personal communication between the author and Caroline Cooper and electronic transmission of data files by Elizabeth Janovski from the Office of Justice Programs Drug Court Clearinghouse and Technical Assistance Project at American University, July 22.

———. 2006. *Frequently asked questions series: State-level approaches and experiences in developing MIS systems for local drug court programs.* Washington, DC: Drug Court Clearinghouse and Technical Assistance Project at American University, Bureau of Justice Assistance, U.S. Department of Justice.

Osborne, David, and Ted Gaebler. 1992. *Reinventing government: How the entrepreneurial spirit is transforming the public sector.* Reading, MA: Addison-Wesley.

O'Toole, Laurence J., Jr. 1988. Strategies for intergovernmental management: Implementing programs in intergovernmental management. *International Journal of Public Administration* 11 (4): 417–41.

———. 1997. Implications for democracy in a networked bureaucratic world. *Journal of Public Administration Research and Theory* 7 (3): 443–59.

O'Toole, Laurence J., Jr., and Kenneth J. Meier. 2004. Desperately seeking Selznick: Co-optation and the dark side of public management in networks. *Public Administration Review* 64 (6): 681–93.

Ott, J. Steven. 2001. Perspectives on organizational governance: Some effects on government–nonprofit relations. In *The nature of the nonprofit sector*, edited by J. Steven Ott, 288–96. Boulder, CO: Westview Press.

Page, Stephen. 2004. Measuring accountability for results in interagency collaboratives. *Public Administration Review* 64 (5): 591–606.

Peters, Jeremy W. 2009. Albany reaches deal to repeal '70s drug laws. *New York Times*, March 26.

Peters, Roger H., and Mary R. Murrin. 2000. Effectiveness of treatment-based drug courts in reducing criminal recidivism. *Criminal Justice and Behavior* 27 (1): 72–96.

Pew Center on the States. 2008. *One in 100: Behind bars in America 2008.* Washington, DC: Pew Charitable Trusts.

———. 2009. *One in 31: The long reach of American corrections.* Washington, DC: Pew Charitable Trusts.

Philadelphia, City of. 2006. *Resolution No. 060348 proclaiming the month of May, 2006 as "National Drug Treatment Court Month" in the City of Philadelphia.* Philadelphia: Council of the City of Philadelphia.

Pressman, Jeffrey L., and Aaron Wildavsky. 1984. *Implementation*, 3rd ed. Berkeley: University of California Press.

Provan, Keith G., and H. Brinton Milward. 1995. A preliminary theory of interorganizational network effectiveness: A comparative study of four community mental health systems. *Administrative Science Quarterly* 40 (1): 1–33.

———. 2001. Do networks really work? A framework for evaluating public sector organizational networks. *Public Administration Review* 61 (4): 414–23.

Putnam, Robert D. 2001. *Bowling alone: The collapse and revival of American community.* New York: Simon & Schuster.

Radin, Beryl. 2000. *Beyond Machiavelli: Policy analysis comes of age.* Washington, DC: Georgetown University Press.

———. 2006. *Challenging the performance movement: Accountability, complexity and democratic values.* Washington, DC: Georgetown University Press.

Rainey, Hal G. 2003. *Understanding and managing public organizations*, 3rd ed. San Francisco: Jossey-Bass.

Rainey, Hal G., and Paula Steinbauer. 1999. Galloping elephants: Developing elements of a theory of effective government organizations. *Journal of Public Administration Research and Theory* 9 (1): 1–32.

Reilly, Dennis A., and Atoundra Pierre-Lawson. 2008. *Ensuring sustainability for drug courts: An overview of funding strategies*. Alexandria, VA: National Drug Court Institute of National Association of Drug Court Professionals.

Rhodes, Ronald A. W. 1996. The new governance: Governing without government. *Political Studies* 44 (3): 652–67.

———. 1997. Foreword to *Managing complex networks: Strategies for the public sector*, 2nd ed., edited by Walter J. M. Kickert, Erik-Hans Klijn, and Joop F. M. Koopenjan. Thousand Oaks, CA: Sage.

Riccio, James, Howard S. Bloom, and Carolyn J. Hill. 2000. Management, organizational characteristics and performance: The case of welfare-to-work programs. In *Governance and performance: New perspectives*, edited by Carolyn Heinrich and Laurence E. Lynn Jr., 166–98. Washington, DC: Georgetown University Press.

Rittel, Horst W. J., and Melvin Webber. 1973. Dilemmas in a general theory of planning. *Policy Sciences* 4 (2): 155–69.

Roderick, Melissa, Brian A. Jacob, and Anthony S. Bryk. 2000. Evaluating Chicago's efforts to end social promotion. In *Governance and performance: New perspectives*, edited by Carolyn Heinrich and Laurence E. Lynn Jr., 34–67. Washington, DC: Georgetown University Press.

Rogers, Everett M. 1995. *Diffusion of innovation*, 4th ed. New York: Free Press.

Roman, John, Wendy Townsend, and Avinash Singh Bhati. 2003. *National estimates of drug court recidivism*. Washington, DC: National Institute of Justice, U.S. Department of Justice.

Rosenthal, John Terrence A. 2002. Therapeutic jurisprudence and drug treatment courts. In *Drug courts in theory and in practice*, edited by James L. Nolan Jr., 145–71. New York: Walter de Gruyter.

Rottman, David B., and William E. Hewitt. 1996. *Trial court structure and performance*. Williamsburg, VA: National Center for State Courts.

Rubin, Herbert J., and Irene S. Rubin. 1995. *Qualitative interviewing: The art of hearing data*. Thousand Oaks, CA: Sage.

Salamon, Lester M. 1995. *Partners in public service: Governmental relations in the modern welfare state*. Baltimore: Johns Hopkins University Press.

———. 2002. The resilient sector: The state of nonprofit America. In *The state of nonprofit America*, edited by Lester M. Salamon, 3–61. Washington, DC: Brookings Institution Press.

Sampson, Robert J., and John H. Laub. 2005. *Crime in the making: Pathways and turning points through life*. Cambridge, MA: Harvard University Press.

Savage, Robert L. 1985. Diffusion research traditions and the spread of policy innovations in a federal system. *Publius, The Journal of Federalism* 15 (4): 1–27.

Schutt, Russell K. 1999. *Investigating the social world: The process and practice of research*, 2nd ed. Thousand Oaks, CA: Pine Forge Press.

Shaffer, Deborah K., Shelley J. Listwan, Edward J. Latessa, and Christopher T. Lowenkamp. 2008. Examining the differential impact of drug court services by court type: Findings from Ohio. *Drug Court Review* 6 (1): 33–66.

Sherman, Lawrence W. 2002. Fair and effective policing. In *Crime: Public policies for crime control*, edited by James Q. Wilson and Joan Petersilia, 383–412. Oakland, CA: ICS Press.

Simon, Herbert A. 1986. Theories of bounded rationality. In *Decision and organization*, 2nd ed., edited by C. B. McGuire and Roy Radner, 161–76. Minneapolis: University of Minnesota Press.

Smith, David Horton. 1973. The impact of the volunteer sector on society. In *The nature of the nonprofit sector*, edited by J. Steven Ott, 79–87. Boulder, CO: Westview Press.

Smith, Stephen Rathgeb. 2006. Government financing of nonprofit activity. In *Nonprofits and government: Collaboration and conflict*, 2nd ed., edited by Elizabeth T. Boris and C. Eugene Steuerle, 219–56. Washington, DC: Urban Institute Press.

Smith, Stephen Rathgeb, and Michael Lipsky. 1995. *Nonprofits for hire: The welfare state in the age of contracting*. Cambridge, MA: Harvard University Press.

Sosin, Michael R., Stephen Rathgeb Smith, Timothy Hilton, and Lucy P. Jordan. 2009. Temporary crisis and priority changes: The case of state substance abuse systems. *Journal of Public Administration and Theory*, advance access published online August 27, Doi 10.1093/jopart/mup022.

Squire, Peverill. 1992. Legislative professionalism and membership diversity in state legislatures. *Legislative Studies Quarterly* 17 (1): 69–79.

Stake, Robert E. 1995. *The logic of case study research*. Thousand Oaks, CA: Sage.

Steen, Sara. 2002. West coast drug courts: Getting offenders morally involved in the criminal justice process. In *Drug courts in theory and in practice*, edited by James L. Nolan Jr., 50–66. Hawthorne, NY: Aldine de Gruyter.

Steuerle, C. Eugene, and Virginia A. Hodgkinson. 2006. Meeting social needs: Comparing independent sector and government resources. In *Nonprofits and government: Collaboration and conflict*, 2nd ed., edited by Elizabeth T. Boris and C. Eugene Steuerle, 81–106. Washington, DC: Urban Institute Press.

Stimson, James. 1985. Regression in space and time: A statistical essay. *American Journal of Political Science* 29 (4): 914–47.

Stone, Deborah. 1997. *The policy paradox: The art of political decision making*, 2nd ed. New York: W. W. Norton.

Sullivan, John. L. 1973. Political correlates of social, economic and religious diversity in the American states. *Journal of Politics* 35 (1): 70–84.

Supreme Court of Florida. 2006. *Administrative Order No. AOSC06-51*. Tallahassee: Supreme Court of Florida.

Supreme Court Task Force on Treatment-Based Drug Courts 2004a. Critical per-
    formance indicators and data elements for adult drug courts in Florida. Talla-
    hassee: Office of the State Courts Administrator, State Courts System of
    Florida.
————. 2004b. Critical performance indicators and data elements for juvenile drug
    courts in Florida. Tallahassee: Office of the State Courts Administrator, State
    Courts System of Florida.
————. 2004c. Critical performance indicators and data elements for dependency
    drug courts in Florida. Tallahassee: Office of the State Courts Administrator,
    State Courts System of Florida.
————. 2004d. Report on Florida's Drug Courts. Tallahassee: Office of the State
    Courts Administrator, State Courts System of Florida.
Tauber, Jeffery. 1998. The future of drug court: Comprehensive drug court systems.
    National Drug Court Institute Review 1 (1): 86–101.
Tennessee Office of Criminal Justice Programs. 2004. Tennessee Mentor Drug Court
    Program. Nashville: Office of Criminal Justice Programs, Department of
    Finance and Administration.
————. 2005. 2004/2005 Tennessee drug court annual report. Nashville: Office of
    Criminal Justice Programs, Department of Finance and Administration.
————. 2007. 2006/2007 Tennessee drug court annual report. Nashville: Office of
    Criminal Justice Programs, Department of Finance and Administration.
————. 2008. The Tennessee Office of Criminal Justice Programs Announces a Drug
    Court Certification Program. Nashville: Office of Criminal Justice Programs,
    Department of Finance and Administration.
Terry, W. Clinton, III. 1999. Broward County's dedicated drug treatment court:
    From postadjudication to diversion. In The early drug courts: Case studies in
    judicial innovation, edited by W. Clinton Terry III, 77–107. Thousand Oaks, CA:
    Sage.
Tittle, Charles R., and David A. Ward. 1993. The interaction of age with the
    correlates and causes of crime. Journal of Quantitative Criminology 9 (1): 3–45.
Tolbert, Caroline J., Karen Mossberger, and Ramona McNeal. 2008. Institutions,
    policy innovation and e-government in the American states. Public Administra-
    tion Review 68 (3): 549–63.
Tonry, Michael. 1998. Intermediate sanctions in sentencing guidelines. Crime and
    Justice: A Review of Research 23: 199–253.
Townsend, Wendy A. 2004. Systems changes associated with criminal justice treat-
    ment networks. Public Administration Review 64 (5): 607–17.
Turner, Susan, and Joan Petersilia. 1996. Work release in Washington: Effects on
    recidivism and correctional costs. Prison Journal 76 (2): 138–64.
University of Alabama. 2008. MIDAS: Alabama's DUI tracking system. Tuscaloosa:
    CARE Research and Development Laboratory, University of Alabama. Avail-
    able at http://care.cs.ua.edu/projects_midas.aspx.
University of Missouri at Columbia School of Social Work. 2001. Composite Report
    on the Ten Key Components in Selected Missouri Drug Court Programs, February

2001. Columbia: School of Social Work, University of Missouri at Columbia. Available at www.courts.mo.gov/.

U.S. Bureau of the Census. Various years. *Statistical Abstract of the United States (1988–2005).* Available at www.census.gov.

U.S. General Accounting Office. 1997. *Drug courts: Overview of growth, characteristics, and results. Report to the Committee on the Judiciary, U.S. Senate, and the Committee on the Judiciary, House of Representatives.* July 1997. GAO/GCD-97-106. Washington, DC: U.S. Government Printing Office.

———. 2002. *Drug Courts: Better DOJ data collection and evaluation efforts needed to measure impact of drug court programs—Report to congressional requesters, April.* GAO-02-434. Washington, DC: U.S. Government Printing Office.

U.S. Government Accountability Office. 2005. *Adult drug courts: Evidence indicates recidivism reductions and mixed results for other outcomes—Report to the Congressional Committees, February.* GAO-05-218. Washington, DC: U.S. Government Printing Office.

U.S. Sentencing Commission. 2007. *Analysis of the impact of the Crack Cocaine Amendment if made retroactive, October 3, 2007.* Washington, DC: U.S. Sentencing Commission.

———. 2008a. *U.S. Sentencing Commission preliminary crack cocaine retroactivity data report.* Washington, DC: U.S. Sentencing Commission.

———. 2008b. *U.S. Sentencing Commission 2008 annual report.* Washington, DC: U.S. Sentencing Commission.

Van Til, Jon. 2000. *Growing civil society: From nonprofit sector to third space.* Bloomington: Indiana University Press.

Votey, Harold L., Jr., and Llad Philips. 2003. Crime, youth and the labor market: Are we any closer to answers? In *Crime control and social justice: The delicate balance,* edited by Darnell F. Hawkins, Samuel L. Myers Jr., and Randolph N. Stone, 67–92. Westport, CT: Greenwood Press.

Walker, Jack L. 1969. The diffusion of innovations among the American states. *American Political Science Review* 63 (3): 880–99.

Weiss, Carol H. 1983. Ideology interests and information: The basis of policy positions. In *Ethics, the social sciences and policy analysis,* edited by Daniel Callahan and Bruce Jennings, 213–45. New York: Plenum Press.

Weiss, Janet. A. 2002. Public information. In *The tools of government: A guide to the new governance,* edited by Lester M. Salamon, 217–54. New York: Oxford University Press.

Welsh, Brandon C., and David P. Farrington. 2000. Monetary costs and benefits of crime prevention programs. In *Crime and justice: A review of research, Vol. 27,* edited by Michael Tonry, 1–79. Chicago: University of Chicago Press.

Wexler, David B. 2004. *Therapeutic jurisprudence: It's not just for problem-solving courts and calendars anymore—Trends.* Williamsburg, VA: National Center for State Courts.

Wildavsky, Aaron. 1972. The self-evaluating organization. *Public Administration Review* 32 (5): 509–20.

Wilson, James Q. 1983. *Thinking about crime*, 2nd ed. New York: Basic Books.

———. 1990. Drugs and crime. In *Drugs and crime, Crime and justice: A review of research, Vol. 26*, edited by Michael Tonry and James Q. Wilson, 521–43. Chicago: University of Chicago Press.

———. 2002. Crime and public policy. In *Crime: Public policies for crime control*, edited by James Q. Wilson and Joan Petersilia, 253–90. Oakland: ICS Press.

Wool, Jon, and Don Stemen. 2004. *Changing fortunes or changing attitudes? Sentencing and corrections reform in 2003*. New York: Vera Institute of Justice.

Wright, Deil S. 1988. *Understanding intergovernmental relations*. Pacific Grove, CA: Brooks/Cole.

Yin, Robert K. 2002. *Case study research: Design and methods*, 3rd ed. Thousand Oaks, CA: Sage.

Yin, Robert K., and Gregory D. Andranovich. 1986. *Increasing states' use of federal statistics about mental health organizations*. Washington, DC: Cosmos Corporation.

———. 1987. *Getting research used in the natural hazards field: The role of professional associations*. Washington, DC: Cosmos Corporation.

Young, Dennis R. 2006. Complementary, supplementary or adversarial? Nonprofit–government relations. In *Nonprofits and government: Collaboration and conflict*, 2nd ed., edited by Elizabeth T. Boris and C. Eugene Steuerle, 37–80. Washington, DC: Urban Institute Press.

INDEX

Page numbers in italics signify illustrations.

226

INDEX

Kllijn, Erik-Hans, 11
Koopenjan, Joop F. M., 11

law enforcement, 37, 54, 171
  collaboration with drug court
    programs, 35, 77, 119, 120–21,
    135, 158
  specialization in, 172
local support and control, 28, 94, 183
Louisiana, 119

management techniques, 113
McCaskill, Claire, 79, 80, 102n2
McGuire, Michael, 11
mental health courts, 165
mentor courts, 116–17, 119, 120, 128
  administrators' observation of,
    117–18
  supporter organizations and, 119
Mexico, 166
Milward, H. Brinton, 11
Missouri, 140, 145–46, 164
Missouri Association of Drug Court
    Professionals, 77, 79–80
Model Integrated Defendant Access
    System (MIDAS), 124
model programs
  as information tool, 3, 69, 177, 183
  and national information network,
    103, 105, 106, 121, 128
Mossberger, Karen, 14
motivation, 23, 28, 76, 176, 179

National Association of Blacks in
    Criminal Justice, 63n4
National Association of Criminal
    Defense Lawyers (NACDL),
    169–71
National Association of Drug and
    Alcohol Abuse Counselors, 59,
    63n4
National Association of Drug Court
    Professionals (NADCP), 31, 66,
    171

and Alabama drug court program,
    125
central leadership position of, 58, 60,
    172
as champion organization, 26–28, 54,
    55, 62, 92–93, 131, 155, 158–59
and collaborative process, 135–36,
    156
diffusion of drug court concept by,
    26, 27, 106, 166
founding of, 38, 43
governing board of, 72, 73, 75–76,
    92, 101
guiding principles of, 27, 28, 109–10,
    130, 137
  and mentor court programs, 116
mission and focus, 42, 47
National Drug Court Institute of, 46,
    47, 121
and professionalization, 134
National Association of Probation
    Executives, 43
mission and focus, 41, 47
as supporter organization, 54, 56–57,
    59
National Association of State Alcohol
    and Drug Abuse Directors, 43, 71
as bystander organization, 54
mission and focus, 41, 45, 47
National Association of State
    Sentencing Commissions, 38
as bystander organization, 54
mission and focus, 41, 47
National Center for Institutions and
    Alternatives
as challenger organization, 54, 56
mission and focus, 41, 50
National Center for State Courts
    (NCSC), 27, 28, 43, 101
governing board of, 72, 74, 76, 92
mission and orientation, 40, 46,
    47, 48
organizational leadership by, 60,
    162–63